MW01516295

Pearson Australia
(a division of Pearson Australia Group Pty Ltd)
707 Collins Street, Melbourne, Victoria 3008
PO Box 23360, Melbourne, Victoria 8012

www.pearson.com.au

First published 2018 by Pearson Australia
2021   2020   2019   2018
10 9 8 7 6 5 4 3 2 1

Lead Publishers: Misal Belvedere and Mal Parsons
Project Manager: Michelle Thomas
Production Editors: Casey McGrath and Virginia O'Brien
Lead Development Editor: Fiona Cooke
Development Editors: Amy Sparkes and Haeyean Lee
Editor: David Meagher
Designers: Anne Donald, iEnergizer Aptara Ltd
Rights and Permissions Editor: Samantha Russell-Tulip
Senior Publishing Services Analyst: Rob Curulli
Proofreader: Right Style Editing
Illustrator: DiacriTech
Printed in Malaysia by Vivar

ISBN 978 1 4886 1934 2

Pearson Australia Group Pty Ltd   ABN 40 004 245 943

Attributions
Cover: ADA_photo/Shutterstock
Science Photo Library: p. 99–101; UK Crown Copyright of Fera,
pp. 158–9.
Shutterstock: ADA_photo, p, I; AG-Photos, pp. 1–2; DoubleO, pp. 48–9.
Wet Tropics Management Authority: pp. 61–2.

All material identified by (AC) is material subject to copyright under
the *Copyright Act 1968* and is owned by the Australian Curriculum,
Assessment and Reporting Authority (ACARA) 2018.

ACARA neither endorses nor verifies the accuracy of the
information provided and accepts no responsibility for incomplete
or inaccurate information. In particular, ACARA does not endorse or
verify that:

- the content descriptions are solely for a particular year
  and subject
- all the content descriptions for that year and subject have
  been used
- the author's material aligns with the Australian Curriculum
  content descriptions for the relevant year and subject.

You can find the unaltered and most up-to-date version of this
material at http://www.australiancurriculum.edu.au/. This material
is reproduced with the permission of ACARA.

Chemistry Stage 6 Syllabus © NSW Education Standards Authority
for and on behalf of the Crown in right of the State of NSW, 2017.

Contents

Contents

How to use this book

The *Pearson Chemistry 12 New South Wales Skills and Assessment* book provides an intuitive, self-paced approach to science education that ensures every student has opportunities to practise, apply and extend their learning through a range of supportive and challenging activities. While offering opportunities for reinforcement of key concepts, knowledge and skills, these activities enable flexibility in the approach to teaching and learning.

Explicit scaffolding makes learning objectives clear, and there are regular opportunities for student reflection and self-evaluation at the end of individual activities throughout the book. Students are also guided in self-reflection at the end of each module. In addition, there are rich opportunities to take the content further with the explicit coverage of Working scientifically skills and key knowledge in the depth studies.

This resource has been written to the new Stage 6 Syllabus for New South Wales Chemistry and addresses the final four modules of the syllabus. Each module consists of five main sections:
- key knowledge
- worksheets
- practical activities
- depth study
- module review questions.

Explore how to use this book below.

Chemistry toolkit

The Chemistry toolkit supports development of the skills and techniques needed to undertake practical investigations, secondary-sourced investigations and depth studies, and covers examination techniques and study skills. It also includes checklists, models, exemplars and scaffolded steps. The toolkit can serve as a reference tool to be consulted as needed.

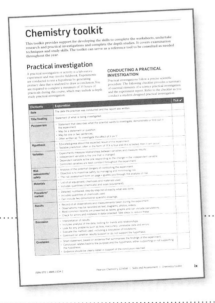

Module opener

Each book is split into the four modules of the syllabus, with the module opener linking the module content to the syllabus.

Key knowledge

Each module begins with a key knowledge section. This consists of a set of succinct summary notes that cover the key knowledge set out in each module of the syllabus. This section is highly illustrative and written in a straightforward style to assist students of all reading abilities. Key terms are bolded for ease of navigation. It also provides a ready reference for completing the worksheets and practical activities.

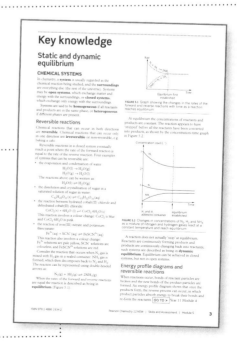

Worksheets

A diverse offering of instructive and self-contained worksheets is included in each module. Common to all modules is the initial 'Knowledge review' worksheet to activate prior knowledge, a 'Literacy review' worksheet to explicitly build understanding and application of scientific terminology, and finally a 'Thinking about my learning' worksheet, which provides a reflection and self-assessment opportunity for students. Each additional worksheet provides opportunities to revise, consolidate and further student understanding.

These worksheets function as formative assessment and are clearly aligned to the syllabus. A range of questions building from foundation to challenging are included within worksheets.

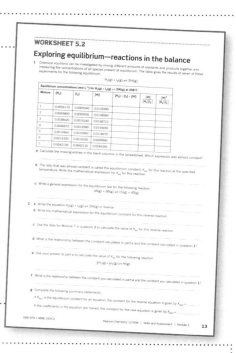

Practical activities

Practical activities provide the opportunity to complete practical work related to the various themes covered in the syllabus. All practical activities referenced in outcomes within the syllabus have been covered. Across the suite of practical activities provided, students are exposed to opportunities where they design, conduct, evaluate, gather and analyse data, appropriately record results and prepare evidence-based conclusions directly into the scaffolded practical activities. Students also have opportunities to evaluate safety and any potential hazards.

Each practical activity includes a suggested duration. Along with the depth studies, the practical activities meet the 35 hours of practical work mandated at Year 12 in the syllabus. Where there is key knowledge that will support the completion of a practical activity, students are referred back to it.

Like the worksheets, the practical activities include a range of questions building from foundation to challenging.

Depth studies

Each module contains one suggested depth study. The depth studies allow further development of one or more concepts found within or inspired by the syllabus. They allow students to acquire a depth of understanding and take responsibility for their own learning. They also promote differentiation and engagement.

Each depth study allows for the demonstration of a range of Working scientifically skills, with all depth studies assessing the Working scientifically outcomes of Questioning and predicting, and Communicating. A minimum of two additional Working scientifically skills and at least one Knowledge and understanding outcome are also assessed.

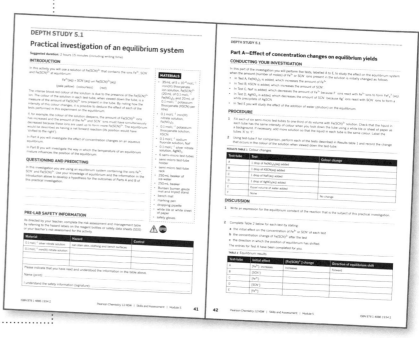

Module review questions

Each module finishes with a comprehensive set of questions, consisting of multiple choice and short answer, that helps students to draw together their knowledge and understanding and apply it to these styles of questions.

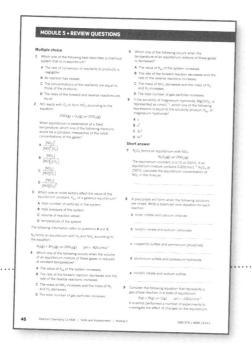

Icons and features

The New South Wales Stage 6 Syllabus Learning across the curriculum content is addressed and identified using the following icons:

 GoTo icons are used to make important links to relevant content within the book.

 The **safety icon** highlights significant hazards indicating caution is needed.

 The **safety glasses icon** highlights that protective eyewear is to be worn during the practical activity.

A **pre-lab safety box** is included. Students are to sign agreeing that they have understood the hazards associated with the material(s) in use and the control measures to be taken.

PRE-LAB SAFETY INFORMATION		
Material	**Hazard**	**Control**
KSCN solution	irritating to the skin and eyes	Wear gloves, lab coat, safety glasses.
$FeSCN^{2+}$ solution	contains nitric acid and is irritating to the skin and eyes	Wear gloves, lab coat, safety glasses.
$Fe(NO_3)_3$ solution	irritating to eyes, respiratory system and skin	Wear gloves, lab coat and safety glasses.
Please indicate that you have understood the information in the safety table.		
Name (print): _____		
I understand the safety information (signature): _____		

Rating my learning

Rating my learning is an innovative tool that appears at the bottom of the final page of most worksheets and all practical activities. It provides students with the opportunity for self-reflection and self-assessment. It encourages students to look ahead to how they can continue to improve, and assists in highlighting focus areas for further skill and knowledge development.

The teacher may choose to use student responses to the 'Rating my learning' feature as a formative assessment tool. At a glance, teachers can assess which topics and which students need intervention for improvement.

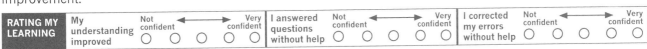

Teacher support

Comprehensive answers and fully worked solutions for all worksheets, practical activities, depth studies and module review questions are provided in the *Pearson Chemistry 12 New South Wales Teacher Support*. An editable suggested assessment rubric for depth studies is also provided.

Pearson Chemistry 12
New South Wales

Student Book

Pearson Chemistry 12 New South Wales has been written to fully align with the 2018 New South Wales Chemistry Stage 6 Syllabus. The Student Book includes the very latest developments and applications of chemistry and incorporates best practice literacy and instructional design to ensure the content and concepts are fully accessible to all students.

Skills and Assessment Book

The Skills and Assessment book gives students the edge in preparing for all forms of assessment. Key features include a toolkit, key knowledge summaries, worksheets, practical activities, suggested depth studies and module review questions. It provides guidance, assessment practice and opportunities to develop key skills.

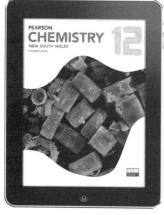

Reader+ the next generation eBook

Pearson Reader+ lets you use your Student Book online or offline on any device. Pearson Reader+ retains the look and integrity of the printed book. Practical activities, interactives and videos are available on Pearson Reader+ along with the fully worked solutions to the Student Book questions.

Teacher Support

Online teacher support for the series includes syllabus grids, a scope and sequence plan, and three practice exams per year level. Fully worked solutions to all Student Book questions are provided, as well as teacher notes for the chapter inquiry tasks. Skills and Assessment book resources include solutions to all worksheets, practical activities, depth studies and module review questions; teacher notes, safety notes, risk assessments and lab technician's checklists and recipes for all practical activities; and assessment rubrics and exemplar answers for the depth studies.

Access your digital resources at **pearsonplaces.com.au**
Browse and buy at **pearson.com.au**

Chemistry toolkit

This toolkit provides support for developing the skills to undertake research and practical investigations, and complete the depth studies. It also covers examination techniques and study skills. The toolkit can serve as a reference tool to be consulted as needed throughout the year.

Practical investigation

A practical investigation or activity is a laboratory experiment and may involve fieldwork. Experiments are conducted to test a hypothesis by generating primary data that is analysed to draw a conclusion. You are required to complete a minimum of 35 hours of practical work during this course, which may include a depth study practical investigation.

CONDUCTING A PRACTICAL INVESTIGATION

Practical investigations follow a precise scientific procedure. The following checklist provides a summary of essential elements of a science practical investigation and the experiment report. Refer to the checklist as you conduct a student-designed practical investigation.

Elements	Explanation	Tick ✔
Date	The date the practical was conducted and the report was written.	
Title/heading	Statement of what is being investigated.	
Purpose/aim	• Statement that describes what the scientist wants to investigate, demonstrate or find out in the experiment. • May be a statement or question. • May be one or two sentences. • Often written as 'To investigate the effect of X on Y.'	
Hypothesis	• Educated guess about the expected result of the experiment. • Testable prediction, often in the form of 'If X is true and this is tested, then Y will occur.'	
Variables	• Experiments measure relationships between variables and measure results. • Independent variable is the one that is changed. • Dependent variable is the one responding to the change in the independent variable. • Controlled variables are kept constant throughout the experiment.	
Risk assessments/safety	• Analysis of the potential dangers of conducting the experiment. • Objective is to maximise safety by managing and minimising risk. • The risk assessment form on page xi guides you through the analysis of risk.	
Materials	• List of all equipment, chemicals and materials used. • Includes quantities (chemicals) and sizes (equipment).	
Procedure/method	• Detailed, numbered, step-by-step list of exactly what was done. • Includes quantities of chemicals used. • Can include two-dimensional scientific drawings.	
Results	• Record of all observations and measurements taken during the experiment. • Observations may be recorded as text, diagrams, photos, videos. • Most common records are presented as tables and graphs, and can include calculations. • Check for errors and mistakes in data collected. Take steps to reduce these.	
Discussion	• Interpretation of results. • Includes analysis of the data, looking for trends and relationships. • Look for any problems such as bias, inaccuracy, unreliable data and errors. • Evaluate the procedure used, including a discussion of limitations. • Comment on whether results support or do not support the hypothesis.	
Conclusion	• Short statement based on evidence that summarises the findings of the experiment. • Conclusion relates back to the purpose and the hypothesis, either supporting or not supporting the hypothesis. • Evidence should be clearly listed in support of the conclusion reached.	

RISK ASSESSMENT FORM

Five levels of safety should be considered in an investigation. The inverted pyramid ranks these levels in order of importance. The school and your teacher are responsible for reducing most of these risks. You as a student scientist can take measures to reduce the risks shown at the bottom of the hierarchy.

Complete a risk assessment form for each activity to identify possible risks for which you can take responsibility and to think of ways you can reduce risks to create a safe experiment environment.

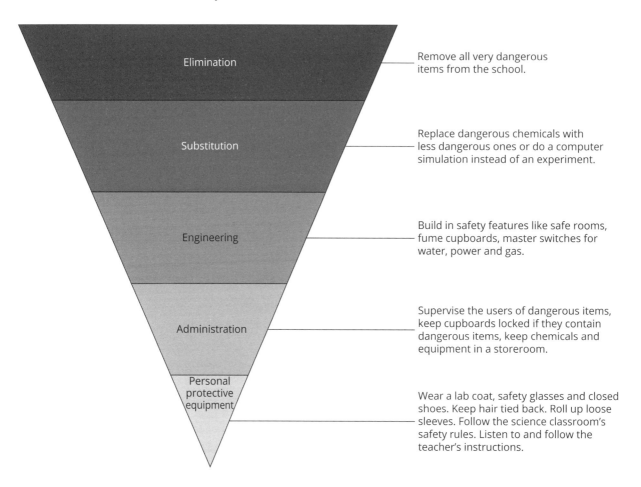

Elimination — Remove all very dangerous items from the school.

Substitution — Replace dangerous chemicals with less dangerous ones or do a computer simulation instead of an experiment.

Engineering — Build in safety features like safe rooms, fume cupboards, master switches for water, power and gas.

Administration — Supervise the users of dangerous items, keep cupboards locked if they contain dangerous items, keep chemicals and equipment in a storeroom.

Personal protective equipment — Wear a lab coat, safety glasses and closed shoes. Keep hair tied back. Roll up loose sleeves. Follow the science classroom's safety rules. Listen to and follow the teacher's instructions.

EXAMPLES OF PRACTICAL REPORTS

It can be difficult to gauge whether you have attained a high standard in your completed practical investigation report. Looking at sample practical reports can help you identify what is required. Two sample practical reports were provided in the Year 11 Skills and Assessment Book. They included annotations to draw your attention to key points to note on each practical report. These points are also reflected in the checklist, so you are able to use this as a tool to evaluate whether all requirements of the practical are complete. GO TO ➤ Year 11 Toolkit

Risk assessment form		
What activity are you doing?		
Title or description of the investigation:		
List ...	**Identify any risks**	**State how you will ...**
equipment you will be using:		safely use each piece of equipment:
chemicals you will be using:		carefully use each chemical: carefully dispose of the chemicals:
ethical issues you need to consider:		ethically use human participants in the investigation:
outdoor or fieldwork activities:		reduce any risks:
any other possible risks:		reduce these risks:

Secondary-sourced investigation

This section guides you in conducting a secondary-sourced investigation. For assistance with conducting a practical investigation, see pages ix–xi.

A major secondary-sourced investigation is also often known as a research project. Such investigations require you to think carefully about the topic; find, collect and organise information; analyse and synthesise findings; and present your ideas. The investigation process is summarised in the following flow chart. An investigation is not necessarily a straightforward linear process as shown in the flow chart. You can move back and forth between steps as needed.

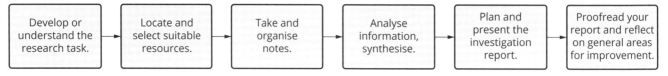

Develop or understand the research task. → Locate and select suitable resources. → Take and organise notes. → Analyse information, synthesise. → Plan and present the investigation report. → Proofread your report and reflect on general areas for improvement.

THE INVESTIGATION TASK

It is important to understand the breakdown of investigation questions or tasks. This helps you to write your own tasks and better understand the requirements of those written by others.

As you develop an investigation task, be aware of the depth of thinking it will require. The following chart provides support in writing tasks at different levels of thinking or complexity. It also provides some key words to help target tasks at these thinking levels and gives some examples of questions.

When developing your question or task, be conscious of the level at which you are pitching it. When you are writing your own questions for a depth study investigation, they should generally be at the analysis level.

Level of question complexity	Type of thinking	Words that may be used		Examples of questions
Simple	**Retrieval:** remembering, producing information on demand	• who • where • list • show • describe • select • complete • define	• what • when • label • demonstrate • name • state • recognise	1 Define the term 'molecule'. 2 What is the function of intermolecular forces? 3 List the metallic elements in order of least to most reactive. 4 What are the products of a neutralisation reaction?
	Comprehension: the ability to understand information	• who • where • explain • represent • show how	• what • when • summarise • draw • describe	1 Represent the Bohr model of the atom with a labelled diagram. 2 Why is the atomic radius of an oxygen atom smaller than the atomic radius of a lithium atom? 3 Explain why the mole concept is useful to chemists.
	Analysis: scrutinising and breaking something into its smaller parts, including: • comparing • classifying • identifying errors • concluding • predicting • judging	• why • categorise • contrast • sort • organise • generalise • evaluate • edit • assess • judge	• how • compare • distinguish • discriminate between • deduce • critique • diagnose • identify errors • identify misunderstandings	1 Categorise the following compounds according to their type of bonding. 2 Compare an exothermic and an endothermic reaction. 3 Compare and contrast alpha and beta decay.
Complex (requiring more thinking)	**Application:** using knowledge in new situations, including: • testing a hypothesis • solving a problem • experimenting and using data • decision making	• why • investigate • find out about • test • solve • develop • decide	• how • research • experiment • predict • adapt • judge	1 Many people believe that fossil fuels should be replaced with biofuels as a source of energy. Construct an argument for or against this statement. 2 Investigate the methods for storing hydrogen in a car powered by a fuel cell. 3 How would different water temperatures affect the rate at which a submerged iron rod rusts?

Pearson Chemistry 12 NSW | Skills and Assessment | Chemistry toolkit ISBN 978 1 4886 1934 2

RESOURCES

The resources you refer to in an investigation may be primary and/or secondary.

Primary sources of information are from investigations that you have conducted yourself. Examples of primary sources are results from your experiments, reports of your scientific investigations, photographs you have taken, and specimens or artefacts that you have collected. Secondary sources of information are from investigations that have been conducted by others. Secondary sources include peer-reviewed articles, textbooks, biographies, documentaries, newspaper articles and many websites.

Refer to the two tables below. The first shows features to look for when assessing and selecting the best sources for your investigation. The second shows the information that is required for the references section of your report.

Always remember to note the reference information for every resource you use. It is very time-consuming and difficult to backtrack later to obtain these details when you need them to write the references.

Selecting resources for the investigation	Tick ✔
The resource is:	
• **credible** and I can identify the author, author's expertise and publisher	
• **current** because the date of publication of the material is provided and is recent	
• **factual** and I know that it is objective material and not biased	
• **accurate** and all information is correct	
• **relevant** and covers the area I am investigating	
• **readable** and neither too simple nor too complex in its coverage of the material.	

Information required for references and examples
Article in scientific magazine   Author, initials. (year). Title of article. *Journal title, volume number*(issue number). Page numbers.   Lee, M. L. (2017). Materials science: Crystals aligned through graphene. *Nature 544*(7650). 301–302.
Book   Author, initials. (year). *Title of book* (edition, if not first). City: publisher.   Rickard, G. *et al.* (2017). *Pearson Science Student Book 9*. Melbourne: Pearson Education.   Where there are more than two authors, list first author then write *et al.* meaning 'and others'.
Internet   Author, initials/name of organisation. (year). *Title of webpage or web document.* Retrieved from <URL>.   Royal Society of Chemistry. (2017). *Periodic table.* Retrieved from http://www.rsc.org/periodic-table.

NOTE-TAKING AND ORGANISING NOTES

Note-taking and organising your notes takes skill. Good note-taking helps you avoid plagiarism and provides excellent information for writing up the investigation. Plagiarism is taking someone else's ideas and words and presenting them as your own work. You plagiarise if you copy sections or sentences from sources or if you cut and paste from the internet. It is acceptable to use the ideas of others but you must state clearly where the information has come from in the body of your report and include the source in your references.

The examples in the table are of original text, plagiarised text and acceptably rephrased text.

Original text	Plagiarised text	Rephrased text
Dogs have sweat glands on their feet. Dogs pant when they are hot because their sweat glands are not sufficient to cool down their bodies. In addition, their tongues allow the water from their bodies to evaporate and cool down their bodies.	Dogs have their sweat glands on their feet. When dogs get hot they pant because their sweat glands are not enough to cool down their bodies. Their tongues let the water from their bodies evaporate and cool their bodies.	Dogs pant in order to cool down. Water evaporates from their tongues and this lowers their body temperature. They can't get cool enough through just the sweat glands on their feet.

There are various approaches to effective note-taking. Whatever technique you use, try to keep notes brief, and focus on key points. Some examples include:

- dot point summary
- underlining or highlighting text
- labelled diagram
- flow chart—show sequences
- concept map—show connections between items
- Venn diagrams—show similarities and differences
- table—may incorporate any of the other note-taking techniques. Tables are useful for summarising longer and more complex information that has subparts. Adapt the table to suit your style and the task. The following sample table (partially completed) shows how this technique can be used to take notes for your secondary-sourced investigation.

Secondary-sourced investigation task			
Many scientists believe that limiting human population growth is necessary to control environmental damage. Construct an argument for or against this statement.			

	Source 1 (e.g. book) Title: Author: Publisher's name: Publisher's location: Date of publication:	**Source 2** (e.g. Internet) Title: Author: URL: Date accessed:	**Source 3** (e.g. science journal) Author: Date: Title of article: Journal title: Volume number: Pages:
Population growth trends			
Impact of population growth on environment	• growth of cities • demand for resources		
Reasons to control and limit population growth	• increased demand for resources for human survival		
Reasons not to limit population growth but to allow natural population growth			• other factors contributing to environment damage; land-use policies, e.g. poor land use

Human population growth graph showing Population/billions vs Year

SCIENTIFIC WRITING

Scientists have a particular writing style. Your investigation should use this distinctive style to communicate your ideas. Writing in the scientific style is:

- objective—describes events rather than what people think or feel
- as free as possible of bias or personal opinion
- precise—avoids exaggeration and uses qualified language
- formal—uses scholarly language rather than colloquial or everyday language
- concise—conveys information in short, clearly understandable sentences without unnecessary information
- simple—uses short sentences where possible
- usually written in passive voice rather than active voice, although sometimes active voice can be used
- structured to include headings, tables, diagrams, mathematical calculations.

Examples of unscientific and scientific writing are shown in the table.

Unscientific writing	Scientific writing
Subjective, biased writing: • The results were fantastic. • This produced a disgusting odour. • The breathtakingly beautiful bowerbird …	**Objective, unbiased writing:** • The results showed … • This produced a pungent odour … • The golden bowerbird …
Exaggerated writing: • The object weighed a huge amount. • The magnesium burst into huge flames. • Millions of ants swarmed over …	**Accurate, precise writing:** • The mass of the object was 250 kg. • The magnesium burnt vigorously. • Ants swarmed all over …

Everyday, informal language:	Formal language:
• The bacteria passed away.	• The bacteria died.
• The results don't ...	• The results do not ...
• We guessed that ...	• It was hypothesised that ...
• Previous researchers were slack and missed ...	• Previous researchers did not perceive that ...
Active voice:	**Passive voice:**
• We recorded oxygen levels every hour.	• The oxygen level was recorded hourly.
• We put 50 g of solute in a conical flask containing distilled water, and then we slowly added $1 \, mol \, L^{-1}$ hydrochloric acid.	• 50 g of solute was placed in a conical flask containing distilled water, and then $1 \, mol \, L^{-1}$ hydrochloric acid was slowly added.

PRESENTING THE INVESTIGATION

Scientific findings may be presented in a variety of ways. A common presentation format at science conferences is a poster. Posters can get ideas across to a large audience in an organised, concise and creative way. Other common presentation formats are essays, reports, oral presentations and articles. Each presentation format has its own conventions. The table summarises characteristics of a number of presentation formats.

Presentation formats and their characteristics		
Format	**Characteristics/inclusions**	
Poster	• Balance of text and visuals • Title, subheadings • Balanced layout • Captions for figures and tables	• References • Hierarchy of font size according to subheading level • Consistent font style—no more than three fonts
Report/article	• Structured with introduction, paragraphs, conclusion • Includes subheadings	• Mainly text • Can include diagrams, graphs, tables
Essay	• Structured with an introduction, paragraphs, conclusion • Introduction states focus of essay • Each paragraph makes a new point supported by evidence	• Each paragraph links back to last paragraph • A text-style presentation format—visuals at end in appendix • Conclusion draws all ideas together but does not include any new information
Oral presentation	• Needs to be engaging • Use cue cards but do not read from them • Watch audience as you speak	• Stand still and don't fidget • Look at audience and appear confident

PROOFREADING

After you have completed the investigation and prepared your presentation, it is important to think about and check what you have done.

Proofread your work to minimise errors and maximise communication of the ideas from your investigation. Use these questions as a proofreading checklist.

Proofreading checklist	Tick ✔
Have I investigated the question fully?	
Have I expressed myself clearly so I communicated my ideas well?	
Have I used the scientific writing style?	
Have I included data analysis?	
Have I checked spelling, punctuation and grammar?	
Have I included references?	
Have I met the requirements of the presentation format?	

Depth study

A depth study is an investigation that allows you to look in more detail into a particular area of interest in the syllabus. A depth study gives you the chance to gain greater understanding of concepts and is designed so you take more responsibility for your own learning.

It is expected that you demonstrate the use of a variety of scientific skills. Depth studies may vary, and may include practical work, fieldwork reports, research assignments, and may be based on primary or secondary data or sources. To fulfil the minimum 15-hour time requirement, your teacher may ask you to complete one very detailed depth study or a number of smaller depth studies.

Your teacher may provide a scaffolded approach with questions that guide you through a depth study, or you may be asked to design it yourself. This section of the toolkit will help you with planning your own depth study.

PLANNING YOUR DEPTH STUDY

Careful planning of the depth study before actually starting the investigation will help you to be clear about what you will do and how you will do it. Think of yourself as taking on the role of your teacher or a scientist: identifying the depth-study investigation topic, deciding how it will be investigated and presented, managing time through the investigation and checking that all syllabus requirements are met.

Clarify your ideas for your depth study, following these steps.

1 List all areas that interest you for your depth study. For example, transition metals, carbon nanomaterials, factors that affect the rate of a reaction, the size of a mole.	**My areas of interest are:** _____ _____ _____ _____
2 Do some quick research into each area of interest. Identify which gives you scope to develop into a depth study.	**My chosen area of investigation is:** _____ _____

3 Decide on the procedure you will use to conduct the depth study:
• a practical investigation:
  - may begin with fieldwork
  - may test a claim or a device
  - may include data analysis
• a secondary-sourced investigation:
  - may begin with fieldwork
  - may be expository (explain something)
  - may be an argument based on evidence
  - may include data analysis
• creating:
  - may be designing and constructing a working model
  - may be creating a portfolio.
	My procedure will be: _____ _____ _____ _____ _____ _____

4 Decide how you will present the depth study. Select a presentation format that suits your type of investigation.
• a practical investigation (practical report)
• a secondary-sourced (research) investigation:
  - documentary
  - media report
  - literature review
  - visual presentation
  - journal article
  - essay
  - environmental management plan
• designing or inventing or creating:
  - portfolio
  - working model.
	I will present my depth study by: _____ _____ _____ _____ _____

Pearson Chemistry 12 NSW | Skills and Assessment | Chemistry toolkit   ISBN 978 1 4886 1934 2

5 Now that you have thought about what and how you will conduct the depth study, think about how you can best use your time. It is tempting to spend most of the time conducting the practical or finding resources for the secondary-sourced investigation. This may leave little time to analyse data and prepare your presentation. Refer to the suggested planning timeline.

Present information and proofread work.

Conduct the investigation.

Organise information and analyse data.

Plan the depth study.

Time allocation   10%   40%   30%   20%

My depth study begins on _____

and is to be completed by _____

Fill in the timeline to plan how you will allocate your time to complete the depth study, including specific dates.

6 Assessment requirements

Depth study must:
- address Working scientifically skills outcomes: Questioning and predicting, and Communicating
- address a minimum of two additional Working scientifically skills outcomes:
  - Planning investigations
  - Conducting investigations
  - Processing data and information
  - Analysing data and information
  - Problem solving
- include at least one Knowledge and understanding outcome.

My depth study will include these Working scientifically skills:
1 Questioning and predicting
2 Communicating
3 _____
4 _____

My depth study covers this/these knowledge and understanding outcome(s):

_____

_____

Study skills

There are a variety of techniques or strategies to help you study. You may find that you use different strategies in different situations. For example, you may prefer to highlight key phrases in your notebook throughout the year but make summaries of topics before an examination. The strategies you choose depend on personal preference and may not be the same as those used by classmates.

Effective study skills involve more than the learning strategies you use. Equally important is when you use skills. It is more effective to apply study skills throughout the year, revising and consolidating your knowledge as you progress through the course, rather than doing a rushed cram just before the examination. Revise work regularly. Being organised is the key to reducing your stress and setting up a study plan.

GETTING ORGANISED

To get yourself organised, try the following steps:
- Use a diary to write down all homework and assessment tasks as soon as you get them. Note due dates and what you have to do.
- Be specific about the tasks you need to do. Rather than writing 'do chemistry' it is more effective to note things such as which questions to answer and which page to look at in your student book.

- Write a list of everything you need to do each day. Tick off or cross out items as you complete them.
- Break down larger tasks into smaller, separate parts that are manageable.
- Make sure your lists and planners are realistic. Do not set yourself more than you can actually do.

STUDY TECHNIQUES

Studying requires concentration. Remove any distractions, and factor in some breaks. Allow a 10-minute break every hour. Vary your study technique depending on the content to be learned and your personal preference. Although you may have already found a study technique that works for you, also consider the options on the next page.

Study technique	Tips
Highlighting Dynamic equilibrium A dynamic equilibrium occurs when the <u>forward and reverse reactions occur simultaneously at the same rate</u>. The reaction is 'incomplete' and <u>all of the substances are present</u> in the mixture. <u>Bonds are constantly being broken and new bonds are constantly being formed</u> as the reactants and products continue to be converted from one to the other.	• Highlight or underline key points as you read your notes or text.
Summary notes *IONIC COMPOUNDS* *Common properties of ionic compounds:* • *brittle, which means they shatter when hit with a hammer* • *hard, which means they are resistant to scratching* • *high melting point* • *unable to conduct electricity in solid state* • *good electrical conductor in liquid or aqueous states*	• Create a list of key headings and add some dot points about each heading. • Write your own summary of the key ideas in each chapter. • Use headings and subheadings. • Underline key words and key phrases. • Use simple diagrams. • The most effective chapter summaries are clear, to the point and uncluttered.
Diagrams 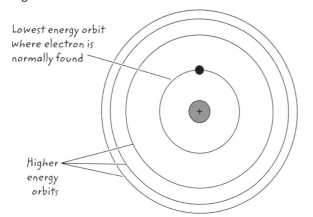 Lowest energy orbit where electron is normally found Higher energy orbits	• Diagrams can be used as a summary of key concepts. • They are useful memory triggers. • Diagrams cover a lot of information in a visual way, with minimal text.
Concept maps 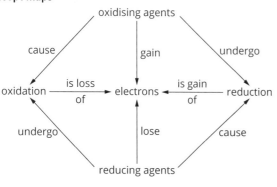	• Concept maps are a great way of connecting key terms and ideas in a simple and ordered way. • Use the lines that connect ideas to note the relationships between the words and phrases. • They may include text and images. • They may be a simple or more complex summary tool. • Concept maps and other graphic organisers such as Venn diagrams and flow charts show how information is connected and help deepen understanding.
Tables	• Tables are useful to show relationships between different factors. • Information is uncluttered.

Subatomic particles

Particle	Relative mass	Charge	Location
neutron	1	neutral	nucleus
proton	1	positive	nucleus
electron	$\frac{1}{1800}$	negative	orbiting nucleus

Mnemonic devices OIL RIG: oxidation is loss; reduction is gain	• Mnemonic tools help you remember information. • To remember the classification of living things, memorise the sentence shown, which contains the initial letters for the classification types.
Glossary *Redox – a reaction where an electron is transferred from the reducing agent to the oxidising agent – both oxidation and reduction occur* *Enthalpy – heat content, symbol H*	• Compile your own glossary—writing the terms and definitions will make them easier to remember. • Add images to help you remember. • Write each term in a sentence. • Memorise these terms and definitions.
Trigger words *Equilibrium* • *reversible and irreversible reactions* • *Le Châtelier's principle*	• Write down the key words associated with a topic or theme. • Trigger words are useful in helping to remember other related words and ideas.
Repeating information aloud	• This is a good way to remember and to force yourself to slow down and absorb the information.
Practice	• Do as many review questions and old exams as possible.
Flash cards What is the Schrödinger model? Identify the states of matter and changes between them.	• Making flash cards helps your understanding. • Make your own cards. • Write a question on one side and the answer on the back. • Cards can include definitions, brief explanations, diagrams, equations and graphs.
Teaching someone	• Teach friends or family members. • Teaching a difficult concept to someone means you must first understand the concept yourself.
Handwriting notes	• Hand-write rather than type summary notes. • Remember, the examination requires you to write answers. • Practise writing for long stretches of time and make sure your writing is legible.
Responding to feedback and self-correcting	• Check through all feedback from your teacher. • Highlight what was right or wrong. • Attempt to identify where you have errors and rework the answer to get it right.

EXAMINATION PREPARATION

In the weeks before the examination, begin your exam preparation. The earlier you begin revising, the easier it will be. It is also helpful to begin practising exam-style questions as early as possible, not just in the weeks ahead of the exam.

Like most skills, practice will improve your ability to do exams and to handle different types of exam question. Doing practice exams is vital because you gain experience in:
• using reading time effectively before starting to write
• allocating the right amount of time to each question
• working to a time limit
• reading and interpreting questions
• understanding what is required by each question
• planning answers
• deciding on relevant information
• proofreading/checking over your own answers
• writing efficiently for the duration of the exam.

Use your practice exam experience not only to revise but also to analyse your strengths and weaknesses, and to assess how you managed your time.

Use the following checklist as a reminder of your study program.

Study program checklist	Tick ✔
Have I revised all areas of the course?	
Have I highlighted important points?	
Have I made a summary of the important points in each topic?	
Have I read over my revision notes?	
Have I looked at and worked through sample exam papers?	
Have I answered practice questions in the appropriate time limit?	

EXAMINATION STRATEGIES

Familiarise yourself with the conditions of the examination well before the day you sit the exam. You should know:

- the number of exams for the subject
- the amount of reading time allowed in the exam before writing begins
- the amount of writing time allocated
- any particular equipment allowed and/or required, such as a calculator, pencils, pens and ruler
- strategies to tackle the exam. Exam strategies are listed in the table.

Exam strategies

Reading time
- You will be given 5 minutes of reading time.
- Remember that no writing at all is allowed during this time—no note-taking, no highlighting, no underlining.
- Read the instructions.
- Read the short-answer questions first—this will give you an overall sense of the themes of questions that require written responses.
- Read the multiple-choice questions next.
- Decide the order in which you will answer questions. Start with what you consider to be the easiest question to build confidence.

Writing time
- You will be given 3 hours of working time.
- Begin with the multiple-choice questions.
- Answer every multiple-choice question, even if you can only make an educated guess.
- If you are unsure of an answer to a multiple-choice question, mark it so you can come back to it if time allows.
- Attempt the short-answer questions next.
- Attempt the easiest short-answer questions first and work your way to the more challenging questions.

Tips for answering questions
- Carefully read each question, underlining key words.
- Be aware that most questions are structured so they become more challenging towards the end. You may not be able to answer the last part of a question but you can earn most of the marks by answering the easier parts of the question.
- Look carefully at any diagrams, pictures, tables and graphs and make sure you understand their relevance to the questions involved.
- For questions with graphs, read the labels on the axes carefully, so that you can establish the relationship the graph is showing.
- For questions with tables, read the headings on the columns and rows carefully, so that you can analyse the content of the table effectively.
- Check for the key words in a question. Highlight them but don't colour the whole question.
- Plan your answers before you write, remembering to address the exam criteria.
- For questions with parts, read the whole question first. This gives you an overall picture of the question. It will also help to ensure that you do not repeat yourself in subsequent parts of the question.
- Make sure you actually answer the question that is asked.
- Once you have answered the question, re-read your answer and then re-read the question, to ensure that you have actually answered the question.
- When writing a definition, don't use the word you are defining in your definition.
- If giving values from a graph, use a ruler to line up points with the axes so you can be accurate, and always include units in your answer.
- Be sure to attempt all questions.
- Read over your answers to pick up careless errors—the mind is faster than the hand, and you may not always write what you intend (especially when you have limited time).
- Write legibly. Exams are scanned and marked online. If the assessor can't read your answer, they can't mark it as correct.
- Keep an eye on the time.
- Never leave an exam early. Use any spare time to re-read and check your answers.

Exam cues
- The number of marks allocated to a question provides a clue about how much you are expected to write. Two marks usually means you need to make a minimum of two points.
- The number of lines allowed for the answer indicates the length of the expected answer. If your writing is large, you may need to turn the page and continue on the back. Make sure you indicate that the examiner must turn to the back of the page for the rest of the answer. Where the answer continues, clearly state that it is the continuation of the question and state the question number.

 Pearson Chemistry 12 NSW | Skills and Assessment | Chemistry toolkit ISBN 978 1 4886 1934 2

HANDLING EXAM QUESTIONS

The exam is divided into two sections: Section I consists of 20 multiple-choice questions and Section II contains a series of short-answer questions.

Multiple-choice questions	Short-answer questions
• In many cases you can use your basic knowledge of the subject to cancel out one or two options. • Mark an answer to every question on your answer sheet as you go through them. This avoids leaving any questions unanswered if you run out of time, and avoids getting out of order by leaving blank rows. You can always go back and change the questions you were unsure about. • Circle the letter of your answer to the question on the exam paper as well, so you can easily check if you get out of sync on the answer sheet. • If you are finding a question very difficult, don't spend too much time on it as it is only worth 1 mark. Guess an answer if necessary then mark the question on your paper and come back to it at the end if you have time. • If you have time at the end of the exam, redo the questions with your original answer covered and compare.	• Be careful to do what the question asks. For example, do you need to identify, describe, explain or compare? Each requires a different response. • When in doubt, point it out, i.e. give a thorough answer. Dot points and labelled diagrams are acceptable as long as you fully address the question. • Tailor your answer specifically to the question being asked. Don't rely on a general answer when given a specific scenario. For example indicate in which direction the equilibrium shifted, don't just say it shifted. • Look at the marks allocated for an indication of the level of detail required. Generally 1 mark = 1 key point, 2 marks = 2 key points, etc. • Set out your answers clearly, stating the formulae you intend to use as this may earn marks, e.g. $n = \frac{m}{M}$. • Show your working because it is easier for you to check and because you often gain part marks and consequential marks if the marker can see where you made an error. • Read over and use any values listed in the data booklet given to you with the exam paper, such as relative atomic masses. • Take care to include units in your answers if they are required. • Use an appropriate number of significant figures in your results. It is important to record data to the number of significant figures available from the equipment or observation. Using either a greater or smaller number of significant figures can be misleading and can lose you marks.

Every year examiners comment that many students fail to answer the question, that is, students' answers are 'not relevant' and are 'off the point'.

Giving a relevant answer to a question is vital and depends on:
• choosing appropriate content
• using content purposefully to do what is asked (see the Key action words list below).

Key action word list	
Analyse	Break down into key points; show the essence of; inquire into; identify components and the relationship between them; draw out and relate implications
Compare	Show points of similarity and points of difference
Describe	Give the general features/characteristics of
Design	Provide steps for an experiment or procedure
Evaluate	Make a judgement based on criteria; determine the value of
Explain	Provide details to give the reader an understanding of; relate cause and effect; make the relationships between things evident; provide why and/or how
Justify	Demonstrate the correctness of (by giving evidence); give evidence in support of an argument or conclusion
Suggest	Put forward ideas, proposals, recommendations
How effective ...?	Make a judgement based on criteria; determine the value of

EXAMPLES OF EXAM RESPONSES

Each year the examiners write an assessment report on the last exam. Reading these reports is a good way to understand what the examiners expected in the answers. The reports show where students showed strong responses and where improvement could be found.

Looking closely at sample responses will help you identify what is required to gain full marks. Two sample responses are provided below: one has room for improvement (low-level response) while the other is well done (high-level response). The annotations draw your attention to key points to note in each response.

High-level responses

Question 1 Carbon disulfide gas (CS_2) is used in the manufacture of rayon. $CS_2(g)$ can be made in an endothermic gas-phase reaction between sulfur trioxide gas (SO_3) and carbon dioxide. Oxygen gas is also produced in the reaction.

a Write a balanced chemical equation for the reaction.

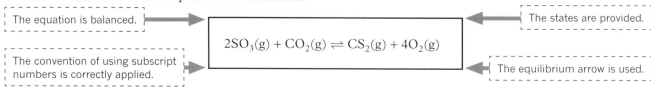

The equation is balanced.

The states are provided.

$$2SO_3(g) + CO_2(g) \rightleftharpoons CS_2(g) + 4O_2(g)$$

The convention of using subscript numbers is correctly applied.

The equilibrium arrow is used.

b Write an expression for the equilibrium constant of the reaction.

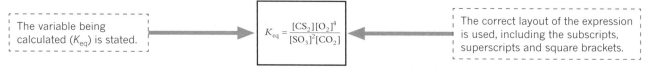

The variable being calculated (K_{eq}) is stated.

$$K_{eq} = \frac{[CS_2][O_2]^4}{[SO_3]^2[CO_2]}$$

The correct layout of the expression is used, including the subscripts, superscripts and square brackets.

c An equilibrium mixture of these gases was made by mixing sulfur trioxide and carbon dioxide. The equilibrium mixture consisted of 0.028 mol of CS_2, 0.022 mol of SO_3, 0.014 mol of CO_2 and an unknown amount of O_2 in a 20 L vessel. Calculate the:

i amount of O_2, in mol, present in the equilibrium mixture

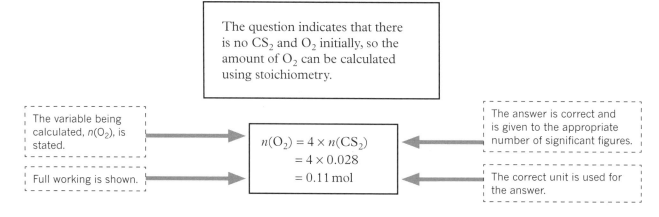

The question indicates that there is no CS_2 and O_2 initially, so the amount of O_2 can be calculated using stoichiometry.

The variable being calculated, $n(O_2)$, is stated.

The answer is correct and is given to the appropriate number of significant figures.

$$n(O_2) = 4 \times n(CS_2)$$
$$= 4 \times 0.028$$
$$= 0.11 \, mol$$

Full working is shown.

The correct unit is used for the answer.

ii value of the equilibrium constant at that temperature.

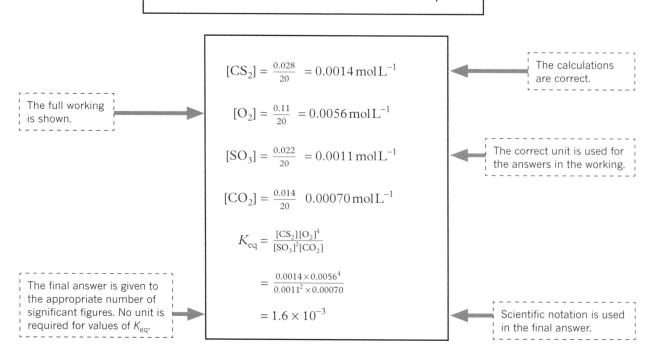

The mole amounts are converted to concentrations using the volume of 20 L and the relationship: $c = \frac{n}{V}$

$$[CS_2] = \frac{0.028}{20} = 0.0014 \, mol \, L^{-1}$$

The calculations are correct.

The full working is shown.

$$[O_2] = \frac{0.11}{20} = 0.0056 \, mol \, L^{-1}$$

$$[SO_3] = \frac{0.022}{20} = 0.0011 \, mol \, L^{-1}$$

The correct unit is used for the answers in the working.

$$[CO_2] = \frac{0.014}{20} \quad 0.00070 \, mol \, L^{-1}$$

$$K_{eq} = \frac{[CS_2][O_2]^4}{[SO_3]^2[CO_2]}$$

The final answer is given to the appropriate number of significant figures. No unit is required for values of K_{eq}.

$$= \frac{0.0014 \times 0.0056^4}{0.0011^2 \times 0.00070}$$

$$= 1.6 \times 10^{-3}$$

Scientific notation is used in the final answer.

Low-level responses

Question 1 Carbon disulfide gas (CS_2) is used in the manufacture of rayon. $CS_2(g)$ can be made in an endothermic gas-phase reaction between sulfur trioxide gas (SO_3) and carbon dioxide. Oxygen gas is also produced in the reaction.

a Write a balanced chemical equation for the reaction.

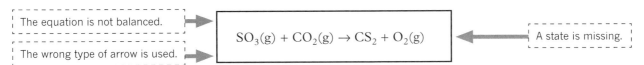

The equation is not balanced.

The wrong type of arrow is used.

$$SO_3(g) + CO_2(g) \rightarrow CS_2 + O_2(g)$$

A state is missing.

b Write an expression for the equilibrium constant of the reaction.

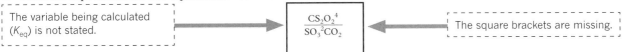

The variable being calculated (K_{eq}) is not stated.

$$\frac{CS_2O_2{}^4}{SO_3{}^2CO_2}$$

The square brackets are missing.

c An equilibrium mixture of these gases was made by mixing sulfur trioxide and carbon dioxide. The equilibrium mixture consisted of 0.028 mol of CS_2, 0.022 mol of SO_3, 0.014 mol of CO_2 and an unknown amount of O_2 in a 20 L vessel. Calculate the:

i amount of O_2, in mol, present in the equilibrium mixture

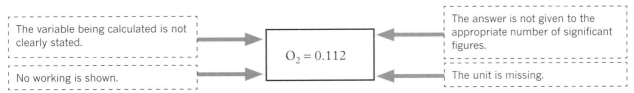

The variable being calculated is not clearly stated.

No working is shown.

$$O_2 = 0.112$$

The answer is not given to the appropriate number of significant figures.

The unit is missing.

ii value of the equilibrium constant at that temperature.

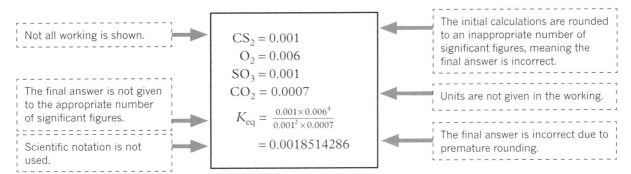

Not all working is shown.

The final answer is not given to the appropriate number of significant figures.

Scientific notation is not used.

$CS_2 = 0.001$
$O_2 = 0.006$
$SO_3 = 0.001$
$CO_2 = 0.0007$

$$K_{eq} = \frac{0.001 \times 0.006^4}{0.001^2 \times 0.0007}$$

$$= 0.0018514286$$

The initial calculations are rounded to an inappropriate number of significant figures, meaning the final answer is incorrect.

Units are not given in the working.

The final answer is incorrect due to premature rounding.

GETTING READY

Once you have finished revising and feel confident with the material, use the checklist below to make sure you are prepared before the exam day arrives.

The exam itself	Tick ✔
Have you:	
• checked the exact exam requirements?	
• obtained and carefully read the instruction cover sheet from previous exams? (Check that there are no changes expected for your exam.)	
• planned how to best use your reading time?	
Practical steps	
Have you:	
• assembled all materials required and allowed? This includes:	
– black pens to write your answers	
– pencils of the correct lead for the multiple choice answer sheet	
– sharpeners, erasers, rulers and other permissible materials like calculators and spare batteries	
– a water bottle (check that your bottle meets the requirements—it may need to be clear with no label)	
– a watch to keep track of the time (you are not permitted to look at mobile phones)	
• double-checked dates, times and locations for each exam?	
• remembered your student number?	
• packed a form of photo ID (if required)?	
• arranged transport, allowing ample time to avoid rushing and to manage possible delays? (Be sure to arrive early to settle nerves and gather thoughts.)	
• planned for appropriate meals and drinks, as exam times vary? (Avoid heavy meals before exams as they make you sleepy.)	

Equilibrium and acid reactions

Outcomes

By the end of this module you will be able to:

- select and process appropriate qualitative and quantitative data and information using a range of appropriate media CH12-4
- analyse and evaluate primary and secondary data and information CH12-5
- solve scientific problems using primary and secondary data, critical thinking skills and scientific processes CH12-6
- communicate scientific understanding using suitable language and terminology for a specific audience or purpose CH12-7
- explain the characteristics of equilibrium systems, and the factors that affect these systems CH12-12

Content

STATIC AND DYNAMIC EQUILIBRIUM

INQUIRY QUESTION What happens when chemical reactions do not go through to completion?

By the end of this module you will be able to:

- conduct practical investigations to analyse the reversibility of chemical reactions, for example:
  - cobalt(II) chloride hydrated and dehydrated
  - iron(III) nitrate and potassium thiocyanate
  - burning magnesium
  - burning steel wool (ACSCH090) ICT
- model static and dynamic equilibrium and analyse the differences between open and closed systems (ACSCH079, ACSCH091)
- analyse examples of non-equilibrium systems in terms of the effect of entropy and enthalpy, for example:
  - combustion reactions
  - photosynthesis
- investigate the relationship between collision theory and reaction rate in order to analyse chemical equilibrium reactions (ACSCH070, ACSCH094) ICT

FACTORS THAT AFFECT EQUILIBRIUM

INQUIRY QUESTION What factors affect equilibrium and how?

By the end of this module you will be able to:

- investigate the effects of temperature, concentration, volume and/or pressure on a system at equilibrium and explain how Le Châtelier's principle can be used to predict such effects, for example:
  - heating cobalt(II) chloride hydrate
  - interaction between nitrogen dioxide and dinitrogen tetroxide
  - iron(III) thiocyanate and varying concentration of ions (ACSCH095)

Module 5 • Equilibrium and acid reactions

- explain the overall observations about equilibrium in terms of the collision theory (ACSCH094)
- examine how activation energy and heat of reaction affect the position of equilibrium

CALCULATING THE EQUILIBRIUM CONSTANT (K_{eq})

INQUIRY QUESTION | How can the position of equilibrium be described and what does the equilibrium constant represent?

By the end of this module you will be able to:

- deduce the equilibrium expression (in terms of K_{eq}) for homogeneous reactions occurring in solution (ACSCH079, ACSCH096) ICT N
- perform calculations to find the value of K_{eq} and concentrations of substances within an equilibrium system, and use these values to make predictions on the direction in which a reaction may proceed (ACSCH096) ICT N
- qualitatively analyse the effect of temperature on the value of K_{eq} (ACSCH093) ICT N
- conduct an investigation to determine K_{eq} of a chemical equilibrium system, for example:
  - K_{eq} of the iron(III) thiocyanate equilibrium (ACSCH096) ICT
- explore the use of K_{eq} for different types of chemical reactions, including but not limited to:
  - dissociation of ionic solutions (ACSCH098, ACSCH099)

SOLUTION EQUILIBRIA

INQUIRY QUESTION | How does solubility relate to chemical equilibrium?

By the end of this module you will be able to:

- describe and analyse the processes involved in the dissolution of ionic compounds in water
- investigate the use of solubility equilibria by Aboriginal and Torres Strait Islander Peoples when removing toxicity from foods, for example: AHC
  - toxins in cycad fruit
- conduct an investigation to determine solubility rules, and predict and analyse the composition of substances when two ionic solutions are mixed, for example:
  - potassium chloride and silver nitrate
  - potassium iodide and lead nitrate
  - sodium sulfate and barium nitrate (ACSCH065)
- derive equilibrium expressions for saturated solutions in terms of K_{sp} and calculate the solubility of an ionic substance from its K_{sp} value ICT N
- predict the formation of a precipitate given the standard reference values for K_{sp}

Chemistry Stage 6 Syllabus © NSW Education Standards Authority
for and on behalf of the Crown in right of the State of NSW, 2017.

Key knowledge

Static and dynamic equilibrium

CHEMICAL SYSTEMS

In chemistry, a **system** is usually regarded as the chemical reaction being studied, and the **surroundings** are everything else (the rest of the universe). Systems may be **open systems**, which exchange matter and energy with the surroundings, or **closed systems**, which exchange only energy with the surroundings.

Systems are said to be **homogeneous** if all reactants and products are in the same phase, or **heterogeneous** if different phases are present.

Reversible reactions

Chemical reactions that can occur in both directions are **reversible**. Chemical reactions that can occur only in one direction are **irreversible** or non-reversible, e.g. baking a cake.

Reversible reactions in a closed system eventually reach a point where the rate of the forward reaction is equal to the rate of the reverse reaction. Four examples of systems that can be reversible are:

- the evaporation and condensation of water:
$$H_2O(l) \rightarrow H_2O(g)$$
$$H_2O(g) \rightarrow H_2O(l)$$
The reactions above can be written as:
$$H_2O(l) \rightleftharpoons H_2O(g)$$

- the dissolution and crystallisation of sugar in a saturated solution of sugar in water:
$$C_{12}H_{22}O_{11}(s) \rightleftharpoons C_{12}H_{22}O_{11}(aq)$$

- the reaction between hydrated cobalt(II) chloride and dehydrated cobalt(II) chloride:
$$CoCl_2(s) + 6H_2O\ (l) \rightleftharpoons CoCl_2{\cdot}6H_2O(s)$$
This reaction involves a colour change: $CoCl_2$ is blue and $CoCl_2{\cdot}6H_2O$ is pink.

- the reaction of iron(III) nitrate and potassium thiocyanate:
$$Fe^{3+}(aq) + SCN^-(aq) \rightleftharpoons FeSCN^{2+}(aq)$$
This reaction also involves a colour change: Fe^{3+} solutions are pale yellow, SCN^- solutions are colourless, and $FeSCN^{2+}$ solutions are red.

Consider the reaction that occurs when N_2 gas is mixed with H_2 gas in a sealed container. NH_3 gas is formed, which then decomposes back to N_2 and H_2. The reaction can be represented using double-headed arrows as:

$$N_2(g) + 3H_2(g) \rightleftharpoons 2NH_3(g)$$

When the rates of the forward and reverse reactions are equal the reaction is described as being in **equilibrium** (Figure 5.1).

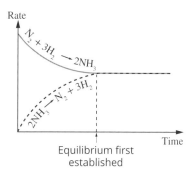

FIGURE 5.1 Graph showing the changes in the rates of the forward and reverse reactions with time as a reaction reaches equilibrium

At equilibrium the concentrations of reactants and products are constant. The reaction appears to have 'stopped' before all the reactants have been converted into products, as shown by the concentration–time graph in Figure 5.2.

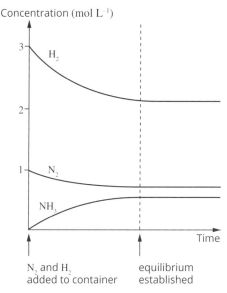

FIGURE 5.2 Changes in concentrations of N_2, H_2 and NH_3 as a mixture of nitrogen and hydrogen gases react at a constant temperature and reach equilibrium

A reaction does not actually 'stop' at equilibrium. Reactants are continuously forming products and products are continuously changing back into reactants; such systems are described as being in **dynamic equilibrium**. Equilibrium can be achieved in closed systems, but not in open systems.

Energy profile diagrams and reversible reactions

When reactions occur, bonds of reactant particles are broken and the new bonds of the product particles are formed. An energy profile diagram shows that once the products form, the reverse process can occur, in which product particles absorb energy to break their bonds and re-form the reactants. GO TO ➤ Year 11 Module 4

In Figure 5.3 the forward reaction is exothermic and the reverse reaction is endothermic. The activation energy for the endothermic reaction is the sum of the ΔH for the reaction and the activation energy for the exothermic reaction.

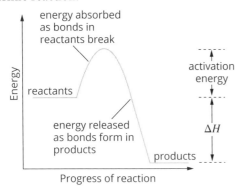

FIGURE 5.3 Energy profile diagram for an exothermic reaction

DYNAMIC EQUILIBRIUM

At equilibrium, the rate of the forward reaction is equal to the rate of the reverse reaction. But the point at which equilibrium is reached is not the same for all reactions. Some reactions go almost to completion, so that when equilibrium is reached almost all the reactants have been converted into products. Other reactions yield almost no products, and most of the reactants are present at any instant. The term **position of equilibrium** is used to describe the extent to which the reaction has proceeded.

The equilibrium law

The relative concentrations of reactants and products at equilibrium can be described using the **equilibrium law**. At a specified temperature, the equilibrium law for the general reaction:

$$a\mathrm{A} + b\mathrm{B} \rightleftharpoons c\mathrm{C} + d\mathrm{D}$$

is given by:

$$K_{eq} = \frac{[C]^c [D]^d}{[A]^a [B]^b}$$

The equilibrium constant, K_{eq}, is the ratio of the equilibrium concentrations of the products to the equilibrium concentrations of the reactants, raised to powers that are their coefficients in the equation. The ratios of reactants to products when equilibrium is reached are different for different reactions.

The ratio of the concentrations of products to reactants can be calculated at any time during the reaction and is called the **reaction quotient**, Q, or concentration fraction.

- If $Q > K_{eq}$ the reaction shifts left to establish equilibrium.
- If $Q < K_{eq}$ the reaction shifts right to establish equilibrium.
- If $Q = K_{eq}$ the reaction is at equilibrium.
  For example, at equilibrium for the reaction:

$$N_2(g) + 3H_2(g) \rightleftharpoons 2NH_3(g)$$

$$Q = K_{eq} = \frac{[NH_3]^2}{[N_2][H_2]^3}$$

You can understand the formation of the equilibrium using **collision theory**, which states that a reaction can occur when reactant particles collide with sufficient energy and have an appropriate molecular orientation.

When the reactants N_2 and H_2 are mixed, initially their particles collide and the reaction commences, producing particles of the product, NH_3. Then, as the concentration of product particles increases and the concentration of reactant particles decreases, the rate of formation of product will decrease and the rate of reformation of reactants will increase. Eventually the rates of the forward and reverse reaction become equal.

The extent of reaction

The value of K_{eq} gives an indication of the **extent of the chemical reaction**, or the position of equilibrium. Different reactions proceed to different extents:

- If $K_{eq} < 10^{-4}$ there is a negligible forward reaction, and mainly reactants are present at equilibrium. The position of equilibrium is 'to the left'.
- If $10^{-4} < K_{eq} < 10^4$ the equilibrium mixture consists of significant amounts of both reactants and products.
- If $K_{eq} > 10^4$ there is an extensive forward reaction, and mainly products are present at equilibrium. The position of equilibrium is 'to the right'.

Factors affecting the value of K_{eq}

The value of the equilibrium constant for a reaction depends on:

- the coefficients in the equation: doubling the coefficients will square the original value of K_{eq}, while halving the coefficients will cause K_{eq} to be the square root of the original
- the direction of the equation: reversing the equation causes K_{eq} to have the inverse value
- the temperature: the effect of change of temperature on the value of K_{eq} is dependent on whether the reaction is exothermic or endothermic (discussed later, see Table 5.3).

Note that the extent of reaction indicates how far the reaction has proceeded when equilibrium is achieved, whereas the rate of reaction indicates how fast the reaction occurred. A reaction can have a large equilibrium constant, K_{eq}, but a very low rate, and vice versa.

STATIC EQUILIBIRUM

Static equilibrium in nature occurs when all forces are in balance; there is no overall force and there is no movement. In chemistry, the term 'static equilibrium' is used to describe chemical reactions in which there is no further conversion of reactants to products or products to reactants and the rates of the forward and reverse reactions are equal to zero. An example of static equilibrium could be considered to be:

$$C(\text{graphite}) \rightleftharpoons C(\text{diamond})$$

Because the activation energy of the reaction for the conversion of diamond to graphite is very high, under normal conditions this reaction would take billions of years. As a result, the rates of the forward and reverse reactions are effectively zero. Table 5.1 summaries the differences between dynamic and static equilibrium in chemical systems.

TABLE 5.1 Differences between dynamic and static equilibrium in chemical systems

Static equilibrium	Dynamic equilibrium
Rates of forward and reverse reactions are equal and almost zero.	Rates of forward and reverse reactions are equal and not zero.
There is no movement of reactant and product particles in either the forward or reverse direction.	Although concentrations do not change, there is an equal rate of reaction of reactants to form products, and vice versa.

NON-EQUILIBRIUM SYSTEMS

Non-equilibrium chemical systems involve reactions that can be considered irreversible and never reach equilibrium. Two examples are combustion and photosynthesis.

For the combustion of hydrocarbons at standard conditions, $\Delta G°$ can be calculated using the equation:

$$\Delta G° = \Delta H° - T\Delta S°$$

$\Delta H°$ is negative and $\Delta S°$ is positive, so $\Delta G°$ is negative, indicating that combustion reactions are spontaneous systems. The products of the reaction, carbon dioxide and water, never recombine to form the hydrocarbon and oxygen so the reaction is described as irreversible.

For photosynthesis, $\Delta H°$ is positive, $\Delta S°$ is negative and $\Delta G°$ is positive. Photosynthesis is therefore a non-spontaneous, endothermic process. It is driven by, or coupled to, spontaneous reactions. The energy released by the spontaneous reactions is used during the many electron transfer steps that occur in photosynthesis.

Heat from these spontaneous reactions is also lost to the surroundings, causing an increase in entropy. Overall, the increase in the entropy of the universe caused by the spontaneous reactions is greater than the decrease in entropy caused by the production of glucose.

Factors that affect equilibrium

LE CHÂTELIER'S PRINCIPLE

Le Châtelier's principle states: 'If a change is imposed on a system at equilibrium, the system will adjust itself to partially oppose the effect of the change'. The equilibrium will not completely return to its original state, but it will tend to oppose the effect.

The effect of a change on an equilibrium can be predicted by Le Châtelier's principle and understood in terms of collision theory and rates of reaction.

Concentration–time graphs and rate–time graphs

Concentration–time graphs and rate–time graphs help to understand the effects of changes to equilibrium. Consider the following equilibrium system:

$$N_2(g) + 3H_2(g) \rightleftharpoons 2NH_3(g)$$

If extra nitrogen gas is added to the container without changing the volume or temperature, the mixture will momentarily not be in equilibrium. The system will adjust to form a new equilibrium with different concentrations of N_2, H_2 and NH_3. Figure 5.4(a) is a concentration–time graph showing this effect.

The rate–time graph in Figure 5.4(b) shows the effects on the rate of the forward and reverse reactions when more nitrogen is added and the system returns to equilibrium. Initially there is a forward reaction. Then the rates of the forward and reverse reaction eventually become equal. The equilibrium position has shifted toward the right.

Because the temperature has not changed, the value of K_{eq} for the equilibrium reaction remains unchanged.

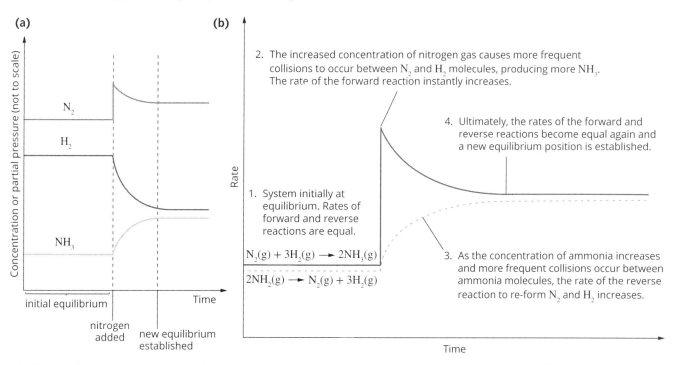

FIGURE 5.4 Concentration–time and rate–time graphs. (a) A representation of changes in concentrations that occur when additional nitrogen gas is added. (b) The effects on the rate of the forward and reverse reactions when more nitrogen is added.

Now consider the aqueous equilibrium system:

$$Fe^{3+}(aq) + SCN^-(aq) \rightleftharpoons FeSCN^{2+}(aq)$$

Figure 5.5 shows the effect of doubling the volume of the system by adding water without any change in temperature.

Although the equilibrium position shifts to the left, the concentrations of Fe^{3+} and SCN^- at the new equilibrium are lower than their concentrations prior to dilution, as the shift in the equilibrium only partially opposes the change.

Adding a catalyst speeds up the rate of the forward and backward reactions equally, so no change in the equilibrium concentrations of the reactants or products occurs. Hence, addition of a catalyst causes no change to the position of the equilibrium and no change in K_{eq}. Table 5.2 summarises the effect of various changes on an equilibrium system when the temperature is kept constant.

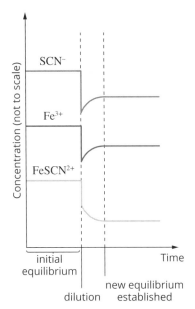

FIGURE 5.5 Effect of dilution on the equilibrium $Fe^{3+}(aq) + SCN^-(aq) \rightleftharpoons FeSCN^{2+}(aq)$

TABLE 5.2 The effect of changes on an equilibrium system when the temperature is constant

Change to system in equilibrium	Effect on equilibrium position predicted by Le Châtelier's principle	Collision theory explanation of effect of change on equilibrium position
Add extra reactant.	Shifts to the right (net forward reaction).	Collisions between reactant molecules are more frequent. Initially the rate of the forward reaction increases. Then there is a gradual increase in the rate of the reverse reaction and a gradual decrease in the rate of the forward reaction until equilibrium is re-established.
Add extra product.	Shifts to the left (net reverse reaction).	The rate of the reverse reaction increases initially. Then there is a gradual increase in the rate of the forward reaction and a gradual decrease in the rate of the reverse reaction until equilibrium is re-established.
Decrease the pressure by increasing the volume (for gases).	Shifts in the direction of the most particles.	Collisions are less frequent overall. The reaction that is less dependent on collisions (fewer particles reacting) occurs to a greater extent.
Add a catalyst.	No change.	No change in either direction, because the rates of the forward and reverse reactions are increased equally. Frequencies of successful collisions are equal.
Add an inert gas (container volume remains constant).	No change.	There is no change in the concentration of reactant or product molecules, so no change in the frequency of collisions between reactants or products or rate of reaction.
Add water (dilution of solutions).	Shifts in the direction of the most particles.	Collisions are less frequent overall. The reaction that is less dependent on collisions (fewer particles reacting) occurs to a greater extent.

Effect of temperature change on equilibrium

Only a change in temperature changes the value of K_{eq}. A rise in temperature decreases the amount of product at equilibrium in an exothermic reaction and increases the amount of product in an endothermic reaction (Table 5.3). These changes are described in Table 5.4 in terms of Le Châtelier's principle and collision theory.

Both the activation energy and heat of reaction affect the position of equilibrium. When the temperature increases, the rates of the forward and reverse reactions increase. The endothermic reaction of an equilibrium system has a greater activation energy and is favoured by an increase in temperature, because a larger proportion of molecules will have sufficient energy to

overcome the activation energy (Figure 5.6). The rate of the endothermic reaction therefore increases more than the rate of the exothermic reaction and the position of equilibrium moves in the direction of the endothermic reaction. The reverse is true for exothermic reactions.

TABLE 5.3 The relationship between K_{eq} and ΔH as temperature increases

Sign of ΔH	Effect on K_{eq} as temperature increases
− (exothermic)	decreases
+ (endothermic)	increases

TABLE 5.4 The effect of a change on an equilibrium system when the temperature is changed

Change to system in equilibrium	Effect on equilibrium position predicted by Le Châtelier's principle	Collision theory explanation of effect of change on equilibrium position
Increasing the temperature for exothermic reactions	Shifts to the left (to absorb some of the added energy) and K_{eq} decreases.	All molecules have more energy and move faster. The direction of the endothermic reaction is favoured because it requires more energy to occur. Hence the reverse reaction is favoured.
Increasing the temperature for endothermic reactions	Shifts to the right (to absorb some of the added energy) and K_{eq} increases.	All molecules have more energy and move faster. The direction of the endothermic reaction is favoured because it requires more energy to occur. Hence the forward reaction is favoured.

(a)

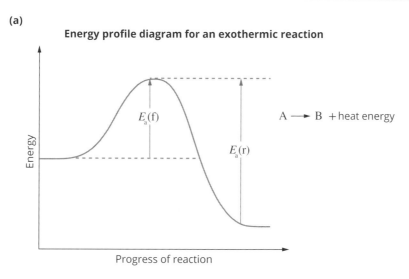

Energy profile diagram for an exothermic reaction

$A \longrightarrow B + \text{heat energy}$

(b)

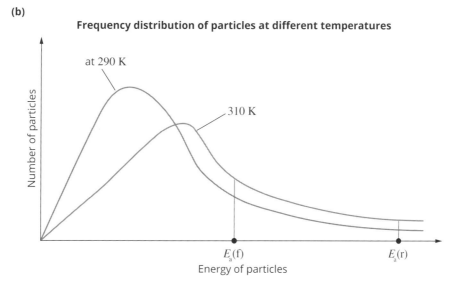

Frequency distribution of particles at different temperatures

FIGURE 5.6 (a) Energy profile diagram for an exothermic reaction. The activation energy, $E_a(f)$, is less than the activation energy of the reverse reaction, $E_a(r)$. (b) The frequency distribution of molecules at two different temperatures. At the higher temperature, a greater proportion of particles have the necessary activation energy for the endothermic reverse reaction.

Consider the exothermic system when brown NO_2 gas is converted to colourless N_2O_4 gas:

$$2NO_2(g) \rightleftharpoons N_2O_4(g) \qquad \Delta H = -58\,\text{kJ}\,\text{mol}^{-1}$$

An increase in temperature will cause the reverse reaction to occur, as indicated in Figure 5.7. The value of the K_{eq} for the new equilibrium will decrease.

In summary, as temperature increases, K_{eq} will:
- increase for an endothermic reaction
- decrease for an exothermic reaction.

The magnitude of ΔH determines the size of the change in K_{eq} for a particular change of temperature.

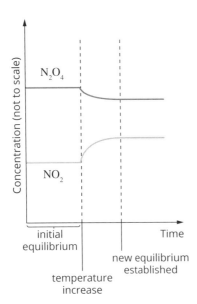

FIGURE 5.7 The effect of increasing the temperature on the equilibrium $2NO_2(g) \rightleftharpoons N_2O_4(g)$

Calculating an equilibrium constant

At a specified temperature, the value of K_{eq} can be calculated from the equilibrium molar concentrations for the reactants and the products. Conversely, the concentration of a particular reactant or product can be calculated if the value of K_{eq} and the concentrations of the other reactants and products are known.

The worksheets in this skills and assessment book will give you practice performing calculations involving equilibrium constants.

Solubility and equilibria

DISSOLUTION OF IONIC COMPOUNDS

The polar nature of water

Water is abundant in the environment. Its unique properties allow it to support life in many different ways. The key points about the structure of water are listed below.

- Each water molecule contains two hydrogen atoms covalently bonded to a single oxygen atom.
- The oxygen atom in each water molecule has two non-bonding electron pairs ('lone pairs').
- The covalent bonds within the molecule are polar; the oxygen atom has a higher electronegativity than the hydrogen atoms. The oxygen has a greater share of the shared electron pair and so carries a negative partial charge. Each hydrogen atom carries a positive partial charge.
- Water molecules are V-shaped and polar.
- The main intermolecular forces between water molecules are **hydrogen bonds** between the partial positive charge on a hydrogen atom on one molecule and a non-bonding pair of electrons on the oxygen atom of another (Figure 5.8).

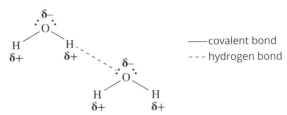

FIGURE 5.8 The structure of water molecules and the bonding between them

Water as a solvent

Solutes dissolve in solvents to form solutions. Figure 5.9 shows the three processes that occur when solutions form.

- In the solute, bonds between particles break.
- In the solvent, intermolecular bonds break.
- In the new solution, bonds form between solvent and solvent particles.

Solvent—particles moving at random

Solute—particles in network

Solution—particles moving at random
- The forces between solute particles have been overcome.
- The forces between some solvent molecules have been overcome.
- New forces formed between solute particles and some solvent particles.

FIGURE 5.9 Rearrangement of particles when a solute dissolves in a solvent

For a solute to dissolve, the force of attraction between the solute and solvent particles must be stronger than or similar to the solute-solute and solvent-solvent interparticle bonds.

The polar nature of water molecules and their ability to form hydrogen bonds enable water to dissolve other polar covalent substances as well as many ionic substances. Water does not readily dissolve non-polar substances.

When the maximum mass of solute dissolves at a specified temperature, the solution is described as **saturated**. **Unsaturated solutions** can dissolve more solute at the specified temperature. Supersaturated solutions are in an unstable state, in which more solute is dissolved than in a saturated solution at that temperature.

Water-soluble substances dissolve in one of three ways (Table 5.5):

- For polar covalent molecules that form hydrogen bonds, the polar molecules of the solute separate from each other and form hydrogen bonds with water molecules. Ethanol is an example.

$$C_2H_5OH(l) \xrightarrow{H_2O} C_2H_5OH(aq)$$

- For polar molecules that ionise, the hydrogen atom has such a strong attraction to water that the polar covalent bond between the hydrogen atom and the rest of the molecule breaks (**dissociates**) and forms ions (**ionises**). The bonding electrons stay with the more electronegative atom, giving it a negative charge, and the hydrogen ion, or proton, bonds to water, forming a hydronium ion, H_3O^+. The resultant ions then become **hydrated**, that is, surrounded by water molecules. Hydrogen chloride is an example.

$$HCl(g) + H_2O(l) \rightarrow H_3O^+(aq) + Cl^-(aq)$$

- For ionic compounds, attraction to the polar water molecules causes the ions in some ionic lattices to dissociate and become hydrated. Sodium chloride is an example:

$$NaCl(s) \xrightarrow{H_2O} Na^+(aq) + Cl^-(aq)$$

Table 5.6 summarises the different ways in which substances dissolve.

TABLE 5.5 Examples of the three ways solutes can dissolve in water

Substance	Bond broken in solute	Bonds formed with water	Arrangement of dissolved particles in solution
ethanol, C_2H_5OH	hydrogen bonds between ethanol molecules	hydrogen bonds between ethanol and water molecules	
hydrogen chloride, HCl	covalent bond between H and Cl atom in the hydrogen chloride molecule	covalent bond between hydrogen atom from HCl and oxygen atom on water molecule forming H_3O^+ ion; ion–dipole bonds between newly formed ions and polar water molecules	
sodium chloride, NaCl	ionic bonds between Na^+ and Cl^- ions	ion-dipole interactions between dissociated ions and polar water molecules	

TABLE 5.6 Summary of the different ways substances dissolve

	Ionic compounds	Non-ionising covalent compounds	Ionising covalent compounds
Examples	$CuSO_4$, NaCl, $Ca(OH)_2$	sugar, glucose, ethanol	HCl, H_2SO_4, HNO_3, CH_3COOH
Name of process	dissociation	—	dissociation and ionisation
Particles present before dissolving occurs	ions	molecules	molecules
Particles present after dissolving occurs	ions	molecules	ions
Example of equation	$NaCl(s) \xrightarrow{H_2O} Na^+(aq) + Cl^-(aq)$	$C_{12}H_{22}O_{11}(s) \xrightarrow{H_2O} C_{12}H_{22}O_{11}(aq)$	$HCl(g) + H_2O(l) \rightarrow H_3O^+(aq) + Cl^-(aq)$

An application of solutions: Detoxifying food

For thousands of years, Aboriginal and Torres Strait Islanders have used different methods to remove toxicity from the cycad seeds, enabling them to be used as a rich food source. One simple way involved the solvent properties of water. The kernels were cut open and left in water so that the soluble toxins dissolved. Once the toxins were removed, the kernels were ground into flour and used to make bread.

SOLUBILITY OF IONIC SUBSTANCES

Not all ionic substances dissolve well in water, although their **solubility** tends to increase with increasing water temperature. Solubility can be measured using different units, but $mol\,L^{-1}$ is common. The solubility table below (Table 5.7) summarises the solubility of many common ionic compounds in water. It is useful to remember that all compounds containing the following ions are soluble:

- sodium
- nitrate
- ammonium
- acetate (also known as ethanoate)
- potassium.

You can remember this as the SNAAP rule (**S**odium, **N**itrate, **A**mmonium, **A**cetate, **P**otassium). (You may also see this written as the SNAPE rule: Sodium, Nitrate, Ammonium, Potassium, Ethanoate.)

TABLE 5.7 Solubility of selected ionic compounds in water

Soluble in water (> 0.1 mol dissolves per L at 25°C)	Exceptions: insoluble (< 0.01 mol dissolves per L at 25°C)	Exceptions: slightly soluble (0.01–0.1 mol dissolves per L at 25°C)
all nitrates, NO_3^-	no exceptions	no exceptions
all salts of ammonium, NH_4^+	no exceptions	no exceptions
all salts of sodium, Na^+, and potassium, K^+	no exceptions	no exceptions
all ethanoates (acetates) CH_3COO^-	no exceptions	no exceptions
most sulfates, SO_4^{2-}	$BaSO_4$, $PbSO_4$, $SrSO_4$	$CaSO_4$, Ag_2SO_4
most chlorides, Cl^-, bromides, Br^-, and iodides, I^-	$AgCl$, $AgBr$, AgI, PbI_2	no exceptions
Insoluble in water	**Exceptions: soluble**	**Exceptions: slightly soluble**
most hydroxides, OH^-	$NaOH$, KOH, $Ba(OH)_2$, NH_4OH	$Ca(OH)_2$, $Sr(OH)_2$
most carbonates, CO_3^{2-}	Na_2CO_3, K_2CO_3, $(NH_4)_2CO_3$	No important exceptions
most phosphates, PO_4^{3-}	Na_2PO_4, K_2PO_4, $(NH_4)_2PO_4$	No important exceptions
most sulfides, S^{2-}	Na_2S, K_2S, $(NH_4)_2S$	No important exceptions

Precipitation reactions

When two aqueous solutions are mixed, an insoluble substance called a **precipitate** sometimes forms (Figure 5.10). The balanced chemical equation for a precipitation reaction has the general form:

ionic compound (aq) + ionic compound (aq) → precipitate (s) + ionic compound (aq)

For example:

$$Pb(NO_3)_2(aq) + 2KI(aq) \rightarrow PbI_2(s) + 2KNO_3(aq)$$

In this case, PbI_2 is the precipitate. K^+ and NO_3^- ions remain dissolved in solution and are termed **spectator ions**.

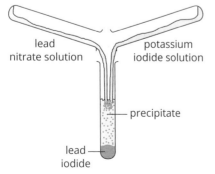

FIGURE 5.10 Mixing solutions of lead nitrate and potassium iodide forms a precipitate of solid lead iodide.

An ionic equation omits spectator ions to give a more accurate picture of the reaction taking place. For example:

$$Pb^{2+}(aq) + 2I^-(aq) \rightarrow PbI_2(s)$$

When writing balanced ionic equations, ensure that:

- species that have (s), (l) or (g) beside them appear in the equation and are not separated into different particles.
- ions with (aq) beside them that appear on both sides of the arrow are omitted from the equation. These are spectator ions.

SOLUBILITY AND EQUILIBRIUM

K_{eq} for heterogeneous equilibria

The expression for K_{eq} for a homogeneous equilibrium includes the molar concentrations (concentrations in $mol\,L^{-1}$) for all the reactants and products in the equilibrium. However, for a heterogeneous equilibrium the concentrations for a pure solid or a pure liquid are assigned the value of 1 in the expression for K_{eq}. These concentrations are constant and can be removed from the expression for the K_{eq}.

ISBN 978 1 4886 1934 2

An example of a heterogenous equilibrium and the associated expression for K_{eq} is the dissolution of an ionic solid in water to form an aqueous solution, e.g for PbI_2:

$$PbI_2(s) \rightleftharpoons Pb^{2+}(aq) + 2I^-(aq) \qquad K_{eq} = [Pb^{2+}][I^-]^2$$

Measuring the solubility of ionic solids

When an ionic solid is added to water, it dissociates into separate hydrated ions. Collisions between the dissolved ions can reform the solid. Eventually the rate of the forward reaction is equal to the rate of the reverse reaction and equilibrium is achieved. The solution becomes saturated.

Consider the saturated solution of solid PbI_2 shown in Figure 5.11 where equilibrium exists between the solid and its ions, Pb^{2+} and I^-. The equation can be written as:

$$PbI_2(s) \rightleftharpoons Pb^{2+}(aq) + 2I^-(aq)$$

Because this is a heterogeneous equilibrium system, the concentration of the solid is 1, and the equilibrium constant is written as:

$$K_{eq} = [Pb^{2+}][I^-]^2$$

An equilibrium constant for a saturated solution is called a **solubility product**, K_{sp}. The smaller the K_{sp}, the less soluble the solid is in water.

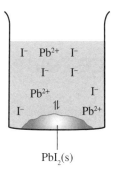

FIGURE 5.11 A saturated solution of solid PbI_2 in equilibrium with its ions, Pb^{2+} and I^-

The solubility product, K_{sp}, of an ionic solid can be used to calculate the solubility, s, of the solid and equilibrium concentrations of the dissolved ions. Solubility, s, is the moles per litre of the solid that has dissolved at that temperature in a saturated solution. Conversely, if the solubility is known then the value of K_{sp} can be determined. Table 5.8 shows the mathematical relationship between K_{sp} and s for two ionic solids.

You can determine whether a solution has reached equilibrium or whether more precipitation or dissolution occurs (Table 5.9) by calculating the reaction quotient, Q, for the system. For the lead iodide solution, Q is equal to $[Pb^{2+}][I^-]^2$. Q is often called the **ionic product** when referring to the dissolution of ionic solids in solution.

TABLE 5.8 Conversion from solubility, s, in $mol\,L^{-1}$ to K_{sp} where s is the amount of an ionic solid that dissolves per litre

Reaction equation	Concentration ($mol\,L^{-1}$) of ions in terms of solubility	K_{sp} expression
$AgCl(s) \rightleftharpoons Ag^+(aq) + Cl^-(aq)$	$[Ag^+] = s$ and $[Cl^-] = s$	$K_{sp} = [Ag^+][Cl^-] = s^2$
$PbI_2(s) \rightleftharpoons Pb^{2+}(aq) + 2I^-(aq)$	$[Pb^{2+}] = s$ and $[I^-] = 2s$	$K_{sp} = [Pb^{2+}][I^-]^2 = s \times (2s)^2 = 4s^3$

TABLE 5.9 The relationship between Q, K_{sp} and the position of equilibrium

$Q > K_{sp}$	Ion concentration is higher than when the system is at equilibrium. The solution is supersaturated. More solid forms (precipitation occurs) to establish equilibrium.
$Q = K_{sp}$	Ion concentration is equal to the equilibrium value, so system is at equilibrium. The solution is saturated.
$Q < K_{sp}$	Ion concentration is lower than when at the system is at equilibrium. The solution is unsaturated. If solid is present, some solid dissolves to establish equilibrium.

WORKSHEET 5.1

Knowledge review—thinking about rates and energy

1. Complete the following table by providing the term to match the definition. This will help you check your knowledge and understanding of the key ideas involved in rates of reaction and energy of reaction, in preparation for your study of equilibrium.

Definition	Correct term
The energy needed to break the bonds between atoms in the reactants to enable a reaction to occur.	
The part of the universe we are studying.	
The name for a theory that accounts for the rates of chemical reactions.	
A system in which only energy is exchanged with the surroundings.	
A substance that increases the rate of reaction but is not consumed in the reaction.	
The speed at which the reaction occurs.	
A reaction that releases energy to the surroundings.	
Name for a chemical equation that includes the enthalpy change of the reaction.	
A reaction for which the ΔH is positive.	
A measure of the number of possible arrangements of a system or the degree of disorder or randomness in the system.	
The quantity that is used to determine if a reaction is spontaneous.	

2. Decide whether each of the following statements is true or false.

Statement	True/False
Rates of reactions can be increased by increasing the concentration of solutions, increasing the surface area of solid reactants and increasing the temperature of the system.	
When ΔG is greater than zero the reaction is non-spontaneous.	
Reactions that are exothermic (ΔH negative) and have an increase in entropy (ΔS positive) are always spontaneous.	
Open systems are only able to exchange matter with the surroundings.	

WORKSHEET 5.2

Exploring equilibrium—reactions in the balance

1 Chemical equilibria can be investigated by mixing different amounts of reactants and products together and measuring the concentrations of all species present at equilibrium. The table gives the results of seven of these experiments for the following equilibrium:

$$H_2(g) + I_2(g) \rightleftharpoons 2HI(g)$$

Equilibrium concentrations (mol L^{-1}) for $H_2(g) + I_2(g) \rightleftharpoons 2HI(g)$ at 458°C

Mixture	$[H_2]$	$[I_2]$	$[HI]$	$[H_2] + [I_2] + [HI]$	$\dfrac{[HI]}{[H_2][I_2]}$	$\dfrac{[HI]^2}{[H_2][I_2]}$
1	0.0056170	0.0005940	0.0126990			
2	0.0045800	0.0009930	0.0148580			
3	0.0038420	0.0015240	0.0168710			
4	0.0046670	0.0010580	0.0154450			
5	0.0016960	0.0016960	0.0118070			
6	0.0014330	0.0014330	0.0099990			
7	0.0042130	0.0042130	0.0294350			

a Calculate the missing entries in the blank columns in the spreadsheet. Which expression was almost constant?

b The ratio that was almost constant is called the equilibrium constant, K_{eq}, for this reaction at the specified temperature. Write the mathematical expression for K_{eq} for this reaction.

c Write a general expression for the equilibrium law for the following reaction:

$$aA(g) + bB(g) \rightleftharpoons cC(g) + dD(g)$$

2 a Write the equation $H_2(g) + I_2(g) \rightleftharpoons 2HI(g)$ in reverse. _____

b Write the mathematical expression for the equilibrium constant for this reverse reaction.

c Use the data for Mixture 1 in question **1** to calculate the value of K_{eq} for this reverse reaction.

d What is the relationship between the constant calculated in part **c** and the constant calculated in question **1**?

e Use your answer to part **c** to calculate the value of K_{eq} for the following reaction:

$$\tfrac{1}{2}H_2(g) + \tfrac{1}{2}I_2(g) \rightleftharpoons HI(g)$$

f What is the relationship between the constant you calculated in part **e** and the constant you calculated in question **1**?

g Complete the following summary statements:

If K_{eq1} is the equilibrium constant for an equation, the constant for the reverse equation is given by K_{eq2} = _____.

If the coefficients in the equation are halved, the constant for the new equation is given by K_{eq3} = _____.

3 a Consider the following solution equilibrium:

$$Fe^{3+}(aq) + SCN^-(aq) \rightleftharpoons FeSCN^{2+}(aq)$$

Sketch concentration–time graphs on the grids provided below if each of the following changes were made to this system at constant temperature.

i A small amount of $Fe^{3+}(aq)$ is added. (Assume the volume change is negligible.)

ii A volume of water is added to the system.

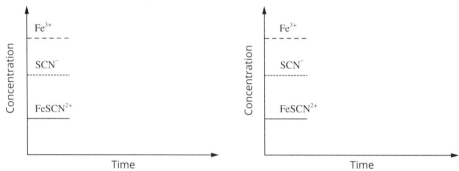

b Sketch the rate–time graph for this system when a small amount of $SCN^-(aq)$ is added, assuming no volume change. Your graph should show what happens to the rates of both the forward and reverse reactions.

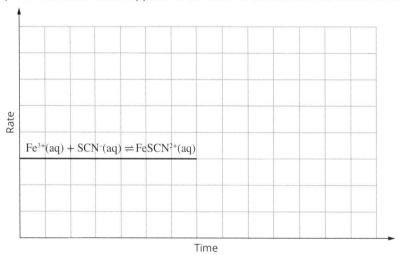

c In terms of collision theory, explain the effects on the rates of the forward and reverse reactions when more SCN^- is added and as the system returns to equilibrium.

_____

_____

_____

4 The following table shows the results of a simple experiment involving temperature changes on the equilibrium at constant volume.

Equilibrium system	Type of reaction	Colour in ice bath	Colour in hot water bath
$Fe^{3+}(aq) + SCN^-(aq) \rightleftharpoons FeSCN^{2+}(aq)$ (pale yellow) (red)	exothermic	red	pale yellow

Complete the table below.

Equilibrium system	Effect of heating on concentration of products	After heating, the position of equilibrium has moved ...	Effect of heating on value of K_{eq}
$Fe^{3+}(aq) + SCN^-(aq) \rightleftharpoons FeSCN^{2+}(aq)$ (pale yellow) (red)			

5 Examine the graph for the following reaction, and answer the questions for the system: $N_2(g) + 3H_2(g) \rightleftharpoons 2NH_3(g)$

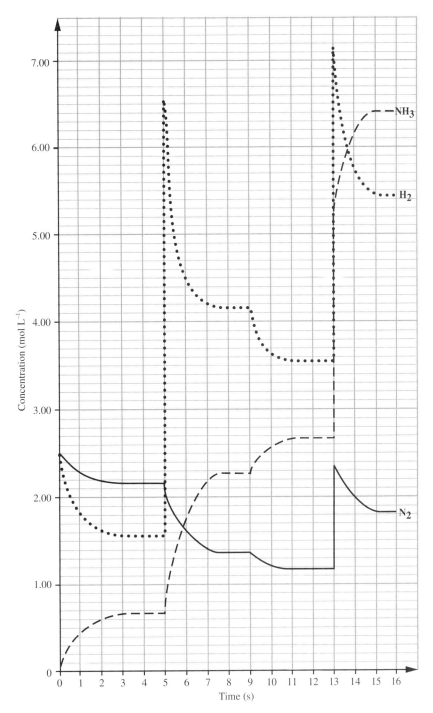

a During which time intervals was the system at equilibrium? _____

b Calculate the equilibrium constant at: **(i)** 4 seconds, **(ii)** 8 seconds, **(iii)** 12 seconds, and **(iv)** 16 seconds.

c Using the answers in part **b** and your knowledge of equilibrium, explain what changes were made to the system at: **(i)** 5 seconds, **(ii)** 9 seconds, and **(iii)** 13 seconds.

| RATING MY LEARNING | My understanding improved | Not confident ⟵ ⟶ Very confident ○ ○ ○ ○ ○ | I answered questions without help | Not confident ⟵ ⟶ Very confident ○ ○ ○ ○ ○ | I corrected my errors without help | Not confident ⟵ ⟶ Very confident ○ ○ ○ ○ ○ |

WORKSHEET 5.3

Calculations—equilibrium constants and concentrations

This worksheet allows you to practise doing calculations involving chemical equilibria.

Steam reforming is used for the large-scale industrial production of hydrogen gas. In this process, methane gas is converted to synthesis gas, which is a mixture of carbon monoxide gas and hydrogen gas. The thermochemical equation is:

$$CH_4(g) + H_2O(g) \rightleftharpoons 3H_2(g) + CO(g) \qquad \Delta H = +206\,kJ\,mol^{-1}$$

The equilibrium constant at 650°C is 2.4×10^{-4}.

1 Write the expression for the equilibrium constant for the equation above.

_____

2 Calculate the equilibrium constant at 650°C and the ΔH value for the equation below.

$$6H_2(g) + 2CO(g) \rightleftharpoons 2CH_4(g) + 2H_2O(g)$$

3 The following gases are added to a sealed 2.00 L container at a constant temperature of 650°C.

- 0.012 mol of methane gas
- 0.0080 mol of water vapour
- 0.016 mol of carbon monoxide gas
- 0.0060 mol of hydrogen gas

a Determine the initial value of the reaction quotient (concentration fraction), Q.

b In which direction would the reaction move to establish equilibrium? Explain.

_____

_____

_____

c The temperature of the equilibrium is increased to 850°C.

i Will the equilibrium constant increase, decrease or remain unchanged? Explain your answer.

_____

_____

_____

ii How will the increased temperature affect the rate and equilibrium yield of the reaction? Explain your answer.

_____

_____

_____

4 An equilibrium mixture of CH_4, H_2O, H_2 and CO was prepared in a 2.00 L flask at another temperature by adding 0.600 mol CH_4 and 0.400 mol of H_2O to the reaction vessel. At equilibrium there was 0.110 mol of CO present.

a Complete the following ICE (Initial, Change, Equilibrium) table to determine the amounts of CH_4, H_2O and H_2 at equilibrium. Let x be the amount of CH_4 used.

	CH_4 +	H_2O ⇌	$3H_2$ +	CO
Initial (mol)	0.600	0.400	0.000	0.000
Change (mol)				
Equilibrium (mol)				0.110

b Calculate the equilibrium concentrations of CH_4, H_2O, H_2 and CO, in mol L^{-1}.

c Calculate the equilibrium constant, K_{eq}, for the reaction at this temperature.

RATING MY LEARNING | My understanding improved — Not confident ◄——► Very confident ○ ○ ○ ○ ○ | I answered questions without help — Not confident ◄——► Very confident ○ ○ ○ ○ ○ | I corrected my errors without help — Not confident ◄——► Very confident ○ ○ ○ ○ ○

ISBN 978 1 4886 1934 2   Pearson Chemistry 12 NSW | Skills and Assessment | Module 5   17

WORKSHEET 5.4

Equilibrium—Le Châtelier's principle and the equilibrium law

1 State Le Châtelier's principle.

_____

_____

2 Consider the following equilibrium system:

$$4HCl(g) + O_2(g) \rightleftharpoons 2H_2O(g) + 2Cl_2(g) \qquad \Delta H = -116\,kJ\,mol^{-1}$$

Predict the effect (increase, decrease, no change) of each of the following changes to the equilibrium system on each quantity in the following table. Briefly explain the reason for your answer by using Le Châtelier's principle.

Predicted effects on equilibrium system			
Quantity	Change	Effect (compared to initial equilibrium)	Reason
$[Cl_2]$	Add O_2 at constant volume and temperature.		
amount of H_2O (in mol)	Decrease the volume of the container at constant temperature.		
$[HCl]$	Decrease the pressure by increasing the volume of the container at constant temperature.		
K_{eq}	Increase the volume of the container at constant temperature.		
K_{eq}	Increase the temperature at constant volume.		
$[O_2]$	Increase the temperature at constant volume.		
$[HCl]$	Add argon gas at constant volume and temperature.		
K_{eq}	Add a catalyst at constant volume and temperature.		

3 Consider the following reaction:

$$2H_2(g) + S_2(g) \rightleftharpoons 2H_2S(g) \qquad K_{eq} = 9.4 \times 10^5 \text{ at } 750°C$$

A mixture of H_2, S_2 and H_2S was allowed to come to equilibrium in a closed 2.0 L container at 750°C. The equilibrium concentrations of H_2 and H_2S gases were analysed and found to be $0.234\,mol\,L^{-1}$ and $0.442\,mol\,L^{-1}$ respectively.

a What does the value of the equilibrium constant for this reaction tell you about the extent of the reaction?

_____

b Write an expression for the equilibrium constant for this reaction.

_____

c Calculate the equilibrium concentration of $S_2(g)$ in the mixture.

ISBN 978 1 4886 1934 2

4 1.364 mol of H_2, 0.682 mol of S_2 and 0.680 mol of H_2S were mixed in another 2.00 L container at 580°C. At equilibrium the concentration of H_2S was measured as 1.010 mol L^{-1}.

a What is the value of the equilibrium constant at this temperature?

b Compare your answer to the value of K_{eq} for this reaction in question **3**. Is this reaction exothermic or endothermic? Give a reason for your answer.

5 Consider the following reaction at equilibrium:

$$N_2O_4(g) \rightleftharpoons 2NO_2(g) \qquad \Delta H = +57 \text{ kJ mol}^{-1} \qquad K_{eq} = 3.62 \times 10^2 \text{ at } 327°C$$

a Calculate the equilibrium constant at 327°C for the following reaction:

$$2NO_2(g) \rightleftharpoons N_2O_4(g)$$

b In terms of Le Châtelier's principle, explain the effect on the position of equilibrium when:

i the temperature is decreased at constant volume

ii the volume of the container is increased at constant temperature.

6 The value of ΔH for a chemical reaction depends on the direction of the equation for the reaction and the coefficients and states of species in the equation. These factors also affect the value of an equilibrium constant. However, when an equation is written in a different way the effects on ΔH and K_{eq} are different.

Complete the following table for the two reactions shown.

Effects on ΔH and K_{eq}					
Equation	ΔH (kJ mol^{-1})	K_{eq} at 527°C	Equation	ΔH (kJ mol^{-1})	K_{eq} at 600°C
$N_2(g) + 3H_2(g) \rightleftharpoons 2NH_3(g)$	–92	0.051	$2SO_2(g) + O_2(g) \rightleftharpoons 2SO_3(g)$	–198	1.56
$2NH_3(g) \rightleftharpoons N_2(g) + 3H_2(g)$				–99	
$2N_2(g) + 6H_2(g) \rightleftharpoons 4NH_3(g)$					2.43
$NH_3(g) \rightleftharpoons \frac{1}{2}N_2(g) + \frac{3}{2}H_2(g)$				+198	

7 Use your results from question **6** to complete the summary statements below.

For ΔH: When equations are reversed, ΔH has the _____ sign and _____ magnitude.

When coefficients are doubled, ΔH has the _____ sign and the magnitude is _____.

When coefficients are halved, ΔH has the _____ sign and the magnitude is _____.

For K_{eq}: When equations are reversed, the value of K_{eq} is _____.

When coefficients are doubled, the value of K_{eq} is _____.

When the coefficients are halved, the value of K_{eq} is _____.

Wonderful water—structure and properties

1   Draw the valence structures of five water molecules as they might appear in a sample of liquid water. Don't forget to show the non-bonding electron pairs (lone pairs) and intermolecular forces.

2   a   What type of bonding holds the oxygen and hydrogen atoms together within the molecule? _____.
        Label one of these bonds on your diagram in question **1**.

    b   Explain why water is a polar molecule.

        _____

        _____

    c   The attraction between different water molecules is mainly due to hydrogen bonding. Label a hydrogen bond on your diagram in question **1**.

    d   Explain what causes hydrogen bonding and why it is stronger than other types of dipole-dipole bonding.

        _____

        _____

3   a   Write a balanced equation to show KI dissolving in water.

        _____

    b   Write a balanced equation for CH_3OH dissolving in water.

        _____

    c   Write a balanced equation for HCl gas dissolving in water.

        _____

4   Sketch the arrangement of water molecules around potassium and iodide ions when KI is dissolved in water.

RATING MY LEARNING	My understanding improved	Not confident ← → Very confident ○ ○ ○ ○ ○	I answered questions without help	Not confident ← → Very confident ○ ○ ○ ○ ○	I corrected my errors without help	Not confident ← → Very confident ○ ○ ○ ○ ○

Solving solubility—predicting precipitation reactions and writing ionic equations

A solubility table summarises the solubility in water of common ionic compounds. Use the solubility data in Table 5.7 on page 10 to answer the questions in this worksheet.

1 The following solutions are mixed together. Indicate whether or not you think a precipitate will form by placing a tick (for yes) or a cross (for no) in each box in the second column. For each predicted precipitate, write a fully balanced chemical equation in the third column.

Solutions mixed	Precipitate? (✓ or ✗)	Balanced chemical equation
potassium chloride + silver nitrate		
copper(II) nitrate + sodium hydroxide		
magnesium nitrate + sodium chloride		
lead nitrate + potassium iodide		
sodium sulfate + barium nitrate		

2 Outline an experimental method a student could follow to obtain a dry sample of silver chloride from solutions of potassium chloride and silver nitrate.

_____

_____

_____

3 Identify the spectator ions in each of the reactions below, and write the ionic equation.

a $2NaBr(aq) + PbCl_2(aq) \rightarrow PbBr_2(s) + 2NaCl(aq)$ Spectator ions: _____

Ionic equation: _____

b $HCl(aq) + KOH(aq) \rightarrow KCl(aq) + H_2O(l)$ Spectator ions: _____

Ionic equation: _____

c $2HCl(aq) + MgO(s) \rightarrow MgCl_2(aq) + H_2O(l)$ Spectator ions: _____

Ionic equation: _____

4 Use the internet to investigate and compare the processes used by Aboriginal and Torres Strait Islanders to remove toxins from foods. Present your findings in a short report below.

_____

_____

_____

_____

_____

_____

RATING MY LEARNING	My understanding improved	Not confident ◄———► Very confident ○ ○ ○ ○ ○	I answered questions without help	Not confident ◄———► Very confident ○ ○ ○ ○ ○	I corrected my errors without help	Not confident ◄———► Very confident ○ ○ ○ ○ ○

WORKSHEET 5.7

Solubility equilibrium—calculating solubility and K_{sp}

A saturated solution forms when the rate of dissolution of an ionic solid equals the rate of precipitation of its ions. This dynamic equilibrium is independent of the amount of solid present, although there must be some solid in equilibrium with the solution. The equilibrium constant for this type of equilibrium is called the solubility product, K_{sp}.

1   For each of the following ionic solids, complete the table by writing the equation for its dissolution in water and the expression for the solubility products.

Solid	Equation for dissolution in water	Expression for K_{sp}
$BaSO_4$		
$AgCl$		
Ag_2CO_3		
$Al(OH)_3$		

2   a   The values of K_{sp} at 25°C for the solids in question 1 are listed in the table below. Calculate the solubility of each substance, in $mol\,L^{-1}$.

Solid	K_{sp}	Calculation of solubility, s (in $mol\,L^{-1}$)
$BaSO_4$	1.08×10^{-10}	
$AgCl$	1.77×10^{-10}	
Ag_2CO_3	8.46×10^{-12}	
$Al(OH)_3$	3.0×10^{-34}	

   b   List these solids in order of solubility, from most soluble to least soluble.

3   Your teeth are composed mainly of the ionic compounds calcium phosphate, $Ca_3(PO_4)_2$ and hydroxyapatite, $Ca_5(PO_4)_3(OH)$.

   a   Given the solubility of $Ca_3(PO_4)_2$ is 7.19×10^{-7}, calculate the K_{sp} of $Ca_3(PO_4)_2$.

   b   Explain why the consumption of carbonated drinks, which have quite a low pH, could increase dental decay.

....

WORKSHEET 5.8

Predicting precipitation using K_{sp}

The reaction quotient, Q, for a system that reaches equilibrium can be determined at any stage during the reaction. By comparing the size of Q with the equilibrium constant, K_{eq}, you can determine which way the reaction will proceed to establish equilibrium, at which point $Q = K_{eq}$.

When an ionic solid forms a saturated solution, the solid is in equilibrium with its ions in solution and $Q = K_{sp}$, where Q is the ion product and K_{sp} is the solubility product. You can predict whether precipitation will occur when two solutions of ions are mixed by comparing Q and K_{sp}. In general, precipitation occurs if the ionic product is greater than the solubility product.

Remember that K_{sp} is the equilibrium constant for the reaction written as the solid in equilibrium with its ions, for example:

$$CaSO_4(s) \rightleftharpoons Ca^{2+}(aq) + SO_4{}^{2-}(aq) \qquad K_{sp} = [Ca^{2+}][SO_4{}^{2-}]$$

1   Consider the following mixtures of chemicals. Complete the table by writing balanced equations and calculating the value of Q. Hence indicate whether precipitation will occur.

Mixture	Balanced equation	K_{sp}	Q	Precipitation occurs (Y or N)?
100 mL 0.5 mol L^{-1} Ca(NO$_3$)$_2$ mixed with 100 mL 0.2 mol L^{-1} Na$_2$SO$_4$		6.1×10^{-5}		
20 mL 0.01 mol L^{-1} AgNO$_3$ mixed with 80 mL 0.05 mol L^{-1} K$_2$CrO$_4$		1.7×10^{-12}		

2   For each of the following 1 L solutions, calculate the minimum concentration of lead ions, Pb^{2+}, in the solution that is needed to cause precipitation of the stated compound.

Precipitate	K_{sp}	Solution	Balanced ionic equation	Calculation of [Pb^{2+}] (in mol L^{-1})
PbS	3×10^{-28}	0.01 mol L^{-1} Na$_2$S		
PbF$_2$	3.3×10^{-8}	0.01 mol L^{-1} NaF		

3   A sample of bore water from a mine contains equal amounts, in mol, of dissolved silver carbonate and iron(II) carbonate. The values of the K_{sp} for these chemicals are:

$K_{sp}(Ag_2CO_3) = 8.10 \times 10^{-12}$

$K_{sp}(FeCO_3) = 3.13 \times 10^{-11}$

Using this data, determine the order in which the ionic solids will precipitate if the water is allowed to evaporate. (Show your calculations below.)

WORKSHEET 5.9

Literacy review—equilibrium terms and expressions

1. Complete the following table to review your understanding of some of the terms in this module.

Term	Meaning
K_{eq}	
Q	
K_{sp}	
equilibrium law	
spectator ions	

2. Select the correct mathematical expressions below and arrange them in order to show how to calculate the solubility of $Ag_3(PO_4)_2$, given the value of the solubility product K_{sp} is 8.89×10^{-17} at 25°C.

   a Let s be the solubility in $mol\,L^{-1}$ of $Ag_3(PO_4)_2$

   b $3s \times 2s = 8.89 \times 10^{-17}$

   c $(3s)^3 \times (2s)^2 = 8.89 \times 10^{-17}$

   d $[Ag^+]^3 \times [PO_4^{3-}]^2 = 8.89 \times 10^{-17}$

   e $[Ag^+] = s$

   f $[Ag^+] = 3s$

   g $[PO_4^{3-}] = 2s$

   h $[Ag^+] \times [PO_4^{3-}] = 8.89 \times 10^{-17}$

3. The following paragraphs about equilibrium contain several factual errors. Highlight the errors and correct them below.

   Dynamic equilibrium occurs when there is a reversible reaction in an open system. In an equilibrium system the rates of the forward and reverse reactions are equal and there is no change in the concentrations of the reactant and product molecules. However, it can be shown that there is continual conversion of reactants to products and vice versa. If the system is closed, it will never achieve equilibrium because only energy is lost to the surroundings.

   The equilibrium law states that at a specific temperature, the equilibrium constant, K_{eq}, is equal to only the concentration of the products divided by the concentration of the reactants. If this concentration ratio, Q, is less than K_{eq} the system will favour the reverse reaction to restore equilibrium.

   When the temperature is decreased for an exothermic reaction, the value of K_{eq}, decreases. When the temperature is increased for an endothermic reaction, K_{eq} increases.

   When reactants are mixed in an open system, collision theory explains that initially, the rate of the forward reaction is low and decreases as the reactants' concentrations decrease. Simultaneously, the reverse reaction is very fast initially and increases as the concentrations of the products increase and collisions between product molecules increase.

   Le Châtelier's principle predicts that when the pressure of a system decreases by increasing the volume, the system will move in the direction of the least particles in order to re-establish equilibrium.

Thinking about my learning

On completion of Module 5: Equilibrium and acid reactions, you should be able to describe, explain and apply the relevant scientific ideas. You should also be able to interpret, analyse and evaluate data.

1   The table lists the key knowledge covered in this module. Read each and reflect on how well you understand each concept. Rate your learning by shading the circle that corresponds to your level of understanding for each concept. It may be helpful to use colour as a visual representation. For example:

   • green—very confident
   • orange—in the middle
   • red—starting to develop.

Concept focus	Rate my learning				
	Starting to develop ⟵⟶ Very confident				
Static and dynamic equilibrium	◯	◯	◯	◯	◯
Factors that affect equilibrium	◯	◯	◯	◯	◯
Calculating the equilibrium constant (K_{eq})	◯	◯	◯	◯	◯
Solution equilibria	◯	◯	◯	◯	◯

2   Consider points you have shaded from starting to develop to middle-level understanding. List specific ideas you can identify that were challenging.

_____

_____

_____

_____

_____

_____

3   Write down two different strategies that you will apply to help further your understanding of these ideas.

_____

_____

_____

_____

PRACTICAL ACTIVITY 5.1

Reversible and irreversible reactions

Suggested duration: 25 minutes

INTRODUCTION

An open system is a system that exchanges matter and energy with the surroundings. A closed system only exchanges energy with the surroundings.

Some reactions only occur in one direction and are described as irreversible, while other reactions are reversible.

In this investigation you will perform reactions in open and closed systems and consider whether the reactions are reversible or irreversible.

PURPOSE

To perform the following reactions and determine which are reversible and which involve open or closed systems. The reactions are:

- formation of hydrated and dehydrated cobalt(II) chloride
- reaction of iron(III) nitrate and potassium thiocyanate
- burning magnesium
- burning steel wool.

MATERIALS

- small bottle of solid hydrated cobalt chloride
- $0.1\,mol\,L^{-1}$ iron(III) nitrate solution, $Fe(NO_3)_3$
- $0.1\,mol\,L^{-1}$ potassium thiocyanate solution, KSCN
- 3–4 cm magnesium ribbon
- steel wool
- 2 semi-micro test-tubes
- semi-micro test-tube rack
- dropping pipette
- white tile
- Bunsen burner
- distilled water
- crucible
- tripod and gauze mat
- lighter
- tongs
- fireproof metal lid
- bench mat
- spatula
- 9 V battery

PRE-LAB SAFETY INFORMATION		
Materials	**Hazard**	**Control**
cobalt chloride	may cause skin, eye and respiratory tract irritation or burns	Wear gloves, lab coat, safety glasses.
$Fe(NO_3)_3$ solution	irritating to the eyes, respiratory system and skin	Wear gloves, lab coat, safety glasses.
KSCN solution	irritating to the skin and eyes	Wear gloves, lab coat, safety glasses.
magnesium ribbon	Burning produces intense white light which can be harmful to eyes; could burn skin and clothing.	Use tongs and eye protection; do not look directly into flame.
iron	Burning iron becomes very hot; could burn.	Use tongs.
Please indicate that you have understood the information in the safety table.		
Name (print): _____		
I understand the safety information (signature): _____		

Part A—Formation of hydrated and dehydrated cobalt(II) chloride

PROCEDURE

1 Set up the Bunsen burner, tripod and gauze mat on bench mat with the crucible on top.

2 Using the spatula, add a small amount of cobalt chloride to the crucible.

3 Light the Bunsen burner and watch the colour changes of the cobalt chloride. Record your observations in Results table 1.

4 Allow the crucible to cool and add a little distilled water, and record any colour change in the table.

5 Heat the crucible again and observe the colour changes of the cobalt chloride.

RESULTS

TABLE 1

Time (mins)	Observations
0 minutes	
1 minute	
2 minutes	
5 minutes	
After adding water	
After further heating	

DISCUSSION

1   The formula of hydrated cobalt chloride is $CoCl_2 \cdot 6H_2O$ and of dehydrated cobalt chloride is $CoCl_2$. Write an equation for this system.

2   What colour is the hydrated form of cobalt chloride?

3   Describe what occurs when you heated the hydrated cobalt chloride.

4   Describe what occurred when you added a little water to the heated cobalt chloride.

Part B—Reaction of iron(III) nitrate and potassium thiocyanate

PROCEDURE

1   Using a dropping pipette, add approx. 2 mL of $Fe(NO_3)_3$ solution to a semi-micro test tube. Clean the pipette and add approx. 2 mL of KSCN solution to the $Fe(NO_3)_3$ solution. The reaction that occurs forms $FeSCN^{2+}$ ions in solution.

2   Note the colours of the $Fe(NO_3)_3$ solution and the KSCN solution and also the colour of $FeSCN^{2+}$ ions in solution in the Results table. In order to produce reliable and accurate results, view the solutions by looking down the test-tubes so you look through the entire solution.

3   Divide the $FeSCN^{2+}$ solution equally into 2 test-tubes.

4   Clean the dropping pipette and add 10 drops of $Fe(NO_3)_3$ solution to one test-tube. Record the changes.

5   Clean the dropping pipette and add 10 drops of KSCN solution to the other test-tube. Record the changes.

RESULTS

TABLE 2

Solution	Colour	Explanation
$Fe(NO_3)_3$		no explanation required
KSCN		no explanation required
$FeSCN^{2+}$		no explanation required
$FeSCN^{2+}$ + $Fe(NO_3)_3(aq)$		
$FeSCN^{2+}$ + KSCN(aq)		

DISCUSSION

1   Write an equation for this system.

_____

2   Explain the colour changes you have observed by completing Results table 2 above.

Part C—Burning magnesium

PROCEDURE

1   Set up a Bunsen burner on a bench mat and light the burner.

2   Record the colour of the magnesium ribbon.

3   Hold one end of the magnesium ribbon with tongs and heat the other end in the flame until it ignites.

4   Hold the burning metal at arm's length over a bench mat. Do not look directly at the light produced.

5   Record the colour of the powder produced.

RESULTS

Colour of magnesium: _____

Colour of product, magnesium oxide: _____

DISCUSSION

Write the equation for this reaction.

Part D—Burning steel wool

PROCEDURE

1   Place the metal lid on the bench mat.

2   Make a small ball of steel wool and place it on the metal lid. Have a spatula nearby in case the steel wool becomes entangled with the battery.

3   Quickly touch the 9 V battery terminals to the steel wool and move it away without allowing it to be caught by the wire wool. Record what you observe.

4   Optional: Place a small, non-flammable board (preferably a cement sheet) on top of a digital balance. Tare the balance (reset the scale to zero). Then perform the experiment on the scales and record your observations.

RESULTS

_____

DISCUSSION

1   Write the equation for this reaction, given that the formula of iron(III) oxide is Fe_2O_3.

2 Explain your observations.

_____

_____

_____

GENERAL DISCUSSION

1 For each of the four reactions, state whether they are reversible or irreversible, and whether they occur in open or closed systems. Explain your answers.

Formation of hydrated and dehydrated cobalt(II) chloride: _____

_____

Reaction of iron(III) nitrate and potassium thiocyanate: _____

_____

Burning magnesium: _____

_____

Burning steel wool: _____

_____

2 Explain the meaning of the term 'dynamic equilibrium'.

_____

_____

CONCLUSION

3 Summarise and explain your results.

_____

_____

_____

_____

_____

_____

_____

RATING MY LEARNING	My understanding improved	Not confident ← → Very confident ○ ○ ○ ○ ○	I answered questions without help	Not confident ← → Very confident ○ ○ ○ ○ ○	I corrected my errors without help	Not confident ← → Very confident ○ ○ ○ ○ ○

PRACTICAL ACTIVITY 5.2

Investigation of the cobalt chloride equilibrium system

Suggested duration: 20 minutes

INTRODUCTION

Cobalt ions, Co^{2+}, react with chloride ions, Cl^-, to form an equilibrium with the cobalt tetrachloride ion, $CoCl_4^{2-}$. The reaction is represented by the equation:

$$Co^{2+}(aq) + 4Cl^-(aq) \rightleftharpoons CoCl_4^{2-}(aq)$$

(pink)   (colourless)   (blue)

If the main species present in an equilibrium mixture is the Co^{2+} ion, then the solution is pink, whereas if the main species present is the $CoCl_4^{2-}$ ion, then the solution is pale blue.

In this experiment you are supplied with a cobalt chloride solution that contains Co^{2+} ions, with lesser amounts of Cl^- and $CoCl_4^{2-}$ ions. The position of the equilibrium (the relative concentrations of ions) in this solution can be changed by altering the temperature, adding more Cl^- ions, or diluting the solution.

PURPOSE

To investigate the position of equilibria established between Co^{2+}, Cl^- and $CoCl_4^{2-}$ ions.

MATERIALS

- $10\,mL \times 0.5\,mol\,L^{-1}$ cobalt chloride solution, $CoCl_2$
- 4 mL saturated sodium chloride solution, NaCl
- 5 mL concentrated hydrochloric acid, HCl
- 10 mL measuring cylinder
- 2 Pyrex® test-tubes
- test-tube rack
- stopper
- stirring rod
- Bunsen burner
- bench mat
- 250 mL beaker of ice-water
- safety gloves
- tongs/wooden peg

PRE-LAB SAFETY INFORMATION		
Material used	**Hazard**	**Control**
concentrated HCl	very corrosive; causes severe burns; harmful by inhalation, ingestion and skin contact	Use small quantities; handle with extreme care and avoid contact; dilute small spills with water. Wear gloves, glasses and a laboratory coat.
$CoCl_2 \cdot 6H_2O$	may cause skin, eye and respiratory tract irritation or burns	Wear gloves, lab coat and safety glasses; wash hands after use.
Please indicate that you have understood the information in the safety table. Name (print): _____ I understand the safety information (signature): _____		

PROCEDURE

Part A—Effect of a change in temperature

1 Note the colour of the cobalt chloride solution supplied. Add 5 mL of this solution and 4 mL of saturated sodium chloride solution to a test-tube. Note the colour of the new solution in the Results table 1.

2 Briefly heat the solution in the test-tube and note any change in its colour.

3 Place the test-tube in a beaker of ice-water. Again note any changes of colour.

Part B—Effect of changes of chloride ion concentration

Slowly and carefully add about 5 mL of concentrated hydrochloric acid to 5 mL of cobalt chloride solution in a test-tube and note the change in colour. Retain this solution for use in Part C.

Part C—Effect of dilution

To the solution you made in Part B, add sufficient water to double its volume. Stopper and invert the test-tube in order to mix. Note the change in the colour of the solution in Results table 1.

RESULTS

TABLE 1

Part	Solutions	Colour
A	$CoCl_2$	
A	$CoCl_2$ + NaCl	
A	$CoCl_2$ + NaCl after heating	
A	$CoCl_2$ + NaCl in ice water	
B	$CoCl_2$ + HCl	
C	$CoCl_2$ + HCl diluted	

DISCUSSION

1   Write an expression for the equilibrium constant, K_{eq}, for this reaction.

2   Use your results from Part A to determine how the value of the equilibrium constant changes as the temperature increases. Explain your reasoning.

3   Is the reaction exothermic or endothermic?

4   Explain why the solution in Part B changes colour when concentrated hydrochloric acid is added.

5   Use Le Châtelier's principle to explain the colour change that occurs in Part C when the solution is diluted.

CONCLUSION

6   Summarise your results and explanations for the effect of changes to the cobalt chloride equilibrium system.

RATING MY LEARNING	My understanding improved	Not confident ← → Very confident ○ ○ ○ ○ ○	I answered questions without help	Not confident ← → Very confident ○ ○ ○ ○ ○	I corrected my errors without help	Not confident ← → Very confident ○ ○ ○ ○ ○

PRACTICAL ACTIVITY 5.3

Effect of temperature on equilibrium yields

Suggested duration: 20 minutes

INTRODUCTION

The effect of temperature on an equilibrium depends on whether the reaction is exothermic or endothermic. For this reason, from the way the temperature influences the equilibrium position, you can determine if ΔH is positive or negative. A change in temperature is the only change to an equilibrium system that causes the equilibrium constant to change.

PURPOSE

To investigate the way in which the temperature of an equilibrium mixture influences the position of the equilibrium.

PRE-LAB SAFETY INFORMATION		
Material	**Hazard**	**Control**
1 mol L^{-1} phosphoric acid	irritating to the eyes and skin	Wear gloves, safety glasses and lab coat.
methyl violet indicator	may irritate the eyes and skin	Wear gloves, safety glasses and lab coat.
Please indicate that you have understood the information in the safety table. Name (print): _____ I understand the safety information (signature): _____		

PROCEDURE

For the exothermic equilibrium system: $H_3PO_4(aq) \rightleftharpoons H_2PO_4^-(aq) + H^+(aq)$

1   Pour 1 mol L^{-1} phosphoric acid into each of two semi-micro test-tubes, to a depth of about 3 cm. Add two drops of methyl violet indicator to each test-tube.

2   Place one test-tube in ice-water. Carefully heat the other test-tube until the solution almost boils. Record the colour of the indicator in the heated and cooled test-tubes in the Results table.

RESULTS

Colour when cold	Colour when hot

DISCUSSION

1   In this experiment the colour of the equilibrium mixture is an indication of the concentration of the H^+ ions in solution, $[H^+]$. Methyl violet indicator is yellow in solutions with a high $[H^+]$. Its colour changes through green to blue and then to violet as the concentration decreases. How does $[H^+]$ in the equilibrium mixture change as the temperature is increased?

2   What does this indicate about the value of the equilibrium constant, K_{eq}, for this reaction as the temperature increases? Explain.

3   Describe how the position of equilibrium has shifted and account for your observations in this experiment.

CONCLUSION

4   Summarise the effects of changes in temperature on an equilibrium system.

PRACTICAL ACTIVITY 5.4

Determination of K_{eq} by colorimetry

Suggested duration: 1 hour 15 minutes (45 minutes for the experiment and 30 minutes for data analysis)

INTRODUCTION

In aqueous solution, Fe^{3+} ions react with SCN^- ions to form the blood-red coloured $FeSCN^{2+}$ ion. The equilibrium is represented by the equation:

$$Fe^{3+}(aq) + SCN^-(aq) \rightleftharpoons FeSCN^{2+}(aq)$$

The colour of the solution is directly proportional to the concentration of $FeSCN^{2+}$ ions present.

Later in the year, in Module 8, you will learn about the analytical technique called colorimetry. This spectroscopic technique is used to determine the concentration of coloured species in an aqueous sample. The absorption of light energy causes electrons in ions or molecules to jump from a lower energy level to a higher one. The amount of light energy absorbed is directly proportional to the concentration of the coloured species.

In this experiment you will use a colorimeter to measure the absorbance of a standard solution with a known concentration of $FeSCN^{2+}$. The concentration of $FeSCN^{2+}$ ions in other equilibrium mixtures can then be found by measuring their absorbance and comparing the absorbance with the absorbance of the standard. Knowing the initial concentration of Fe^{3+} and SCN^- in each mixture, the equilibrium concentration of Fe^{3+} and SCN^- can be calculated and a value for the equilibrium constant, K_{eq}, for the reaction can be determined.

PURPOSE

To determine the value of the equilibrium constant for the equilibrium system involving Fe^{3+} ions, SCN^- ions and $FeSCN^{2+}$ ions by colorimetric analysis.

MATERIALS

- 20 mL × 0.0020 mol L^{-1} potassium thiocyanate solution, KSCN
- 30 mL × 0.0020 mol L^{-1} iron(III) nitrate solution, $Fe(NO_3)_3$
- 15 mL × 0.00020 mol L^{-1} iron(III) thiocyanate ion solution
- 15 mL deionised water
- graduated pipette
- pipette filler
- 5 × 100 mL beakers
- 4 test-tubes
- test-tube rack
- stirring rod
- colorimeter and data collection device
- colorimeter cell
- marking pen
- tissues
- safety gloves

PRE-LAB SAFETY INFORMATION		
Material	**Hazard**	**Control**
KSCN solution	irritating to the skin and eyes	Wear gloves, lab coat, safety glasses.
$FeSCN^{2+}$ solution	contains nitric acid and is irritating to the skin and eyes	Wear gloves, lab coat, safety glasses.
$Fe(NO_3)_3$ solution	irritating to eyes, respiratory system and skin	Wear gloves, lab coat and safety glasses.
Please indicate that you have understood the information in the safety table. Name (print): _____ I understand the safety information (signature): _____		

PROCEDURE

1   Label four test-tubes A to D.

2   Using a graduated pipette, place volumes of 0.0020 mol L^{-1} $Fe(NO_3)_3$ solution, 0.0020 mol L^{-1} KSCN solution and water into each test-tube as indicated in the table below. Mix each solution thoroughly with a stirring rod. Be careful to clean and dry the stirring rod after each mixing.

Test-tube	Fe(NO$_3$)$_3$ (aq) (mL)	KSCN(aq) (mL)	H$_2$O (mL)
A	5.0	2.0	3.0
B	5.0	3.0	2.0
C	5.0	4.0	1.0
D	5.0	5.0	0.0

3 Prepare a reference cell or 'blank' by filling the colorimeter cell to three-quarters of its volume with deionised water. Wipe the outside of the cell with a tissue. By following the manufacturer's instructions, calibrate the colorimeter to read zero transmittance when no light passes through the cell and 100% transmittance when blue light (470 nm) passes through the blank. Use blue light for the remainder of this experiment.

4 Discard the deionised water from the cell, rinse the cell twice with the standard 0.00020 mol L^{-1} FeSCN^{2+} solution and fill the cell to three-quarters of its volume. Measure the absorbance and record the results in the Results table.

5 Repeat the procedure in step 4 to measure the absorbance of the solutions in each of test-tubes A–D.

RESULTS

Solution	Absorbance
FeSCN^{2+}	
test-tube A	
test-tube B	
test-tube C	
test-tube D	

DISCUSSION

1 Write an expression for the equilibrium law for the reaction.

2 Use the following table to enter the results of the calculations in questions **3**–**8** below.

	Test-tube			
	A	B	C	D
[Fe^{3+}]$_{initial}$				
[SCN$^-$]$_{initial}$				
[FeSCN^{2+}]$_{equilibrium}$				
[Fe^{3+}]$_{equilibrium}$				
[SCN$^-$]$_{equilibrium}$				
K_{eq}				

3 Calculate the initial concentration of Fe^{3+} in each of the test-tubes A–D and fill it in the appropriate space in the table. The $[Fe^{3+}]$ in each tube is given by the expression:

$$[Fe^{3+}]_{initial} = \frac{0.0020 \times \text{volume of } Fe(NO_3)_3 \text{ in the tube in mL}}{\text{total volume in mL}}$$

4 Calculate the initial concentration of SCN^- in each of test-tubes A–D and put this in the table. $[SCN^-]$ in each tube is given by the expression:

$$[SCN^-]_{initial} = \frac{0.0020 \times \text{volume of KSCN in the tube in mL}}{\text{total volume in mL}}$$

5 The absorbance of light by a solution is directly proportional to the concentration of the absorbing chemical in solution. As a result, you can calculate the concentration of $FeSCN^{2+}$ at equilibrium in each test-tube by comparing the absorbance of each solution with the absorbance of the standard solution.

$$[FeSCN^{2-}]_{equilibrium} = 0.00020 \times \frac{\text{absorbance of solution}}{\text{absorbance of standard}}$$

6 Calculate the $[Fe^{3+}]_{equilibrium}$ in each of the tubes:

$$[Fe^{3+}]_{equilibrium} = [Fe^{3+}]_{initial} - [FeSCN^{2+}]_{equilibrium}$$

7 Calculate the $[SCN^-]_{equilibrium}$ in each of the tubes:

$$[SCN^-]_{equilibrium} = [SCN^-]_{initial} - [FeSCN^{2+}]_{equilibrium}$$

8 Using the equilibrium law from question **1**, calculate a value for the equilibrium constant, K_{eq}, for each set of data.

CONCLUSION

9 Calculate an average value for K_{eq}. Comment on the reliability and accuracy of K_{eq} determined from each set of data.

RATING MY LEARNING	My understanding improved	Not confident ← → Very confident ⭘ ⭘ ⭘ ⭘ ⭘	I answered questions without help	Not confident ← → Very confident ⭘ ⭘ ⭘ ⭘ ⭘	I corrected my errors without help	Not confident ← → Very confident ⭘ ⭘ ⭘ ⭘ ⭘

PRACTICAL ACTIVITY 5.5

Precipitation reactions

Suggested duration: 50 minutes

INTRODUCTION

When two solutions containing dissolved ionic salts are mixed together, an insoluble product called a precipitate may form and settle out of the mixture. Knowing which ions form precipitates is essential in many industrial processes, and in monitoring and maintaining the health of natural waterways.

PURPOSE

Part A: To observe reactions that involve the formation of a precipitate.

Part B: To distinguish between ions that form precipitates and those that are always soluble.

To write net ionic equations to represent the formation of precipitates.

PRE-LAB SAFETY INFORMATION		
Material	**Hazard**	**Control**
sodium hydroxide	corrosive to skin and eyes	Wear eye and skin protection.
sodium carbonate	slightly toxic if ingested	Wear eye and skin protection.
calcium nitrate	slightly toxic if ingested	Wear eye and skin protection.
copper(II) nitrate	slightly toxic if ingested and by skin contact	Wear eye and skin protection.
zinc nitrate	slightly toxic if ingested	Wear eye and skin protection.
silver nitrate	toxic if ingested, stains skin black	Wear eye and skin protection.
barium nitrate	toxic if ingested	Wear eye and skin protection.
potassium nitrate	may irritate eyes and skin	Wear eye and skin protection.
Please indicate that you have understood the information in the safety table. Name (print): _____ I understand the safety information (signature): _____		

Part A—Solubility of ionic compounds

PROCEDURE

1   Using a marker pen, write the anions you are testing along the top of the plastic well tray. Write the cations you are testing down the side of the wells. (Results table 1 below shows how your grid should look.) Place the well tray on a dark background for easier observation.

2   Place two drops of the appropriate cation solution and one drop of the appropriate anion solution into the wells, according to the labels you have written. Be careful not to allow any contamination, in order to produce reliable and accurate results.

3   If no precipitate is formed, record 's' for soluble.

4   If a precipitate forms, record 'ppt' (for precipitate) and record its colour.

MATERIALS

- dropper bottles, each containing 10 mL of the following 0.5 mol L^{-1} solutions:
  - sodium sulfate, Na_2SO_4
  - sodium chloride, NaCl
  - sodium hydroxide, NaOH
  - sodium carbonate, Na_2CO_3
- dropper bottles, each containing 10 mL of the following 0.1 mol L^{-1} solutions:
  - magnesium nitrate, $Mg(NO_3)_2$
  - calcium nitrate, $Ca(NO_3)_2$
  - copper(II) nitrate, $Cu(NO_3)_2$
  - zinc nitrate, $Zn(NO_3)_2$
  - potassium nitrate, KNO_3
  - silver nitrate, $AgNO_3$
  - barium nitrate, $Ba(NO_3)_2$
- plastic well tray or plastic grid
- marker pen
- 5 dropper bottles, randomly labelled A–E, containing 10 mL of the following 0.1 mol L^{-1} solutions:
  - potassium nitrate, KNO_3
  - sodium chloride, NaCl
  - sodium sulfate, Na_2SO_4
  - sodium hydroxide, NaOH
  - sodium carbonate, Na_2CO_3
- safety gloves

RESULTS

Ion	Nitrate (NO)	Chloride (Cl⁻)	Sulfate (SO_4^{2-})	Hydroxide (OH⁻)	Carbonate (CO_3^{2-})
Mg^{2+}					
K^+					
Ca^{2+}					
Cu^{2+}					
Zn^{2+}					
Ag^+					
Ba^{2+}					

DISCUSSION

1   What generalisations can you make about the solubilities of:

   a nitrates?

   b chlorides?

   c hydroxides?

   d sulfates?

   e carbonates?

2   Which cation(s) did not form any precipitates when combined with the anions?

3   Write a balanced ionic equation to represent the formation of each precipitate observed.

PART B—Identifying unknown solutions

PROCEDURE

You have been given one of five unknown solutions in dropper bottles. Your dropper bottle may contain a solution of potassium nitrate (KNO_3), sodium chloride (NaCl), sodium sulfate (Na_2SO_4), sodium hydroxide (NaOH) or sodium carbonate (Na_2CO_3).

1   Record the label on your unknown sample: _____

2   Select your own set of reagents that will enable you to identify the given unknown sample.

3   Record your results in the Results table below.

RESULTS

Reagent	Observations

DISCUSSION

1   Write the chemical formula for each precipitate formed in your investigation.

_____

_____

2   Identify your unknown sample. Support your answer with experimental evidence.

_____

_____

_____

3   It is often possible to convert one ionic compound to another by exploiting solubility differences. Briefly describe, in a series of steps, how you could convert calcium chloride to potassium chloride.

_____

_____

CONCLUSION

4   Summarise your results in this experiment by writing a series of solubility rules based on your observations.

_____

_____

_____

_____

_____

5   Explain the benefits of writing an ionic equation for each of these reactions.

_____

_____

_____

_____

_____

RATING MY LEARNING	My understanding improved	Not confident ← → Very confident ○ ○ ○ ○ ○	I answered questions without help	Not confident ← → Very confident ○ ○ ○ ○ ○	I corrected my errors without help	Not confident ← → Very confident ○ ○ ○ ○ ○

Practical investigation of an equilibrium system

Suggested duration: 2 hours 15 minutes (including writing time)

INTRODUCTION

In this activity you will use a solution of $Fe(SCN)^{2+}$ that contains the ions Fe^{3+}, SCN^- and $Fe(SCN)^{2+}$ at equilibrium:

$$Fe^{3+}(aq) + SCN^-(aq) \rightleftharpoons Fe(SCN)^{2+}(aq)$$

(pale yellow)   (colourless)   (red)

The intense blood-red colour of the solution is due to the presence of the $Fe(SCN)^{2+}$ ion. The colour of the solution in each test-tube, when viewed down the tube, is a measure of the amount of $Fe(SCN)^{2+}$ ions present in the tube. By noting how the intensity of this colour changes, it is possible to deduce the effect of each of the tests performed in this experiment on the equilibrium.

If, for example, the colour of the solution deepens, the amount of $Fe(SCN)^{2+}$ ions has increased and the amount of the Fe^{3+} and SCN^- ions must have simultaneously decreased because these ions are used up to form more $Fe(SCN)^{2+}$. The equilibrium would be described as having a net forward reaction (its position would have 'shifted to the right').

In Part A you will investigate the effect of concentration changes on an aqueous equilibrium.

In Part B you will investigate the way in which the temperature of an equilibrium mixture influences the position of the equilibrium.

QUESTIONING AND PREDICTING

In this investigation you are using an equilibrium system containing the ions Fe^{3+}, SCN^- and $Fe(SCN)^{2+}$. Use your knowledge of equilibrium and the information in the Introduction above to develop a hypothesis for the outcomes of Parts A and B of this practical investigation.

PRE-LAB SAFETY INFORMATION

As directed by your teacher, complete the risk assessment and management table by referring to the hazard labels on the reagent bottles or safety data sheets (SDS) or your teacher's risk assessment for the activity.

Material	Hazard	Control
$0.1\,mol\,L^{-1}$ silver nitrate solution	can stain skin, clothing and bench surfaces	
$0.1\,mol\,L^{-1}$ iron(III) nitrate solution		

Please indicate that you have read and understood the information in the table above.
Name (print): _____
I understand the safety information (signature): _____

MATERIALS

- 35 mL of $5 \times 10^{-4}\,mol\,L^{-1}$ iron(III) thiocyanate ion solution, $Fe(SCN)^{2+}$ (20 mL of $0.1\,mol\,L^{-1}$ $Fe(NO_3)_3$ and 20 mL of $0.1\,mol\,L^{-1}$ potassium thiocyanate (KSCN) per litre)
- $0.1\,mol\,L^{-1}$ iron(III) nitrate solution, $Fe(NO_3)_3$
- $0.1\,mol\,L^{-1}$ potassium thiocyanate solution, KSCN
- $0.1\,mol\,L^{-1}$ sodium fluoride solution, NaF
- $0.1\,mol\,L^{-1}$ silver nitrate solution, $AgNO_3$
- 6 semi-micro test-tubes
- semi-micro test-tube holder
- semi-micro test-tube rack
- 250 mL beaker of ice-water
- 250 mL beaker
- Bunsen burner, gauze mat and tripod stand
- bench mat
- marking pen
- dropping pipette
- white tile or white sheet of paper
- safety gloves

Part A—Effect of concentration changes on equilibrium yields

CONDUCTING YOUR INVESTIGATION

In this part of the investigation you will perform five tests, labelled A to E, to study the effect on the equilibrium system when the amount (number of moles) of Fe^{3+} or SCN^- ions present in the solution is initially changed as follows.

- In Test A, $Fe(NO_3)_3$ is added, which increases the amount of Fe^{3+}.
- In Test B, KSCN is added, which increases the amount of SCN^-.
- In Test C, NaF is added, which decreases the amount of Fe^{3+} because F^- ions react with Fe^{3+} ions to form FeF_6^{3-}(aq).
- In Test D, $AgNO_3$ is added, which decreases the amount of SCN^- because Ag^+ ions react with SCN^- ions to form a white precipitate of AgSCN.
- In Test E you will study the effect of the addition of water (dilution) on the equilibrium.

PROCEDURE

1   Fill each of six semi-micro test-tubes to one-third of its volume with $Fe(SCN)^{2+}$ solution. Check that the liquid in each tube has the same intensity of colour when you look down the tube using a white tile or sheet of paper as a background. If necessary, add more solution so that the liquid in each tube is the same colour. Label the tubes 'A' to 'F'.

2   Using test-tube F for comparison, perform each of the tests described in Results table 1 and record the change that occurs in the colour of the solution when viewed down the test-tube.

RESULTS TABLE 1 Colour changes

Test-tube	Test	Colour change
A	1 drop of $Fe(NO_3)_3$(aq) added	
B	1 drop of KSCN(aq) added	
C	1 drop of NaF(aq) added	
D	1 drop of $AgNO_3$(aq) added	
E	Equal volume of water added	
F	None	No change

DISCUSSION

1   Write an expression for the equilibrium constant of the reaction that is the subject of this practical investigation.

2   Complete Table 2 below for each test by stating:

a   the initial effect on the concentration of Fe^{3+} or SCN^- of each test

b   the concentration change of $Fe(SCN)^{2+}$ after the test

c   the direction in which the position of equilibrium has shifted.

The entries for Test A have been completed for you.

TABLE 2 Equilibrium results

Test-tube	Initial effect	[Fe(SCN)$^{2+}$] change	Direction of equilibrium shift
A	[Fe^{3+}]: increases	Increases	Forward
B	[SCN$^-$]:		
C	[Fe^{3+}]:		
D	[SCN$^-$]:		
E	[Fe^{3+}]:		

3 Sketch concentration–time graphs to show how the concentration of each ion has changed during each test.

4 Sketch rate–time graphs to show how the rates of the forward and reverse reactions have changed during each test.

5 Use Le Châtelier's principle to account for the way in which the position of equilibrium shifts in Test A.

_____

_____

_____

_____

6 Account for the way in which the position of equilibrium shifts in Test E, using Le Châtelier's principle.

_____

_____

_____

7 Use collision theory to explain the way in which the position of equilibrium shifts in Test B.

_____

_____

_____

_____

Part B—Effect of temperature on equilibrium yields

1 Design an investigation that will allow you to determine the effect of a change in temperature on the following equilibrium system:

$$Fe^{3+}(aq) + SCN^-(aq) \rightleftharpoons Fe(SCN)^{2+}(aq)$$

Write your method in the space below.

_____

_____

_____

2 From the list of materials provided above, select and record the ones you will require for your investigation.

_____

_____

_____

3 Check your method and materials with your teacher and then carry out your investigation. Record your results below in a suitable table.

Sketch one or more concentration-time graphs to show how the concentration of each ion has changed during your investigation.

Use Le Châtelier's principle and the collision theory to explain the effects of a change in temperature on the equilibrium system. In your explanation, state how the value of the equilibrium constant, K_{eq}, for this reaction changes as the temperature changes and whether the reaction is endothermic or exothermic.

COMMUNICATING YOUR FINDINGS AND PRESENTING THE REPORT

Write a practical report for this investigation as a Word document or similar. The questions you have answered above and the sections below will guide your report, but you can also add further to your discussion. You can refer to the Toolkit on page ix for what should be included in each section of a practical report. Don't forget to include a conclusion and references.

Processing data and information

Devise appropriate tables and graphs for inclusion in your final report that record all of the raw data you collected in Parts A and B of the investigation.

Analysing data and information

Devise tables, graphs or flow charts as appropriate in which you can make generalisations about the effects of the changes to the equilibrium system. You should add additional analyses of your results and/or the investigation as you see fit.

Discuss any errors or limitations in the data you have collected in this investigation. What modifications, if any, can you make to your hypothesis based on the new evidence collected in this investigation? You should consider the accuracy and reliability of your results and suggest improvements that could be made to this investigation.

Multiple choice

1 Which one of the following best describes a chemical system that is in equilibrium?

  A The rate of conversion of reactants to products is negligible.

  B All reaction has ceased.

  C The concentrations of the reactants are equal to those of the products.

  D The rates of the forward and reverse reactions are equal.

2 NO reacts with O_2 to form NO_2 according to the equation:

$$2NO(g) + O_2(g) \rightleftharpoons 2NO_2(g)$$

When equilibrium is established at a fixed temperature, which one of the following fractions would be a constant, irrespective of the initial concentrations of the gases?

  A $\dfrac{[NO_2]^2}{[NO]^2[O_2]}$

  B $\dfrac{[NO_2]}{[NO][\frac{1}{2}O_2]}$

  C $\dfrac{[NO_2]}{[NO][O_2]}$

  D $\dfrac{[NO_2]}{[NO][O_2]^2}$

3 Which one or more factors affect the value of the equilibrium constant, K_{eq}, of a gaseous equilibrium?

  A total number of particles in the system

  B total pressure of the system

  C volume of reaction vessel

  D temperature of the system

The following information refers to questions 4 and 5.

N_2 forms an equilibrium with H_2 and NH_3 according to the equation:

$$N_2(g) + 3H_2(g) \rightleftharpoons 2NH_3(g) \qquad \Delta H = -92\,kJ\,mol^{-1}$$

4 Which one of the following occurs when the volume of an equilibrium mixture of these gases is reduced at constant temperature?

  A The value of K_{eq} of the system increases.

  B The rate of the forward reaction decreases and the rate of the reverse reactions increases

  C The mass of NH_3 increases and the mass of N_2 and H_2 decreases.

  D The total number of gas particles increases.

5 Which one of the following occurs when the temperature of an equilibrium mixture of these gases is decreased?

  A The value of K_{eq} of the system increases.

  B The rate of the forward reaction decreases and the rate of the reverse reactions increases.

  C The mass of NH_3 decreases and the mass of N_2 and H_2 increases.

  D The total number of gas particles increases.

6 If the solubility of magnesium hydroxide, $Mg(OH)_2$, is represented as $s\,mol\,L^{-1}$, which one of the following expressions is equal to the solubility product, K_{sp}, of magnesium hydroxide?

  A s

  B s^2

  C $3s^2$

  D $4s^3$

Short answer

7 N_2O_4 forms an equilibrium with NO_2:

$$N_2O_4(g) \rightleftharpoons 2NO_2(g)$$

The equilibrium constant is 0.72 at 250°C. If an equilibrium mixture contains $0.020\,mol\,L^{-1}$ N_2O_4 at 250°C, calculate the equilibrium concentration of NO_2 in the mixture.

8 A precipitate will form when the following solutions are mixed. Write a balanced ionic equation for each reaction.

  a silver nitrate and calcium chloride

  b lead(II) nitrate and sodium carbonate

  c copper(II) sulfate and ammonium phosphate

  d aluminium sulfate and potassium hydroxide

  e iron(III) nitrate and sodium sulfide

9 Consider the following equation that represents a gas-phase reaction in a state of equilibrium:

$$A(g) + B(g) \rightleftharpoons C(g) \qquad \Delta H = -100\,kJ\,mol^{-1}$$

A scientist performed a number of experiments to investigate the effect of changes on the equilibrium.

a In one experiment, after time, t_1, more reactant A was added rapidly to an equilibrium mixture at a constant temperature.

  i Complete the graph below to show the effect of this change on the rates of the forward and reverse reactions as the system returned to equilibrium.

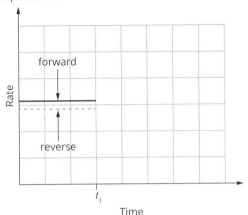

  ii Explain what happened to the rates of the forward and reverse reactions in this experiment in terms of collision theory.

  _____

  _____

  _____

b In another experiment, at time t_2 a catalyst was added to an equilibrium mixture at a constant temperature.

  i Complete the graph below to show the effect of the catalyst on the rates of the forward and reverse reaction.

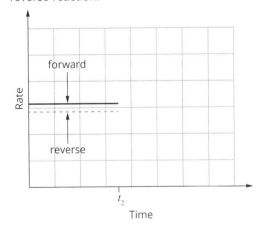

  ii Explain, in terms of collision theory, what happened to the rates of the forward and reverse reactions in this experiment.

  _____

  _____

  _____

c In a third experiment, after time t_3 the temperature was rapidly increased to a new, constant value and equilibrium was re-established.

  Complete the concentration–time graph below to show the effect of the temperature change on the concentration of C.

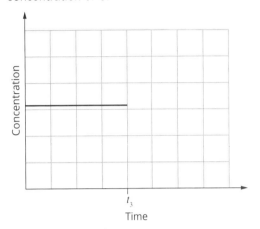

d 2.00 mol of HI was placed in a 1.00 L container at 600 K. The HI decomposed, forming 0.22 mol of H_2 and 0.22 mol of I_2 at equilibrium. Calculate the value of the equilibrium constant, K_{eq}, for the reaction:

$$H_2(g) + I_2(g) \rightleftharpoons 2HI(g)$$

at this temperature.

  _____

  _____

  _____

10 A yellow precipitate of lead iodide forms when a solution of lead nitrate is mixed with a solution of potassium iodide.

  a Name the spectator ions in this reaction.

  _____

  b Write a balanced ionic equation for the formation of the precipitate.

  _____

  c Write an expression for the solubility product, K_{sp}, of the yellow solid that is formed in this reaction.

  _____

  d At 25°C, 1.00 L of water can dissolve 1.26×10^{-3} mol of lead iodide. Calculate the solubility product, K_{sp}, for lead iodide at this temperature.

  _____

  _____

MODULE
6 Acid/base reactions

Outcomes

By the end of this module you will be able to:

- develop and evaluate questions and hypotheses for scientific investigation CH12-1
- design and evaluate investigations in order to obtain primary and secondary data and information CH12-2
- conduct investigations to collect valid and reliable primary and secondary data and information CH12-3
- analyse and evaluate primary and secondary data and information CH12-5
- describe, explain and quantitatively analyse acids and bases using contemporary models CH12-13

Content

PROPERTIES OF ACIDS AND BASES

INQUIRY QUESTION | What is an acid and what is a base?

By the end of this module you will be able to:

- investigate the correct IUPAC nomenclature and properties of common inorganic acids and bases (ACSCH067)
- conduct an investigation to demonstrate the preparation and use of indicators as illustrators of the characteristics and properties of acids and bases and their reversible reactions (ACSCH101)
- predict the products of acid reactions and write balanced equations to represent: ICT
  - acids and bases
  - acids and carbonates
  - acids and metals (ACSCH067)
- investigate applications of neutralisation reactions in everyday life and industrial processes
- conduct a practical investigation to measure the enthalpy of neutralisation (ACSCH093)
- explore the changes in definitions and models of an acid and a base over time to explain the limitations of each model, including but not limited to:
  - Arrhenius' theory
  - Brønsted–Lowry theory (ACSCH064, ACSCH067) ICT

USING BRØNSTED-LOWRY THEORY

INQUIRY QUESTION | What is the role of water in solutions of acids and bases?

By the end of this module you will be able to:

- conduct a practical investigation to measure the pH of a range of acids and bases
- calculate pH, pOH, hydrogen ion concentration ($[H^+]$) and hydroxide ion concentration ($[OH^-]$) for a range of solutions (ACSCH102) ICT N

- conduct an investigation to demonstrate the use of pH to indicate the differences between the strength of acids and bases (ACSCH102)
- write ionic equations to represent the dissociation of acids and bases in water, conjugate acid/base pairs in solution and amphiprotic nature of some salts, for example:
  - sodium hydrogen carbonate
  - potassium dihydrogen phosphate
- construct models and/or animations to communicate the differences between strong, weak, concentrated and dilute acids and bases (ACSCH099) ICT
- calculate the pH of the resultant solution when solutions of acids and/or bases are diluted or mixed ICT N

QUANTITATIVE ANALYSIS

INQUIRY QUESTION | How are solutions of acids and bases analysed?

By the end of this module you will be able to:
- explore the use of K_{eq} for different types of chemical reactions, including but not limited to:
  - dissociation of acids and bases (ACSCH098, ACSCH099)
- conduct practical investigations to analyse the concentration of an unknown acid or base by titration ICT N
- investigate titration curves and conductivity graphs to analyse data to indicate characteristic reaction profiles, for example: ICT
  - strong acid/strong base
  - strong acid/weak base
  - weak acid/strong base (ACSCH080, ACSCH102)
- model neutralisation of strong and weak acids and bases using a variety of media ICT
- calculate and apply the dissociation constant (K_a) and pK_a ($pK_a = -\log10 (K_a)$) to determine the difference between strong and weak acids (ACSCH098) ICT N
- explore acid/base analysis techniques that are applied:
  - in industries
  - by Aboriginal and Torres Strait Islander peoples AHC
  - using digital probes and instruments ICT
- conduct a chemical analysis of a common household substance for its acidity or basicity, for example: (ACSCH080) ICT N
  - soft drink
  - wine
  - juice
  - medicine
- conduct a practical investigation to prepare a buffer and demonstrate its properties (ACSCH080) ICT N
- describe the importance of buffers in natural systems (ACSCH098, ACSCH102)

Key knowledge

Properties of acids and bases

Acids and bases are substances that have characteristic properties (Table 6.1). There are two widely used definitions of acids and bases, **Arrhenius' theory** and the **Brønsted–Lowry theory**.

TABLE 6.1 Properties of acids and bases

Properties of acids	Properties of bases
Taste sour.	Taste bitter.
Turn litmus paper red.	Turn litmus paper blue.
Solutions conduct an electric current.	Solutions conduct an electric current.
Solutions have a relatively low pH.	Solutions have a relatively high pH.
React with bases to produce salt and water.	React with acids to produce salt and water.
Can be corrosive.	Can be corrosive.

In 1922 Arrhenius proposed that acids are substances that produce H^+ ions in water and bases are substances that produce OH^- ions in water. Arrhenius' theory can be used for reactions in water. In 1923 Brønsted and Lowry proposed a new theory that defined acids and bases in terms of proton transfer. This theory can be applied to a broader range of reactions than Arrhenius' theory, including reactions in non-aqueous solvents. The two theories are summarised in Table 6.2.

TABLE 6.2 Acid–base theories

Definition	Limitations
Arrhenius	**Arrhenius**
Acids ionise in water and produce H^+ ions (protons). Bases ionise or dissociate and produce OH^- ions (hydroxide ions). The products of an acid-base reaction are a salt and water.	Only applies to reactions in aqueous solutions. Does not explain the strengths of acids and bases. The substances must produce H^+ ions and OH^- ions.
Brønsted–Lowry	**Brønsted–Lowry**
Acids are proton donors. Bases are proton acceptors. An acid–base reaction involves an exchange of protons from an acid to a base.	To be classed as an acid, a substance must have a proton (H^+) to lose. Does not explain the reaction between acidic oxides and basic oxides.

ACIDS

According to the Brønsted–Lowry theory, an acid is a proton donor. A molecule of an acid in water can donate a proton to a water molecule to form a hydronium ion, H_3O^+ (Figure 6.1).

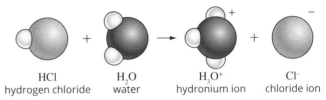

HCl	H_2O	H_3O^+	Cl^-
hydrogen chloride	water	hydronium ion	chloride ion

FIGURE 6.1 Reaction between HCl and water: hydrogen chloride is acting as an acid by donating a proton.

The HCl molecule undergoes **ionisation** (because it forms ions) and **dissociation** (because it breaks apart). Acids which ionise completely are called **strong acids**; acids that do not readily donate protons and ionise incompletely in water are called **weak acids** (Figure 6.2). Examples of the reactions of strong and weak acids are shown below.

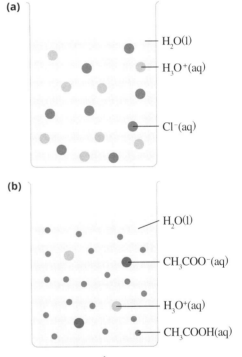

FIGURE 6.2 (a) In a $0.1\,mol\,L^{-1}$ solution of HCl, the acid molecules ionise completely in water. HCl is a strong acid. (b) However, in a $0.1\,mol\,L^{-1}$ solution of CH_3COOH only a small proportion of the CH_3COOH molecules ionise in water. CH_3COOH is a weak acid.

Strong acid: $HCl(aq) + H_2O(l) \rightarrow H_3O^+(aq) + Cl^-(aq)$

Weak acid: $CH_3COOH(aq) + H_2O(l) \rightleftharpoons$
$H_3O^+(aq) + CH_3COO^-(aq)$

Table 6.3 summaries the difference between the strengths of acids.

TABLE 6.3 Strong and weak acids

Type of acid	Definition
strong acid	Readily donates protons and completely ionises in water (Figure 6.2a).
weak acid	Does not readily donate protons and incompletely ionises in water (Figure 6.2b).

Strength versus concentration

Acids can be described as either strong or weak and also as **concentrated** or **dilute** (Figure 6.3). The strength of an acid is determined by its ability to ionise in solution, whereas the concentration of an acid refers to the amount of acid present in a given volume of solution.

The concentration of an acid (or any solute in solution) is calculated using the formula:

$$c = \frac{n}{V}$$

where n is the amount in mol of the acid, c is the concentration in $mol\,L^{-1}$ and V is the volume of the solution in L.

When solutions are diluted, the number of moles of solute does not change but the volume of water is increased, which causes the concentration to decrease. A handy formula for calculating the concentration of a diluted solution is:

$$c_1 \times V_1 = c_2 \times V_2$$

where c_1 and V_1 are the initial concentrations and volume and c_2 and V_2 are the final concentrations and volume.

Polyprotic acids

Some acids are able to donate more than one proton per molecule and are referred to as **polyprotic acids** (Table 6.4). However, having more than one hydrogen atom in the formula does not make an acid polyprotic. For example, although ethanoic acid, CH_3COOH, has four protons, it is a **monoprotic acid** because only one of its H atoms can be donated to a base. This hydrogen atom is called the **acidic proton**.

Acids undergo characteristic reactions with many substances, as shown in Table 6.5.

BASES

The Brønsted–Lowry theory defines a base as a proton acceptor. When a molecule acts as a base in water, it accepts a proton from a water molecule and produces a hydroxide ion, OH^- (Figure 6.4 on page 52). The molecules can be said to ionise (because they form ions) and dissociate (because they break up) (Figure 6.5 on page 52).

Soluble ionic compounds that contain the OH^- ion, such as NaOH, dissociate in water and release the OH^- ion, producing a strongly basic solution.

Like acids, bases can be classed as strong or weak, as defined in Table 6.6 on page 52.

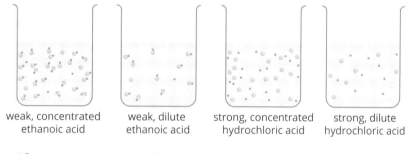

weak, concentrated ethanoic acid   weak, dilute ethanoic acid   strong, concentrated hydrochloric acid   strong, dilute hydrochloric acid

acid (CH_3COOH, HCl)   conjugate base (CH_3COO^-(aq), Cl$^-$(aq))   H$^+$(aq)

FIGURE 6.3 The concentration of ions in an acid solution depends on both the concentration and the strength of the acid.

TABLE 6.4 Monoprotic and polyprotic acids

Type of acid	No. of protons available to donate	Example	Equation
monoprotic acid	1	nitric acid, HNO_3, ethanoic acid, CH_3COOH	$HNO_3(aq) + H_2O(l) \rightarrow NO_3^-(aq) + H_3O^+(aq)$
diprotic acid	2	sulfuric acid, H_2SO_4	$H_2SO_4(aq) + H_2O(l) \rightarrow HSO_4^-(aq) + H_3O^+(aq)$ $HSO_4^-(aq) + H_2O(l) \rightleftharpoons SO_4^{2-}(aq) + H_3O^+(aq)$
triprotic acid	3	phosphoric acid, H_3PO_4	$H_3PO_4(aq) + H_2O(l) \rightleftharpoons H_2PO_4^-(aq) + H_3O^+(aq)$ $H_2PO_4^-(aq) + H_2O(l) \rightleftharpoons HPO_4^{2-}(aq) + H_3O^+(aq)$ $HPO_4^{2-}(aq) + H_2O(l) \rightleftharpoons PO_4^{3-}(aq) + H_3O^+(aq)$

TABLE 6.5 Some common reactions of acids

Reactants	Products	Example
acid + metal hydroxide	salt + water	$HCl(aq) + NaOH(aq) \rightarrow NaCl(aq) + H_2O(l)$
acid + reactive metal	salt + hydrogen gas	$2HCl(aq) + Mg(s) \rightarrow MgCl_2(aq) + H_2(g)$
acid + metal carbonate acid + metal hydrogen carbonate	salt + water + carbon dioxide gas	$2HCl(aq) + Na_2CO_3(aq) \rightarrow 2NaCl(aq) + CO_2(g) + H_2O(l)$ $HCl(aq) + NaHCO_3(aq) \rightarrow NaCl(aq) + CO_2(g) + H_2O(l)$

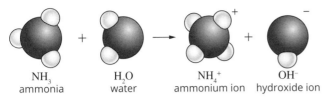

NH₃ ammonia   H₂O water   NH₄⁺ ammonium ion   OH⁻ hydroxide ion

FIGURE 6.4 Reaction between ammonia and water: ammonia acts as a base and accepts a proton.

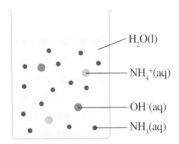

FIGURE 6.5 Only a small proportion of NH_3 molecules in an ammonia solution are ionised at any given time. NH_3 is a weak base.

TABLE 6.6 Strong and weak bases

Type of base	Definition and example	Equation
strong	Readily accepts protons: O^{2-} and OH^-.	$KOH(aq) \xrightarrow{H_2O} K^+(aq) + OH^-(aq)$
weak	Does not readily accept protons: NH_3 (Figure 6.5).	$NH_3(aq) + H_2O(l) \rightleftharpoons NH_4^+(aq) + OH^-(aq)$

NAMING ACIDS AND BASES

- To name a simple acid composed of hydrogen and another element, take the element's name and change the 'ide' ending to 'ic acid'. For example:
  - hydrogen chloride becomes hydrochloric acid and the anion is the chloride ion.
- For acids that contain oxygen (oxyacids), the acid name often ends in 'ic acid'. The name of the anion of the acid often ends in 'ate'. For example:
  - sulfuric acid, H_2SO_4, and the anion, sulfate, SO_4^{2-}
  - nitric acid, HNO_3, and the anion, nitrate, NO_3^-

- ethanoic acid (acetic acid), CH_3COOH and the anion, ethanoate (acetate), CH_3COO^-
- For some oxyacids, the acid name ends in 'ous acid'. These oxyacids have fewer O atoms than the corresponding 'ic acid'. The anion name will end in 'ite'. For example:
  - sulfurous acid, H_2SO_3, and the anion, sulfite, SO_3^{2-}
  - nitrous acid, HNO_2, and the anion, nitrite, NO_2^-.

REACTIONS OF ACIDS AND BASES

The Brønsted–Lowry theory describes an acid–base reaction as a reaction in which proton transfer occurs. This reaction is also referred to as a **neutralisation reaction** and can be represented by a formula or an ionic equation.

In an acid–base reaction, the acid donates a proton to form its **conjugate base** and the base accepts a proton and becomes its **conjugate acid**. A **conjugate acid–base pair** is two species that differ by a single H^+ ion. For example:

$$HCl(aq) + OH^-(aq) \rightarrow Cl^-(aq) + H_2O(l)$$
acid   base   conjugate base   conjugate acid

Cl^- is the conjugate base of HCl and H_2O is the conjugate acid of OH^-. Table 6.7 shows some the conjugate pairs in some acid–base reactions.

TABLE 6.7 Conjugate pairs in some acid–base reactions

Ionic equation	Conjugate pairs
$NH_3(aq) + H_2O(l) \rightleftharpoons NH_4^+(aq) + OH^-(aq)$	NH_3 and NH_4^+ H_2O and OH^-
$HCl(aq) + OH^-(aq) \rightarrow Cl^-(aq) + H_2O(l)$	HCl and Cl^- OH^- and H_2O
$H_2SO_4(aq) + H_2O(l) \rightarrow$ $HSO_4^-(aq) + H_3O^+(aq)$	H_2SO_4 and HSO_4^- H_2O and H_3O^+
$CH_3COOH(aq) + OH^-(aq) \rightarrow$ $CH_3COO^-(aq) + H_2O(l)$	CH_3COOH and CH_3COO^- OH^- and H_2O

An **amphiprotic** substance can act as either an acid or a base depending on the substance with which it is reacting, i.e. it is able to donate or accept protons. The HCO_3^- and $H_2PO_4^-$ ions are examples of amphiprotic substances, as shown in Table 6.8.

TABLE 6.8 Amphiprotic substances

Ionic equation	Conjugate pairs
HCO_3^- acting as an acid: $HCO_3^-(aq) + H_2O(l) \rightleftharpoons CO_3^{2-}(aq) + H_3O^+(aq)$	HCO_3^- and CO_3^{2-}, H_2O and H_3O^+
HCO_3^- acting as a base: $HCO_3^-(aq) + H_2O(l) \rightleftharpoons H_2CO_3(aq) + OH^-(aq)$	HCO_3^- and H_2CO_3, OH^- and H_2O
$H_2PO_4^-$ acting as an acid: $H_2PO_4^-(aq) + H_2O(l) \rightleftharpoons HPO_4^{2-}(aq) + H_3O^+(aq)$	$H_2PO_4^-$ and HPO_4^{2-}, H_2O and H_3O^+
$H_2PO_4^-$ acting as a base: $H_2PO_4^-(aq) + H_2O(l) \rightleftharpoons H_3PO_4(aq) + OH^-(aq)$	$H_2PO_4^-$ and H_3PO_4, OH^- and H_2O

Enthalpy of neutralisation

Neutralisation reactions release energy. This energy is called the **enthalpy of neutralisation** and can be measured experimentally. For example:

Formula equation:

$$HCl(aq) + NaOH(aq) \rightarrow NaCl(aq) + H_2O(l)$$

   acid   base   salt   water

                           (neutral products)

Ionic equation: $H^+(aq) + OH^-(aq) \rightarrow H_2O(l)$

ΔH (enthalpy of neutralisation) = $-57.6\,kJ\,mol^{-1}$ at 25°C

Note that the value of the enthalpy of neutralisation is the same if HNO_3 reacts with NaOH, or if HCl reacts with KOH; it is independent of the spectator ions that are present in the solution.

Applications of neutralisation reactions

There are many applications of neutralisation reactions in everyday life and industry. Table 6.9 lists some examples.

TABLE 6.9 Applications of neutralisation reactions

Where?	Examples
agriculture	Neutralising acidic soils using powdered lime, CaO, limestone, $CaCO_3$, or ashes of burnt wood. Neutralising basic soils using decomposing compost, which releases acidic CO_2 gas.
industry	Neutralising acidic emissions from factories and power plants. Preventing the coagulation of latex. Using acid–base analysis when testing for quality control in medicines. Using acid–base analysis to determine the acid concentration in wine, fruit juices and vinegar.
health	Treating patients who have indigestion. Treating wasp and bee stings.
home	Preventing tooth decay by neutralising food acids. Using baking powder in food preparation. Adding chemicals to shampoos and washing powders.

Using the Brønsted-Lowry theory

pH AND pOH

The **acidity** of a solution is conveniently measured using the quantity called **pH**. The pH of a solution is a function of the concentration of hydronium ions present in the solution:

$$pH = -\log_{10}[H_3O^+]$$

This equation can be rearranged and written as:

$$[H_3O^+] = 10^{-pH}$$

The pH scale is shown in Figure 6.6. As you can see, the more acidic a solution becomes, the lower its pH. The more basic a solution becomes, the higher its pH. In general, at 25°C:

- pH < 7 is an acidic solution
- pH = 7 is a neutral solution
- pH > 7 is a basic solution.

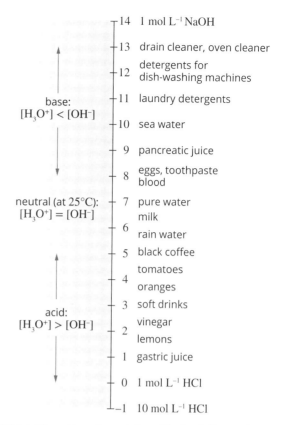

FIGURE 6.6 The pH scale and the pH of solutions of some common household substances

The **basicity** of a solution can be measured using the quantity called **pOH**. The pOH of a solution is a function of the concentration of hydroxide ions present in the solution:

$$pOH = -\log_{10}[OH^-]$$

This equation can be rearranged and written as $[OH^-] = 10^{-pOH}$.

IONISATION CONSTANT OF WATER (K_w)

In an aqueous solution, water molecules react to a very slight extent to form H_3O^+ and OH^- ions:

$$H_2O(l) + H_2O(l) \rightleftharpoons H_3O^+(aq) + OH^-(aq)$$
$$\Delta H = +57.6\ kJ\ mol^{-1}$$

This reaction is called the **self-ionisation** of water, and an equilibrium constant can be written as:

$$K_{eq} = \frac{[H_3O^+][OH^-]}{[H_2O]^2}$$

Because the concentration of water in aqueous solutions, $[H_2O]$, is approximately $55\,mol\,L^{-1}$ and relatively constant, it is convenient to include the $[H_2O]^2$ term as part of the equilibrium constant.

So:

$$K_{eq} \times [H_2O]^2 = K_w = [H_3O^+][OH^-]$$
$$= 1.0 \times 10^{-14}\ at\ 25°C$$

where K_w is the **ionisation constant of water** (also called the ionic product of water).

In pure water at 25°C, $[H_3O^+] = [OH^-]$, so the concentration of both H_3O^+ and OH^- is $1.0 \times 10^{-7}\,mol\,L^{-1}$.

If the concentration of OH^- in a solution is known, the concentration of H_3O^+ in the solution can be calculated, and vice versa.

Since $K_w = [H_3O^+][OH^-]$, you can see that as $[H_3O^+]$ increases the $[OH^-]$ decreases, and vice versa. At 25°C, pH + pOH = 14.

K_w is an equilibrium constant, so it is temperature-dependent. The ionisation constant of water is 1.0×10^{-14} only at 25°C. Because the self-ionisation reaction between water molecules is an endothermic reaction, we know from Le Châtelier's principle that as the temperature increases, K_w will also increase. As a consequence, $[H_3O^+]$ will increase and the pH of water will decrease as the temperature increases.

CALCULATING THE pH OF DILUTIONS AND MIXTURES

The following flow chart (Figure 6.7) shows how to calculate pH when a strong acid or a strong base is diluted, or when a strong acid and a strong base are mixed together. The worksheets in this book will give you practice in these calculations.

Quantitative analysis

ACID-BASE TECHNIQUES USED BY ABORIGINAL AND TORRES STRAIT ISLANDER PEOPLES

Aboriginal and Torres Strait Islander peoples have always used bush plants for medicines. Some are heated and applied to the skin, others are boiled and inhaled and occasionally drunk. These medicines may be acidic or basic.

An example of the use of acids as a food is the Billy-goat plum or Kakadu plum. This plant is found in the woodland regions of Western Australia and the Northern Territory. The vitamin C (ascorbic acid) concentration in the plums is more than 50 times higher than that found in oranges, and they are used as a major food source. A fruit called quinine berry has acid properties and is used for treating toothache by holding the berries in the mouth.

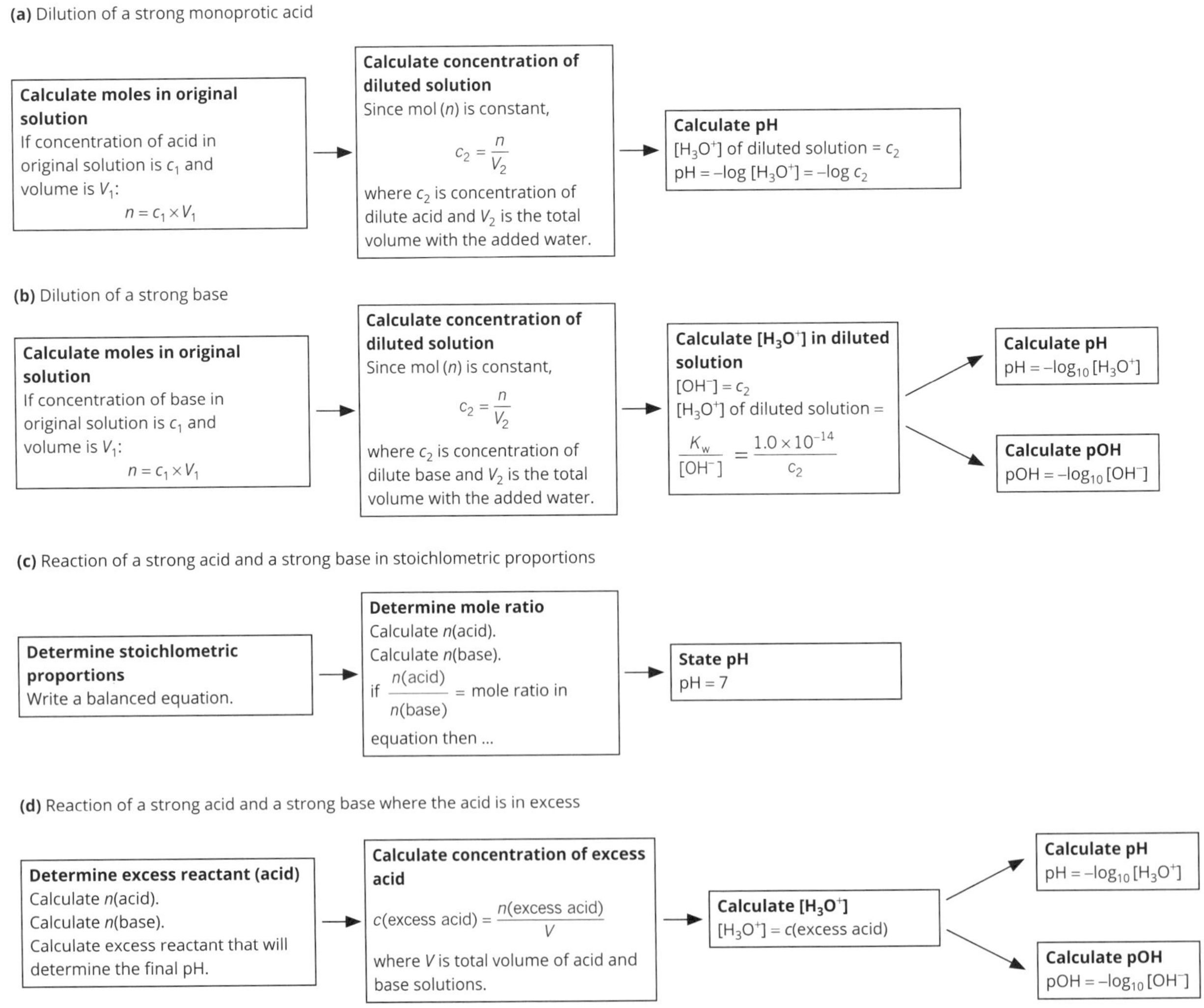

(a) Dilution of a strong monoprotic acid

Calculate moles in original solution
If concentration of acid in original solution is c_1 and volume is V_1:
$$n = c_1 \times V_1$$

Calculate concentration of diluted solution
Since mol (n) is constant,
$$c_2 = \frac{n}{V_2}$$
where c_2 is concentration of dilute acid and V_2 is the total volume with the added water.

Calculate pH
$[H_3O^+]$ of diluted solution = c_2
pH = $-\log [H_3O^+]$ = $-\log c_2$

(b) Dilution of a strong base

Calculate moles in original solution
If concentration of base in original solution is c_1 and volume is V_1:
$$n = c_1 \times V_1$$

Calculate concentration of diluted solution
Since mol (n) is constant,
$$c_2 = \frac{n}{V_2}$$
where c_2 is concentration of dilute base and V_2 is the total volume with the added water.

Calculate $[H_3O^+]$ in diluted solution
$[OH^-] = c_2$
$[H_3O^+]$ of diluted solution =
$$\frac{K_w}{[OH^-]} = \frac{1.0 \times 10^{-14}}{c_2}$$

Calculate pH
pH = $-\log_{10}[H_3O^+]$

Calculate pOH
pOH = $-\log_{10}[OH^-]$

(c) Reaction of a strong acid and a strong base in stoichiometric proportions

Determine stoichiometric proportions
Write a balanced equation.

Determine mole ratio
Calculate n(acid).
Calculate n(base).
if $\dfrac{n(acid)}{n(base)}$ = mole ratio in equation then ...

State pH
pH = 7

(d) Reaction of a strong acid and a strong base where the acid is in excess

Determine excess reactant (acid)
Calculate n(acid).
Calculate n(base).
Calculate excess reactant that will determine the final pH.

Calculate concentration of excess acid
$$c(\text{excess acid}) = \frac{n(\text{excess acid})}{V}$$
where V is total volume of acid and base solutions.

Calculate $[H_3O^+]$
$[H_3O^+] = c$(excess acid)

Calculate pH
pH = $-\log_{10}[H_3O^+]$

Calculate pOH
pOH = $-\log_{10}[OH^-]$

FIGURE 6.7 Calculating pH for (a) dilution of a strong monoprotic acid, (b) dilution of a strong base, (c) the reaction of a strong acid and a strong base in stoichiometric proportions, and (d) the reaction of a strong acid and a strong base where the acid is in excess

TITRATIONS

Acid–base titrations can be used to determine the concentration of an acid or a base in a water sample. Acid–base titrations are a type of volumetric analysis and can be used to determine the concentrations of ingredients in common household substances, such as soft drink, wine, juice and medicine. The analysis involves performing volume–volume stoichiometry calculations.

To calculate an unknown concentration of an acid or a base using volume–volume stoichiometry, you need to know the volumes of both reactants in the titration, as well as the concentration of one reactant. The calculation requires a balanced equation, the use of stoichiometric ratios and the formula $n = c \times V$ (Figure 6.8). The worksheets in this book provide you with practice in performing these calculations.

In a simple acid–base titration (Figure 6.9), one solution is dispensed from a **burette** into a conical flask that contains a volume of another solution, which has been precisely measured using a **pipette**. These solutions are usually colourless, so an acid–base **indicator** is added to the conical flask. The indicator selected must be one that changes colour when stoichiometric amounts of reactants have been added, making it possible to see when the reaction is complete.

Instead of using an indicator, a titration can also be monitored using a pH meter or conductivity meter, as described below.

TERMINOLOGY IN VOLUMETRIC ANALYSIS

Some of the terms used in volumetric analysis are listed in Table 6.10 on page 56.

DETERMINING THE pH CHANGE DURING A TITRATION

Indicators

An acid–base indicator is a weak acid that has a conjugate base of a different colour. The colour of an indicator in solution depends on the relative concentrations of the acid and base, and therefore depends on the pH of the solution. Table 6.11 on page 56 lists the source of some common indicators and their pH range (the pH over which they change colour).

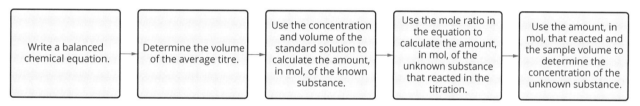

FIGURE 6.8 Flow chart summarising the steps in the calculation of the concentration of an unknown substance using data from a titration

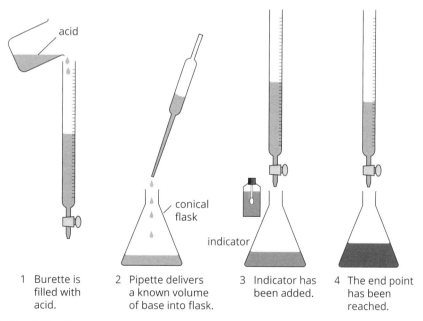

FIGURE 6.9 Steps in a direct titration

Indicators undergo reversible reactions between their acid and base forms. If the acid form is represented by the general formula HIn and the base form as In$^-$, the reaction can be represented as:

$$HIn(aq) + H_2O(l) \rightleftharpoons In^-(aq) + H_3O^+(aq)$$

with an acidity constant given by:

$$K_a = \frac{[H_3O^+][In^-]}{[HIn]}$$

Indicators are used in acid–base titrations to indicate the equivalence point of the reaction. If an indicator is selected carefully, the end point and the equivalence point of the reaction will occur at nearly the same pH.

Several plants contain compounds that act as indicators, such as lichens (the source of litmus), red cabbage, hydrangeas and beetroot. However, the indicators used for titrations usually have synthetic origins.

TABLE 6.10 Terms used in volumetric analysis

Term	Description
primary standard	A substance so pure that the amount can be accurately calculated from its mass. For a chemical to be a primary standard, it should be easily obtained, have a known formula and be easily stored without reacting with water or gases in the atmosphere. Na_2CO_3 is an example of a primary standard.
standard solution	A solution with an accurately known concentration. This illustration shows a standard solution being made from a primary standard. 1 Place weighed sample in volumetric flask. 2 Half fill with water. Shake to dissolve the sample. 3 Add water to the calibration line. Shake again.
burette	A calibrated glass tube that delivers variable volumes accurately.
titre	The volume delivered by a burette.
pipette	A calibrated glass tube that delivers a fixed volume accurately.
aliquot	Volume delivered by a pipette.
end point	The point at which the indicator changes colour.
equivalence point	The point in the titration when stoichiometric proportions of the reactants have been mixed.
indicator	A weak acid that has a conjugate base of a different colour.

TABLE 6.11 Some indicators and their origin, colour and pH range

Indicator	Origin	Colour in acid	Colour in base	pH range
phenolphthalein	synthetic	colourless	pink	8.2–10.0
methyl orange	synthetic	pink	yellow	3.2–4.4
bromothymol blue	synthetic	yellow	blue	6.0–7.6

Conductivity graphs

An alternative to using an indicator to determine an equivalence point is to measure the conductivity of the solution in the flask. When titrating a strong acid with a strong base, a graph of the conductivity of the acid solution against the volume of base added shows a sharp dip at the equivalence point.

The conductivity of the solution is largely dependent on the concentration of H_3O^+ and OH^- ions, which are small and mobile. Table 6.12 shows the conductivity graphs that are observed for titrations of different combinations of strong and weak acids and bases, and explains the reasons for the shapes of the graphs. The equivalence point is indicated by the dashed grey line.

TABLE 6.12 Explanation of shapes of conductivity graphs

Reaction	Conductivity graph	Stages	Concentration of mobile ions, H_3O^+ and OH^-	Conductivity
strong acid, HCl, with strong base, NaOH	Volume of NaOH (mL)	initially	high $[H_3O^+]$	high
		gradual addition of base	decrease in $[H_3O^+]$ due to neutralisation by OH^- ions	decreases
		at equivalence point	$[H_3O^+] = [OH^-]$	at a minimum; only larger, slow-moving ions are present
		continued addition of base after equivalence point	high $[OH^-]$	increases
strong acid, HCl, with weak base, NH_3	Volume of NH_3 (mL)	initially	high $[H_3O^+]$	high
		gradual addition of base	decrease in $[H_3O^+]$ due to neutralisation by the added base	decreases
		at equivalence point	$[H_3O^+] = [OH^-]$	at a minimum; only larger, slow-moving ions are present
		continued addition of base after equivalence point	low $[OH^-]$	remains approximately constant because of the partial ionisation of the weak base and minimal concentration of mobile OH^- ions
weak acid, CH_3COOH, with strong base, NaOH	Volume of NaOH (mL)	initially	low $[H_3O^+]$	low; the partial ionisation of the weak acid produces a low concentration of mobile H_3O^+ ions
		gradual addition of base	neutralises weak acid to produce less mobile conjugate base ions	gradually increases due to increasing concentration of conjugate base ions
		at equivalence point	$[H_3O^+] = [OH^-]$	significant because of a high concentration of the conjugate base ions
		continued addition of base after equivalence point	high $[OH^-]$	increases

Titration curves

If a pH meter is used for a titration, a titration curve can be plotted of pH against volume of base added and the equivalence point identified from the shape of the curve. Table 6.13 shows the titration curves for different reactions with explanations of the pH at different points along the curves.

Figure 6.10 on the next page compares the titration curves of a strong acid and a strong base with a strong acid and a weak base, and also a strong acid and a strong base with a weak acid and a strong base. In summary:

- in a strong acid–strong base titration, pH = 7 at equivalence point
- in a weak acid–strong base titration, pH > 7 at equivalence point
- in a strong acid–weak base titration, pH < 7 at equivalence point.

TABLE 6.13 Explanation of shape of pH curves

Reaction	pH curve	Stages	pH	Explanation of shape and pH
strong acid, HCl, with strong base, NaOH		1	very low	High [H_3O^+] due to complete ionisation of strong acid
		2	7	Equivalence point, where [H_3O^+] = [OH^-] because moles of strong acid equal moles of strong base. Neutral salt and water are products.
		3	very high	Excess OH^- ions as more base is added
strong acid, HCl, with weak base, NH_3		1	very low	High [H_3O^+] due to complete ionisation of strong acid
		2	<7	Equivalence point, where moles of HCl equals moles of NH_3. The conjugate acid of the weak base ionises slightly, producing some H_3O^+ so the pH is less than 7.
		3	high	[OH^-] ions from ionisation of excess NH_3, causes pH to increase slowly to produce a moderately basic solution
weak acid, CH_3COOH, with strong base, NaOH		1	low	pH below 7, due to partial ionisation of weak acid
		2	>7	Equivalence point, where moles of CH_3COOH equals moles of NaOH. The conjugate base of the weak acid ionises slightly, producing OH^-, so the pH is more than 7.
		3	very high	Excess OH^- ions as more base is added

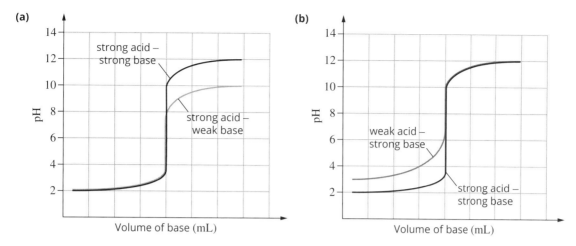

FIGURE 6.10 Comparison of titration curves: (a) pH curve of a strong acid and a strong base with a strong acid and a weak base, and (b) pH curve of a strong acid and a strong base with a weak acid and a strong base

DISSOCIATION CONSTANTS

Acidity constant, K_a and pK_a

Consider the ionisation of the weak acid, ethanoic acid, in water:

$$CH_3COOH(aq) + H_2O(l) \quad H_3O^+(aq) + CH_3COO^-(aq)$$

An equilibrium constant can be written as:

$$K_{eq} = \frac{[H_3O^+][CH_3COO^-]}{[CH_3COOH][H_2O]}$$

Because $[H_2O]$ is almost constant, you can write:

$$K_{eq}[H_2O] = K_a = \frac{[H_3O^+][CH_3COO^-]}{[CH_3COOH]}$$

$$= 1.75 \times 10^{-5} \text{ at } 25°C$$

The constant K_a is called the **acidity constant** of the acid. An acidity constant is a measure of the strength of an acid. The small value of K_a for CH_3COOH indicates that the extent of the reaction is limited and that CH_3COOH is a weak acid. By comparison, the K_a for HCl is 10^7 at 25°C. The reaction of HCl with water is almost complete at equilibrium and HCl is classed as a strong acid.

Just as pH is defined as $-\log[H_3O^+]$, **pK_a** is defined as $-\log_{10}K_a$.

Table 6.14 summarises the key formulae you need to know for your study of acids and bases.

TABLE 6.14 Acid–base formulae

pH = $-\log_{10}[H_3O^+]$	$[H_3O^+] = 10^{-pH}$
pH + pOH = 14 (at 25°C)	$[H_3O^+] \times [OH^-] = 1.00 \times 10^{-14}$ (at 25°C)
pOH = $-\log_{10}[OH^-]$	$[OH^-] = 10^{-pOH}$
pK_a = $-\log_{10}(K_a)$	$K_a = 10^{-pK_a}$

BUFFERS

Buffers are solutions that contain appreciable amounts of a weak acid and its conjugate weak base. Buffers resist changes to pH. A buffer may be prepared by mixing a weak acid with a soluble salt of its conjugate base.

The most effective buffers have approximately equal amounts of the conjugate acid and base. To make a buffer of a particular pH, the conjugate acid–base pair that is chosen should have a pK_a of the acid as close as possible to the desired pH.

Table 6.15 describes how a buffer made from ethanoic acid and sodium ethanoate resists a change in pH when HCl is added. The acid and its conjugate base are in equilibrium:

$$CH_3COOH(aq) + H_2O(l) \rightleftharpoons H_3O^+(aq) + CH_3COO^-(aq)$$

TABLE 6.15 How a buffer consisting of ethanoic acid and ethanoate ions resists change to pH

Stage	Explanation
initial	Equilibrium between buffer acid and buffer base. Equal amounts of both the acid and base are present in the buffer.
addition of a small amount of HCl	As Le Châtelier's principle predicts, the added H$^+$ favours the reverse reaction; the reaction between the added acid and buffer base produces more buffer acid.
final	Equilibrium is restored between buffer acid and buffer base. Most of the added H$^+$ has been neutralised and so there is little decrease in pH.

Similarly, the addition of a small amount of a strong base will favour the forward reaction. Most of the added OH$^-$ will be neutralised by reaction with the buffer acid and again there will be little increase in pH.

Buffers in natural systems

Buffers are essential in many natural systems. Two examples are described below.

- Seawater contains an equilibrium mixture of CO_2, H_2CO_3, HCO_3^- and CO_3^{2-} ions (Figure 6.11). This mixture acts as a buffer, preventing significant changes of pH that would be detrimental to marine life.

The reactions that form a buffer in sea water can be written as:

$$H_2CO_3(aq) + H_2O(l) \rightleftharpoons H_3O^+(aq) + HCO_3^-(aq)$$
$$HCO_3^-(aq) + H_2O(l) \rightleftharpoons H_3O^+(aq) + CO_3^{2-}(aq)$$

The addition of acid shifts the equilibria to the left, minimising the change in pH. Similarly, addition of a base shifts the equilibria to the right with little effect on pH.

At present the pH of sea water is 8.1, but because of the increased levels of atmospheric CO_2 it is expected to decrease in the future. This effect is referred to as 'ocean acidification'.

- The human body has a number of buffer systems that control pH. Enzymes are biological catalysts that play a vital role by ensuring different biochemical reactions proceed at the required rate. Enzyme activity is optimum within a narrow pH range.

CO_2 is produced during the process of respiration. It dissolves in blood to form carbonic acid, which tends to reduce the pH. A buffer system counteracts this effect and assists in maintaining the pH in blood at almost constant levels. The buffer is made from H_2CO_3 and HCO_3^-:

$$H_2CO_3(aq) + H_2O(l) \rightleftharpoons H_3O^+(aq) + HCO_3^-(aq)$$

The same buffer resists potentially fatal pH changes in blood when diseases produce acidosis (a decrease in pH) or alkalosis (an increase in pH).

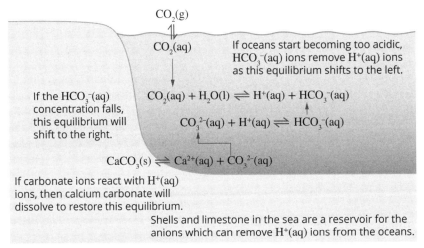

FIGURE 6.11 Sea water contains an equilibrium mixture of CO_2, H_2CO_3, HCO_3^- and CO_3^{2-} ions.

. . . .

WORKSHEET 6.1

Knowledge review—acids and bases

1 Define the following terms. This will help you check your knowledge and understanding of the key ideas involved in acid–base theory and the dilution of solutions.

Weak acid:

_____

Strong base:

_____

Dilute solution:

_____

Concentrated solution:

_____

2 Write balanced equations for the reactions that occur when the following substances dissolve in water. Include states of matter in the equations.

$HCl(g)$ _____

$NaOH(s)$ _____

$NH_3(g)$ _____

$CH_3COOH(l)$ _____

3 Which of the following statements about standard solutions are true?

A A standard solution has an accurately known concentration.

B A standard solution always has a neutral pH.

C A standard solution always has a concentration of $1.0\,mol\,L^{-1}$.

D A standard solution can have any concentration, as long as it is accurately known.

E A standard solution must be pure and not react with the atmosphere.

4 Calculate the concentration of a standard solution prepared by dissolving 3.65 g of sodium carbonate, Na_2CO_3, in water and making the volume up to 250.0 mL in a volumetric flask.

5 Determine the mass of sodium carbonate, Na_2CO_3, you would need to dissolve in a 500 mL volumetric flask to make up 500 mL of a $1.00\,mol\,L^{-1}$ solution.

6 Medicines have been developed over the years as scientists learn more about diseases. Since ancient times people have used different plants as medicines and health treatments, without necessarily understanding how they worked on a chemical level. More recently, in their search for new medicines, international pharmaceutical companies have used traditional knowledge of the indigenous people in many parts of the world to guide them.

In order to extract the active chemical for use as a new medicine, it saves significant time and money if the companies use bush medicine to locate the active chemical from which a new drug can be made. However, this often results in huge profits for the companies who have a patent on the new drug, and nothing for the indigenous people whose intellectual property has been passed down for generations. This is often referred to as biopiracy. Read the following extract from the Wet Tropics Management Authority in Cairns about bush medicine.

Hyoscine is the chemical which achieved sudden notoriety recently when larger than normal doses in Travacalm tablets caused severe illness in a number of people. Interestingly, this chemical is found in a common rainforest tree known as soft corkwood (*Duboisia myoporoides*). Indeed, when this tree was hybridised with a closely related species last century the result contained more hyoscine than any other known plant. It was grown commercially to make ophthalmic and sedative drugs, before synthetic versions of the compound were developed. Extracts from the plant dilate the pupil – useful in eye surgery – and during World War II considerable quantities of hyoscine were exported to treat travel sickness in troops and shell shock. In 1989, 500 tonnes of dried and powdered leaves were exported to pharmaceutical companies in Germany and Switzerland.

Soft corkwood is poisonous to stock and has been blamed for at least one human death, in 1987, when a man experimentally ate some leaves. Interestingly, it is closely related to a desert shrub, pituri (*Duboisia hopwoodii*) which was valued as a narcotic and widely traded by Aboriginal people in days gone by.

(Source: 'Bush medicine', Wet Tropics Management Authority.)

a Travacalm is an antihistamine that contains a mixture of drugs, including hyoscine. The hyoscine molecule has an –OH group and other polar groups, and acts as a base (see the figure below). Consider the structure and bonding of hyoscine below and discuss whether it is likely to dissolve well in water.

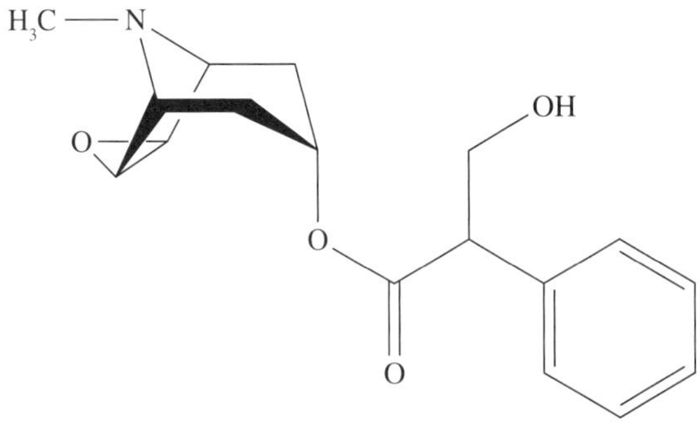

b What is a narcotic?

_____

_____

c Research online to find the names of three other traditional bush medicines.

_____

_____

d What is meant by a component of a medicine that is 'active'?

_____

_____

e What is meant by 'biopiracy'?

_____

_____

_____

WORKSHEET 6.2

Concentration and strength—modelling acids and bases and calculating pH

1   Complete the following table by listing the types of particles present in each solution. Draw a model or represent the relative numbers of particles in solution. The first row has been completed for you.

Solution and chemical formula	Weak or strong acid or base?	Particles present in solution	Model of the relative proportions of particles
concentrated hydrochloric acid, HCl	strong acid	H_2O molecules Cl^- ions H_3O^+ ions OH^- ions	 concentrated HCl(aq) or H_2O molecules: ✓✓✓✓✓✓✓✓✓✓✓✓✓✓ Cl^- ions: ✓✓✓✓✓✓ H_3O^+ ions: ✓✓✓✓✓✓ OH^- ions: negligible HCl molecules: none where ✓ represents millions of particles
dilute nitric acid			
concentrated ethanoic acid			
dilute sodium hydroxide			
concentrated ammonia			

ISBN 978 1 4886 1934 2

2 Complete the following table by calculating the pH of different types of strong acids and strong bases from their concentrations.

Solution	Relationship of $[H_3O^+]$ to [acid] or $[OH^-]$ to [base]	Calculation of pH
$0.10\,mol\,L^{-1}$ HCl	$[H_3O^+]$ = [acid]	
$0.10\,mol\,L^{-1}$ H_2SO_4 (assume fully ionised)	$[H_3O^+]$ =	
$0.10\,mol\,L^{-1}$ NaOH	$[OH^-]$ = [base]	
$0.010\,mol\,L^{-1}$ $Ca(OH)_2$	$[OH^-]$ =	

3 What is the key difference between an acid and a base according to the Brønsted–Lowry theory?

_____

_____

4 Explain the differences between a monoprotic acid and a diprotic acid.

_____

_____

_____

5 Scientists develop models to understand and explain natural phenomena. While they may not always be able to see or fully understand a phenomenon, the models provide representations and theories consistent with the observations the scientists make.

The models of acids and bases have changed over time as chemists developed a better understanding of the properties of matter. Two models for acids and bases are Arrhenius' theory and the Brønsted–Lowry theory.

Read the following statements and discuss their accuracy.

a Despite a fundamental difference between these two theories, they both explain acids and bases.

_____

_____

_____

b Use of the Brønsted–Lowry theory of acids and bases offers no advantages over Arrhenius' theory.

_____

_____

_____

RATING MY LEARNING	My understanding improved	Not confident ← → Very confident ○ ○ ○ ○ ○	I answered questions without help	Not confident ← → Very confident ○ ○ ○ ○ ○	I corrected my errors without help	Not confident ← → Very confident ○ ○ ○ ○ ○

WORKSHEET 6.3

Acid-base relationships—calculating pH and pOH

1 Complete the following statements about the strength of acids using the terms and expressions given below. Some terms may not be used, and others may be used more than once.

$[H_3O^+]$	acidity	$[OH^-]$	$[A^-]$	forward	pOH	$[HA][H_2O]$	constant
pK_a	pH	higher	lower	ionises	reverse	temperature	[HA]

Consider the general ionisation reaction of an acid in water:

$$HA(aq) + H_2O(l) \rightleftharpoons H_3O^+(aq) + A^-(aq)$$

The strength of the acid (the extent to which it _____) is measured by the equilibrium constant for the reaction, K_{eq} = _____ / _____ . Because the $[H_2O]$ is nearly _____ in an aqueous solution, this expression is simplified to K_a = _____ / _____ . This expression is called the _____ constant.

We define _____ as $-\log_{10} [H_3O^+]$ and _____ as $-\log_{10}[OH^-]$. K_a can also be expressed as a logarithmic term, _____ = $-\log_{10}K_a$. Like all equilibrium constants, K_a is _____ dependent. The larger its value, the _____ the concentration of the products, indicating that the extent of reaction is in the _____ direction, favouring the products.

2 Complete the calculations of pH and pOH for each of the following solutions and enter your answers in the table.

Solution	Calculation
0.010 mol L^{-1} HCl (a strong monoprotic acid)	$[HCl] = 0.010\,mol\,L^{-1} = 1.0 \times 10^{-2}\,mol\,L^{-1}$ $[H_3O^+]$ = _____ $[OH^-]$ = _____ pH = _____ pOH = _____
0.050 mol L^{-1} H$_2$SO$_4$ (a diprotic strong acid; assume fully ionised)	$[H_2SO_4] = 0.050\,mol\,L^{-1}$ $[H_3O^+]$ = _____ $[OH^-]$ = _____ pH = _____ pOH = _____
0.010 mol L^{-1} CH$_3$COOH (a weak monoprotic acid)	$[CH_3COOH] = 0.010\,mol\,L^{-1} = 1.0 \times 10^{-2}\,mol\,L^{-1}$ $K_a = 1.75 \times 10^{-5}$ $[H_3O^+]$ = _____ $[OH^-]$ = _____ pH = _____ pOH = _____
0.010 mol L^{-1} NaOH (a strong base)	$[NaOH] = 0.010\,mol\,L^{-1} = 1.0 \times 10^{-2}\,mol\,L^{-1}$ $[OH^-]$ = _____ $[H_3O^+]$ = _____ pOH = _____ pH = _____
0.00050 mol L^{-1} Mg(OH)$_2$ (a strong base)	$[Mg(OH)_2] = 0.00050\,mol\,L^{-1} = 5.0 \times 10^{-4}\,mol\,L^{-1}$ $[OH^-]$ = _____ $[H_3O^+]$ = _____ pOH = _____ pH = _____

3 Some interesting differences in the change in pH occur when a strong acid is diluted compared to the dilution of a weak acid.

a Calculate the pH for each of the following solutions, given HNO$_3$ is a strong acid and $K_a(CH_3COOH) = 1.75 \times 10^{-5}$.

Strength of acid	Concentrated solution	Dilute solution
strong	1.0 mol L^{-1} HNO$_3$ pH = _____	0.010 mol L^{-1} HNO$_3$ pH = _____
weak	1.0 mol L^{-1} CH$_3$COOH pH = _____	0.010 mol L^{-1} CH$_3$COOH pH = _____

b Using the answers from part a to help you, complete the following summary.

For a strong acid, when the acid is diluted by a factor of 100, $[H_3O^+]$ decreases by a factor of _____ and the pH *increases/decreases* (circle the correct one) by _____ units. The effect of dilution on the pH of a weak acid is greater/less (circle the correct one) than for a strong acid.

RATING MY LEARNING	My understanding improved	Not confident ← → Very confident ○ ○ ○ ○ ○	I answered questions without help	Not confident ← → Very confident ○ ○ ○ ○ ○	I corrected my errors without help	Not confident ← → Very confident ○ ○ ○ ○ ○

WORKSHEET 6.4

Indicators and K_a—colourful considerations

Acid–base indicators are weak acids or bases. In solution, the acid form of an indicator forms an equilibrium with its conjugate base. The acid form of the indicator is a different colour to the base form and different indicators change colour at different pH.

Bromothymol blue is an indicator that is yellow in its acid form and blue in its base form. Because indicators are large molecules, we often abbreviate their names instead of writing their full formulae. For bromothymol blue we can use HBm for the acid form and Bm^- for the base form. The equilibrium that forms in solution can be represented as:

$$HBm(aq) + H_2O(l) \rightleftharpoons H_3O^+(aq) + Bm^-(aq) \qquad K_a \text{ at } 25°C = 1.0 \times 10^{-7}$$

When $[H_3O^+]$ is greater than $10 \times K_a$, the yellow colour of HBm dominates, and when $[H_3O^+]$ is less than $\frac{K_a}{10}$, the blue colour of Bm^- dominates.

1 Write an expression for the acidity constant for the above reaction.

2 What is the pH of the indicator when the acid and base forms are present in equal concentrations, i.e. $[HBm] = [Bm^-]$?

3 Predict the colour of the solution at this point.

4 What is the value of the fraction $\frac{[Bm^-]}{[HBm]}$ at pH 5?

5 Predict the colour of the solution at this point.

6 What is the value of the fraction $\frac{[Bm^-]}{[HBm]}$ at pH 8?

7 Predict the colour of the solution at this point.

8 For an acid–base titration that has an equivalence point of pH 5, is bromothymol blue likely to be suitable to use as the indicator? Explain.

9 The purple colour in grapes and the red colour in cabbage are two natural indicators found in plants. Suggest one reason that fruits change colour when they ripen.

RATING MY LEARNING	My understanding improved	Not confident ◄—► Very confident O O O O O	I answered questions without help	Not confident ◄—► Very confident O O O O O	I corrected my errors without help	Not confident ◄—► Very confident O O O O O

ISBN 978 1 4886 1934 2

WORKSHEET 6.5

Calculating the pH of mixtures and dilutions

Mixing acids and bases and diluting solutions causes the pH to change.

1 Complete the following mathematical relationships to remind yourself of the connections between pH, pOH, K_w, $[H_3O^+]$ and $[OH^-]$.

   a pH =

   b $[H_3O^+]$ =

   c pOH =

   d $[H_3O^+] \times [OH^-]$ =

   e At 25°C, the value of K_w =

   f At 25°C, pH + pOH =

2 **a** Given the molar mass of sodium hydroxide is $40.0\,g\,mol^{-1}$, what mass of sodium hydroxide must be dissolved in 500.0 mL of water to give a pH of 11.0?

   b What will be the pH of the solution when an extra 500.0 mL of water is added?

3 Calculate the pH of a solution formed by mixing 20.00 mL of $0.30\,mol\,L^{-1}$ HCl with 30.00 mL of $0.15\,mol\,L^{-1}$ HNO_3.

4 HI is a strong acid. 6.4 g of HI is dissolved to give 2.0 L of solution.

   a Calculate the pH of the solution.

   b When a 20.00 mL aliquot is diluted to a volume of 250 mL, what is the pH of this diluted solution?

5 A NaOH solution has a pH of 12.0. A 60.00 mL volume of the NaOH solution is added to 4.0×10^{-3} mol of HCl in water. What volume of $0.200\,mol\,L^{-1}$ KOH must be added to bring the pH of the solution to 7.0?

6 Calculate the pH of the final solution obtained by mixing 20 mL of $0.20\,mol\,L^{-1}$ KOH solution with 80 mL of $0.20\,mol\,L^{-1}$ HCl solution.

RATING MY LEARNING	My understanding improved	Not confident	← →	Very confident	I answered questions without help	Not confident	← →	Very confident	I corrected my errors without help	Not confident	← →	Very confident
			○ ○ ○ ○ ○				○ ○ ○ ○ ○				○ ○ ○ ○ ○	

Acid–base curves—detecting an equivalence point

1 To assist in the selection of an appropriate indicator for an acid–base titration, it is useful to examine the pH changes that occur during the titration. For example, when a weak acid is titrated with a strong base the equivalence point occurs when enough strong base has been added to react exactly with all the weak acid present. The equivalence point will have a pH greater than 7 because the conjugate base of the weak acid will ionise, producing OH^- ions.

Some common indicators and their colour ranges are listed below.

Indicator	pH range	Colour of acid form of indicator	Colour of base form of indicator
methyl orange	3.1–4.4	red	yellow
bromophenol blue	3.0–4.6	yellow	blue
methyl red	4.2–6.3	red	yellow
bromothymol blue	6.0–7.6	yellow	blue
phenolphthalein	8.3–10.0	colourless	red

a Use the table of indicators above to decide which indicator, methyl orange or phenolphthalein, would be more suitable for detecting the equivalence point of a titration of a strong base and a weak acid.

b Which indicator would be more suitable for a strong acid titrated against a strong base, bromothymol blue or methyl orange?

2 A volumetric analysis was carried out in which 100.0 mL of 0.050 mol L^{-1} ammonia solution was titrated with 0.10 mol L^{-1} hydrochloric acid.

a Write a balanced equation for this reaction.

b Complete the following table.

Total volume of HCl added (mL)	n(HCl) added (mol)	n(NH$_3$) remaining (mol)	[NH$_3$] remaining (mol L^{-1})	[NH$_4^+$] (mol L^{-1})	[H$_3$O$^+$] (mol L^{-1})	pH
0.0	0.00	0.0050	0.050	0.00	1.1×10^{-11}	
10.0	0.0010	0.0040	0.0040/0.110	0.0010/0.110	1.4×10^{-10}	
25.0					5.6×10^{-10}	
40.0					1.0×10^{-8}	
50.0					4.3×10^{-6}	
60.0					6.2×10^{-3}	

c Use the data in the table above to sketch the titration curve (a graph of pH versus volume of HCl added) for this reaction.

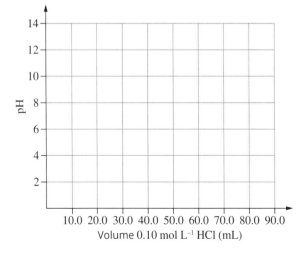

Volume 0.10 mol L^{-1} HCl (mL)

d Label the equivalence point on your curve. What is the pH at this point?

_____

e Briefly explain why the pH is not 7 at the equivalence point.

_____

_____

3 Instead of using an indicator, another way to detect the equivalence point of a titration is to measure the conductivity of the solution. The conductivity of the solution mainly depends on the concentration of the small, mobile H_3O^+ ions or OH^- ions that are present.

a Draw the conductivity curve that you would expect for the reaction between ammonia and hydrochloric acid in question **2** above. Remember that a weak acid or base does not ionise to the same extent as a strong acid or base and therefore the concentration of H_3O^+ ions or OH^- ions will be less. This will affect the conductivity at the starting and finishing points of the curve.

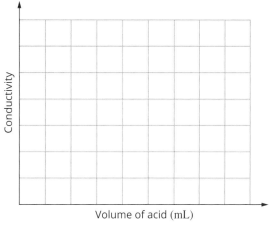

Volume of acid (mL)

b Label the equivalence point on your curve.

c Briefly explain the shape of the conductivity curve for this titration.

_____

_____

_____

| RATING MY LEARNING | My understanding improved | Not confident ⟵ ⟶ Very confident ○ ○ ○ ○ ○ | I answered questions without help | Not confident ⟵ ⟶ Very confident ○ ○ ○ ○ ○ | I corrected my errors without help | Not confident ⟵ ⟶ Very confident ○ ○ ○ ○ ○ |

ISBN 978 1 4886 1934 2   Pearson Chemistry 12 NSW | Skills and Assessment | Module 6   **69**

....

WORKSHEET 6.7

Volumetric analysis—finding the fizz in soda water

The steps to determine the concentration of carbon dioxide dissolved in soda water are listed below.

1 Write numbers beside each step to indicate the order in which they should be performed.

A Add phenolphthalein indicator. _____

B Stir the soda water well and then pipette 20.00 mL of soda water into a 100 mL conical flask. _____

C Record the final burette reading. _____

D Fill the burette with 0.100 mol L^{-1} sodium hydroxide solution. _____

E Record the initial burette reading. _____

F Titrate until the first permanent pink colour is observed. _____

2 Draw a diagram to show each of the main steps in the experiment. Your diagram should include sketches of the following pieces of equipment: burette, conical flask and pipette.

3 A student recorded the results below for the analysis. Use these data to answer the questions and calculate the concentration of carbon dioxide in the soda water.

Experiment number	Initial burette reading (mL)	Final burette reading (mL)	Titre (mL)
1	0.00	10.25	
2	10.25	20.24	
3	20.24	30.19	
4	30.19	40.29	

a At the end point of this titration the carbon dioxide has formed the hydrogen carbonate, HCO_3^-, ion. Write a balanced equation for the reaction between aqueous carbon dioxide and sodium hydroxide solution.

_____

b Calculate the average titre. Use only concordant values.

_____

_____

_____

c Freshly opened soda water is supersaturated. What is the advantage of stirring the solution before taking an aliquot of the soda water?

_____

_____

d Calculate the number of moles of sodium hydroxide used to reach the end point.

_____

_____

_____

_____

e Calculate the number of moles of carbon dioxide present in the aliquot.

_____

_____

f Calculate the concentration of the carbon dioxide as a saturated solution in the bottle of soda water.

_____

_____

_____

_____

g The equipment used in the titration was washed immediately before use. Complete the following table by stating whether the equipment should be washed with water, sodium hydroxide solution or soda water. Explain the reason for your choice.

Equipment	Wash with ...	State the reason for your choice.
conical flask		
pipette		
burette		

h Explain the reason for using an indicator in the titration. Include the terms _end point_ and _equivalence point_ in your answer.

_____

_____

_____

_____

RATING MY LEARNING | My understanding improved — Not confident ◄——► Very confident ○ ○ ○ ○ ○ | I answered questions without help — Not confident ◄——► Very confident ○ ○ ○ ○ ○ | I corrected my errors without help — Not confident ◄——► Very confident ○ ○ ○ ○ ○

ISBN 978 1 4886 1934 2   Pearson Chemistry 12 NSW | Skills and Assessment | Module 6   **71**

WORKSHEET 6.8

Buffers—keeping pH in control

Buffers resist changes in pH by neutralising either an excess of acid or base that is added to the system. There are a number of different buffer systems in the environment and in the human body that maintain pH within the narrow ranges that are critical for life.

The action of a buffer can be understood using Le Châtelier's principle, where the addition of an acid (or base) to a buffer increases the $[H_3O^+]$ (or $[OH^-]$) and causes the reaction to move in the direction that consumes H_3O^+ (or OH^-).

The most effective buffers have approximately equal amounts of the conjugate acid and base. To make a buffer of a particular pH, the pK_a of the acid of the conjugate acid–base pair that is chosen should be as close as possible to the desired pH.

1   Explain why a buffer system is made from a weak acid and its conjugate base, but not from a strong acid and its conjugate base.

2   State whether the following solutions would act as buffers for the pH indicated. Explain your answers.

   a   For pH 1, 1 L of a solution is prepared containing 0.05 mol HNO_3 and 0.05 mol of NO_3^- ions. K_a (HNO_3) = 2.4×10^1.

   b   For pH 4.9, 1 L of a solution is prepared containing 0.05 mol CH_3CH_2COOH and 0.05 mol of CH_3COO^- ions. K_a (CH_3CH_2COOH) = 1.3×10^{-5}.

   c   For pH 4.8, 1 L of a solution is prepared containing 0.6 mol CH_3COOH and 0.006 mol of CH_3COO^- ions. K_a (CH_3COOH) = 1.7×10^{-5}.

   d   For pH 4.9, 1 L of a solution is prepared containing 0.07 mol CH_3CH_2COOH and 0.07 mol of $CH_3CH_2COO^-$ ions. K_a (CH_3CH_2COOH) = 1.3×10^{-5}.

3   The oceans contain the following equilibrium systems:

$CO_2(g) \rightleftharpoons CO_2(aq)$

$CO_2(aq) + H_2O(l) \rightleftharpoons H_2CO_3(aq)$

$H_2CO_3(aq) \rightleftharpoons HCO_3^-(aq) + H^+(aq)$

$HCO_3^-(aq) \rightleftharpoons CO_3^{2-}(aq) + H^+(aq)$

$Ca^{2+}(aq) + CO_3^{2-}(aq) \rightleftharpoons CaCO_3(s)$

Choose the correct alternative from each pair of terms in italics to complete the sentences about these equilibria.

As more CO_2 is released into the atmosphere, a *greater/lesser* amount of CO_2 is dissolving in the oceans. An increased concentration of CO_2 causes the oceans to become more *acidic/basic*. The H^+ ions combine with CO_3^{2-} ions to produce a *higher/lower* concentration of HCO_3^- ions, *reducing/increasing* the CO_3^{2-} concentration, and causing $CaCO_3$ to be *more/less* soluble. As a consequence, marine corals have difficulty producing exoskeletons, which are made from $CaCO_3$.

WORKSHEET 6.9

Literacy review—acids, bases and volumetric analysis

1 Consider the definitions and recall the correct term or expression.

Statement	Term or expression
The point in the titration when the reactants have been mixed in stoichiometric proportions.	
A calibrated glass tube that delivers variable volumes accurately.	
The mathematical expression to calculate the amount, in mole, of a stated volume of a solution whose concentration is given.	
A weak acid with a conjugate base of a different colour.	
The point at which an indicator changes colour.	
A piece of glassware that features a flat base and a cylindrical neck, used to prepare standard solutions.	
Volume delivered by a pipette.	
A calibrated glass tube that delivers a fixed volume accurately.	
The volume delivered by a burette	
A solution that resists changes in pH.	
An acid–base theory that defines a base as a proton acceptor.	
A term equal to the negative log to base 10 of K_a.	
An acid–base pair whose formulae differ by one H^+ unit.	

2 The following questions require you to apply the concepts you have learned in this module.

a Using the hydrogen carbonate ion as an example, write reactions to show a species acting as an acid and a species acting as a base, and to show how an amphiprotic substance behaves.

_____

_____

_____

b Haemoglobin, which can be represented as Hb, and its conjugate acid, HbH^+, act as a buffer system in blood. Is haemoglobin a strong or weak base? Explain briefly how a buffer works.

_____

_____

_____

c For a $0.010\,mol\,L^{-1}$ solution of CH_3COOH, show the steps involved in finding the pH, pOH, pK_a. (The K_a of CH_3COOH is 1.78×10^{-5}.)

_____

_____

_____

_____

RATING MY LEARNING	My understanding improved	Not confident ◯ ◯ ◯ ◯ ◯ Very confident	I answered questions without help	Not confident ◯ ◯ ◯ ◯ ◯ Very confident	I corrected my errors without help	Not confident ◯ ◯ ◯ ◯ ◯ Very confident

WORKSHEET 6.10

Thinking about my learning

On completion of Module 6: Acid/base reactions, you should be able to describe, explain and apply the relevant scientific ideas. You should also be able to interpret, analyse and evaluate data.

1 The table lists the key knowledge covered in this module. Read each and reflect on how well you understand each concept. Rate your learning by shading the circle that corresponds to your level of understanding for each concept. It may be helpful to use colour as a visual representation. For example:

- green—very confident
- orange—in the middle
- red—starting to develop.

Concept focus	**Rate my learning**				
	Starting to develop ◄				► Very confident
Properties of acids and bases	○	○	○	○	○
Using Brønsted–Lowry theory	○	○	○	○	○
Quantitative analysis	○	○	○	○	○

2 Consider the points you have shaded, from starting to develop to middle-level understanding. List specific ideas you can identify that were challenging.

____

____

____

____

____

____

3 Write down two different strategies that you will apply to help further your understanding of these ideas.

____

____

____

____

____

 ISBN 978 1 4886 1934 2

PRACTICAL ACTIVITY 6.1

Comparing the strengths of acids and bases

Suggested duration: 20 minutes

INTRODUCTION

Acids and bases ionise and/or dissociate when they dissolve in water. Covalent compounds that act as acids ionise (form ions) by reacting with water and dissociate (break apart). Ionic compounds that act as bases dissociate when dissolved with water, releasing the ions present in the solid.

The extent to which different acids and bases ionise and/or dissociate depends on whether they are strong or weak acids or bases. A strong acid ionises fully in solution whereas a weak acid only partially ionises. If the concentrations of the acids are equal, the solution of the weak acid has a much lower concentration of H_3O^+ ions. Similarly, a solution of a weak base has a lower concentration of OH^- ions than a solution of a strong base of the same concentration.

PURPOSE

To compare the relative strengths of some acids and bases in order to:

* relate the measured pH of acids to the concentration of H_3O^+ ions
* relate the measured pH of bases to the concentration of H_3O^+ and therefore to OH^- ions
* distinguish between strong and weak acids and bases
* distinguish between monoprotic and polyprotic acids

PRE-LAB SAFETY INFORMATION

Material used	Hazard	Control
0.1 mol L^{-1} hydrochloric acid	corrosive to eyes and skin	Wear safety glasses and lab coat.
0.1 mol L^{-1} sulfuric acid	corrosive to eyes and skin	Wear safety glasses and lab coat.
0.1 mol L^{-1} phosphoric acid	corrosive to eyes and skin	Wear safety glasses and lab coat.
0.1 mol L^{-1} sodium hydroxide solution	may irritate eyes and skin	Wear safety glasses and lab coat.
0.1 mol L^{-1} potassium hydroxide solution	may irritate eyes and skin	Wear safety glasses and lab coat.
0.1 mol L^{-1} ammonia solution	may irritate respiratory system	Wear safety glasses and lab coat.
ethanoic acid solution	may irritate respiratory system	Wear safety glasses and lab coat.

Please indicate that you have understood the information in the safety table.

Name (print): _____

I understand the safety information (signature): _____

PROCEDURE

1   Add about 20 mL of each solution to a small beaker.

2   Use the pH meter to record the pH of each solution in Table 1.

3   Calculate the concentration of H_3O^+ ions in each of the solutions.

4   Use the concentrations of H_3O^+ ions to calculate the concentrations of OH^- ions and pOH for each of solution. Remember that pH + pOH = 14 at 25°C.

RESULTS

TABLE 1 pH, $[H_3O^+]$, pOH and $[OH^-]$ of each solution

Acid	pH	$[H_3O^+]$ (in mol L^{-1})	pOH	$[OH^-]$ (in mol L^{-1})
0.1 mol L^{-1} hydrochloric acid				
0.1 mol L^{-1} ethanoic acid				
0.1 mol L^{-1} sulfuric acid				
0.1 mol L^{-1} phosphoric acid				
0.1 mol L^{-1} sodium hydroxide solution				
0.1 mol L^{-1} potassium hydroxide solution				
0.1 mol L^{-1} ammonia solution				

DISCUSSION

1   Rank the acids from most acidic to least acidic.

2   Account for the difference between the measured pH of ethanoic acid and hydrochloric acid.

3   Explain why 0.1 mol L^{-1} sulfuric acid has a lower pH than 0.1 mol L^{-1} HCl.

4   a   Phosphoric acid is a triprotic acid. Write chemical equations for the three ionisation stages of phosphoric acid.

   b   On the basis of the measured pH of a 0.1 mol L^{-1} solution, is phosphoric acid a weak or strong acid? Explain your answer.

5   Classify the bases as strong or weak.

6 Account for the difference between the measured pH of ammonia solution and sodium hydroxide solution.

_____

_____

_____

7 Explain why $0.1\,mol\,L^{-1}$ KOH solution and $0.1\,mol\,L^{-1}$ NaOH solution have the same pH and pOH.

_____

_____

8 Write chemical equations for the reactions of KOH(s), NaOH(s) and NH_3(aq) solutions with water.

_____

_____

_____

CONCLUSION

9 Discuss the reasons why solutions of acids (or bases) that have the same concentration may not have the same pH.

_____

_____

_____

| RATING MY LEARNING | My understanding improved | Not confident ◄————► Very confident ○ ○ ○ ○ ○ | I answered questions without help | Not confident ◄————► Very confident ○ ○ ○ ○ ○ | I corrected my errors without help | Not confident ◄————► Very confident ○ ○ ○ ○ ○ |

PRACTICAL ACTIVITY 6.2

Amphiprotic substances in water

Suggested duration: 20 minutes

INTRODUCTION

Amphiprotic substances can act as both acids and bases. In aqueous solution, an amphiprotic substance will undergo two hydrolysis reactions, one as an acid and one as a base. In most cases, one of these reactions will predominate. If the acid reaction proceeds to a greater extent than the base reaction, $[H_3O^+] > [OH^-]$ and the pH of the solution will be less than 7. If the base reaction proceeds further than the acid reaction, then the pH of the solution will be greater than 7.

In this experiment, the sodium or potassium salt of the amphiprotic anion is used. The Na^+(aq) ion and K^+(aq) ion do not hydrolyse to any appreciable extent in water. Any change of pH can therefore be attributed to the acid–base reactions of the amphiprotic anion in each solution.

PURPOSE

To determine the relative acid and base strengths of some amphiprotic substances.

To write equations representing the behavior of acids and bases in water and their amphiprotic nature.

PRE-LAB SAFETY INFORMATION		
Material used	**Hazard**	**Control**
universal indicator	irritant to eyes and skin	Wear eye and skin protection.

Please indicate that you have understood the information in the safety table.

Name (print): _____

I understand the safety information (signature): _____

PROCEDURE

1   Place 20 drops of each solution into separate semi-micro test-tubes. Add one drop of universal indicator to each solution. Record the colour of each solution in Table 1. Alternatively, a pH meter can be used.

2   Use the indicator chart to determine the pH of each solution.

RESULTS

TABLE 1 Colour and pH of amphiprotic substances

Solution	Amphiprotic anion	Colour of universal indicator	pH
$0.1 \, mol \, L^{-1}$ $NaHCO_3$			
$0.1 \, mol \, L^{-1}$ $NaHSO_4$			
$0.1 \, mol \, L^{-1}$ K_2HPO_4			
$0.1 \, mol \, L^{-1}$ KH_2PO_4			

DISCUSSION

1 In Table 2, write equations for the acid and base hydrolysis reaction undergone by each of the amphiprotic anions tested in Table 1. In each case, indicate which reaction predominates.

TABLE 2 Acid and base hydrolysis reactions

Solution	Formula of anion	Equations	Does acid or base reaction predominate?
0.1 mol L^{-1} NaHCO$_3$		As acid: As base:	
0.1 mol L^{-1} NaHSO$_4$		As acid: As base:	
0.1 mol L^{-1} K$_2$HPO$_4$		As acid: As base:	
0.1 mol L^{-1} KH$_2$PO$_4$		As acid: As base:	

CONCLUSION

2 Summarise the similarities and differences in behaviour of amphiprotic substances in water.

PRACTICAL ACTIVITY 6.3

Reactions of hydrochloric acid

Suggested duration: 60 minutes

INTRODUCTION

Acids show similar chemical behaviour. They react with many metals and metal compounds in common ways. The following tests can be used to look for common products.

- A lighted taper is used to test for the presence of hydrogen gas. When a lighted taper is placed into a sample of H_2 gas, a 'pop' sound is heard.
- Limewater is used to test for the presence of carbon dioxide. When CO_2 gas is bubbled through limewater (a dilute calcium hydroxide solution) the solution becomes cloudy.
- Methyl violet is an indicator that is yellow at pH of 1 or below and violet at higher pH values.

PURPOSE

To investigate some common reactions of hydrochloric acid, in particular with bases, carbonates and metals.

To write equations to represent these reactions.

PRE-LAB SAFETY INFORMATION		
Material used	**Hazard**	**Control**
$0.1\,mol\,L^{-1}$ hydrochloric acid	corrosive to eyes and skin	Wear eye and skin protection.
$1\,mol\,L^{-1}$ hydrochloric acid	toxic by all routes of exposure; lung irritant	Wear eye and skin protection.
$10\,mol\,L^{-1}$ hydrochloric acid	highly corrosive; lung irritant	Wear eye and skin protection; mop up spills immediately, washing with copious amounts of water; use in fume cupboard.
concentrated ammonia	vapour irritates eyes, skin and lungs	Use in fume cupboard. Wear eye and skin protection.
$0.1\,mol\,L^{-1}$ sodium hydroxide	corrosive to skin and eyes	Wear eye and skin protection.
universal indicator	may irritate the eyes and skin	Wear eye and skin protection.
silver nitrate	toxic if ingested; stains skin black	Wear eye and skin protection.
limewater	slightly toxic if ingested; can burn skin and eyes	Wear eye and skin protection.
methyl violet indicator	may irritate the eyes and skin	Wear eye and skin protection.
copper oxide solid	low toxicity	Wear eye and skin protection.
magnesium solid	burns with a white-hot flame	Wear eye and skin protection.
Please indicate that you have understood the information in the safety table. Name (print): _____ I understand the safety information (signature): _____		

PROCEDURE

Carry out each of the following tests and record your observations in the Results table.

1 Add about 1 mL of $1.0\,mol\,L^{-1}$ HCl to a test-tube containing a small amount of solid $CaCO_3$. Test the gas evolved with limewater.

2 Add about 5 mL of $1.0\,mol\,L^{-1}$ HCl to a small amount of solid CuO in a test-tube. Shake the test-tube and allow it to stand for 5 minutes.

3 Add about 10 mL of $1.0\,mol\,L^{-1}$ HCl to a test-tube containing a 1 cm strip of magnesium. Use an inverted test-tube to collect the gas evolved and test it with a lighted taper.

4 Add 1 mL of $0.1\,mol\,L^{-1}$ HCl to a small amount of solid $NaHCO_3$ in a test-tube. Test the gas evolved with limewater.

5 In the fume cupboard, open a bottle of concentrated ammonia and a bottle of $10\,mol\,L^{-1}$ hydrochloric acid next to each other. (Do not pour one solution into the other; allow only their fumes to react.)

6 Add 1 mL of $0.1\,mol\,L^{-1}$ HCl to 1 mL of $0.1\,mol\,L^{-1}$ $AgNO_3$ in a test-tube.

7 Add one drop of methyl violet indicator to a test-tube containing 20 drops of $1.0\,mol\,L^{-1}$ HCl.

RESULTS AND DISCUSSION

1 Write balanced full and ionic equations for each reaction in the table below.

Test	Observations	Equations
1 $HCl(aq) + CaCO_3(s)$		full: ionic:
2 $HCl(aq) + CuO(s)$		full: ionic:
3 $HCl(aq) + Mg(s)$		full: ionic:
4 $HCl(aq) + NaHCO_3(s)$		full: ionic:
5 $HCl(g) + NH_3(g)$		full: ionic:
6 $HCl(aq) + AgNO_3(s)$		full: ionic:
7 $HCl(aq) + $ methyl violet	colour: pH:	ionisation reaction:

2 Explain what the pH value recorded in Test 7 tells you about the extent of hydrolysis of HCl. Is hydrochloric acid a strong or weak acid?

_____

_____

_____

3 Explain how the reaction between HCl(g) and NH_3(g) in Test 5 can be regarded as an acid–base reaction using the Brønsted–Lowry theory.

_____

_____

_____

_____

CONCLUSION

4 Summarise the reactions of acids you have observed in this activity. Comment on the reliability of your conclusion.

_____

_____

_____

_____

_____

_____

RATING MY LEARNING	My understanding improved	Not confident ← → Very confident ○ ○ ○ ○ ○	I answered questions without help	Not confident ← → Very confident ○ ○ ○ ○ ○	I corrected my errors without help	Not confident ← → Very confident ○ ○ ○ ○ ○

PRACTICAL ACTIVITY 6.4

Measuring the enthalpy of neutralisation

Suggested duration: 20 minutes

INTRODUCTION

The energy change that occurs when one mole of an acid reacts with one mole of a base is called the enthalpy of neutralisation. Since energy is released during a neutralisation reaction, the reaction is exothermic. This experiment determines the enthalpy of neutralisation for hydrochloric acid reacting with sodium hydroxide.

Calorimeters can be used to measure enthalpy changes that occur for reactions in solution. While a calorimeter can be calibrated electrically, in this experiment the specific heat capacity of water is used to estimate the enthalpy change.

PURPOSE

To determine the enthalpy of neutralisation of an acid and a base, using specific heat capacity to calculate the value.

PRE-LAB SAFETY INFORMATION		
Material used	**Hazard**	**Control**
$1.0\,mol\,L^{-1}$ hydrochloric acid	irritating to eyes, respiratory system	Wear safety glasses and lab coat.
$1.0\,mol\,L^{-1}$ sodium hydroxide solution	corrosive; causes burns	Wear safety glasses and lab coat.

Please indicate that you have understood the information in the safety table.

Name (print): _____

I understand the safety information (signature): _____

MATERIALS

- $50\,mL \times 1.0\,mol\,L^{-1}$ sodium hydroxide, NaOH
- $150\,mL \times 1.0\,mol\,L^{-1}$ hydrochloric acid, HCl
- $2 \times 100\,mL$ measuring cylinders
- calorimeter (alternatively, make a simple calorimeter by inserting one polystyrene cup inside another and use foil as a lid)
- thermometer, $-10°C$ to $50°C$
- spatula

PROCEDURE

1 Pour 50 mL of $1.0\,mol\,L^{-1}$ sodium hydroxide solution into a calorimeter. Stir and record the temperature of the solution in Table 1.

2 Pour 50 mL of $1.0\,mol\,L^{-1}$ hydrochloric acid into a measuring cylinder and record its temperature.

3 Add the hydrochloric acid to the calorimeter.

4 Stir the mixture and record the highest temperature the solution reaches.

RESULTS

TABLE 1 Quantities measured to determine the enthalpy of neutralisation

Quantity	Measured value and unit
volume of acid	
concentration of acid	
volume of base	
concentration of base	
total volume of the solution	
initial temperature of each solution (average)	
highest temperature of the solution when they have reacted	

DISCUSSION

1 Write a balanced chemical equation for the reaction that has occurred in this experiment.

_____

2 Using your measurements of the change in temperature, the final volume of the solution and the specific heat capacity of water ($4.18\,J\,g^{-1}\,K^{-1}$), calculate the energy change, in joules, that occurred during the reaction. Assume that the density of water is $1\,g\,mL^{-1}$.

3 Calculate the change in enthalpy, ΔH, for the reaction, in $kJ\,mol^{-1}$. This is the enthalpy of neutralisation. Include a sign to indicate whether the reaction is exothermic or endothermic.

4 Energy is neither created nor destroyed in a chemical reaction. Explain where the energy released (or absorbed) by the reaction goes to (comes from).

_____

_____

_____

5 For the calculations for this experiment, it is assumed that all the heat released by the reaction is absorbed by the water in the calorimeter. Comment on the accuracy of this assumption. Is the actual value for the energy released likely to be higher or lower than your experimental value?

_____

_____

_____

_____

CONCLUSION

6 Write a thermochemical equation for this reaction.

_____

RATING MY LEARNING	My understanding improved	Not confident ← → Very confident ⃝ ⃝ ⃝ ⃝ ⃝	I answered questions without help	Not confident ← → Very confident ⃝ ⃝ ⃝ ⃝ ⃝	I corrected my errors without help	Not confident ← → Very confident ⃝ ⃝ ⃝ ⃝ ⃝

PRACTICAL ACTIVITY 6.5

Beetroot—a natural indicator

Suggested duration: 40 minutes

INTRODUCTION

Some flowers, such as hydrangeas, change colour according to the acidity of the soil. The reason for this is that the flowers contain natural indicators (dyes) which change colour as a consequence of the concentration of H^+ in the soil.

PURPOSE

To extract a natural indicator from beetroot and test its colours in acidic, neutral and basic solutions. The colours of another natural indicator, litmus, and several synthetic indicators in these solutions are also tested.

PRE-LAB SAFETY INFORMATION		
Material used	**Hazard**	**Control**
$0.10 \, mol \, L^{-1}$ hydrochloric acid	irritating to eyes, respiratory system	Wear safety glasses and lab coat.
$0.10 \, mol \, L^{-1}$ sodium hydroxide solution	irritating to skin and eyes	Wear safety glasses and lab coat.
beetroot	stains clothes, hands and benches	Wear gloves, safety glasses and lab coat.
indicators	may cause skin and eye irritation	Wear safety glasses and lab coat.

Please indicate that you have understood the information in the safety table.

Name (print): _____

I understand the safety information (signature): _____

MATERIALS

- 100 mL deionised water
- food processor
- fine strainer
- 4 test-tubes
- 250 mL beaker
- 15 mL of the following solutions:
  - $0.1 \, mol \, L^{-1}$ sodium chloride, NaCl
  - $0.1 \, mol \, L^{-1}$ hydro-chloric acid, HCl
  - $0.1 \, mol \, L^{-1}$ sodium hydroxide, NaOH
- 3 teat pipettes
- glass rod
- small beaker
- dropper bottles (optional, for Part B) containing:
  - blue litmus
  - phenolphthalein
  - methyl orange
  - bromothymol blue
- pH meter or data logger with pH probe (optional, for Part B)

PROCEDURE

Part A—Colour changes of indicators

1. Peel and chop the beetroot. Place it in a blender with 100 mL distilled water and blend the mixture.

2. Strain the mixture into a beaker.

3. To each of four test-tubes, add about 3 mL of one of the following liquids: water, NaCl solution, HCl solution, NaOH solution.

4. Add three drops of beetroot juice to each of the test-tubes and stir. Record your results in Table 1.

5. In the same way, test the other indicators provided.

Part B—pH ranges of indicators

For beetroot, phenolphthalein and bromothymol blue

1. Add three drops of indicator to 10 mL of deionised water in a small beaker.

2. Measure the pH of the solution using a probe and record your measurement in Table 2. Add NaOH solution to the beaker, drop-wise while stirring, until the first colour change is observed. Insert the pH probe and record the pH of this solution.

3. Add a few more drops of NaOH to determine any further change, until the colour remains constant. Again, insert the pH probe and record the pH of this solution.

. . . .

PRACTICAL ACTIVITY 6.5

For blue litmus and methyl orange

4   Add three drops of indicator to 10 mL of deionised water in a small beaker.

5   Measure the pH of the solution using a probe and record your measurement in Table 2. Add HCl drop-wise (instead of NaOH) while stirring, until the first colour change is observed. Insert the pH probe and record the pH of this solution.

6   Add a few more drops of HCl to determine any further change, until the colour remains constant. Again, insert the pH probe and record the pH of this solution.

RESULTS

Part A—Colour changes of indicators

TABLE 1 Indicator colours in different solutions

Indicator	Colour in water	Colour in NaCl solution	Colour in HCl solution	Colour in NaOH solution
beetroot				
litmus				
phenolphthalein				
methyl orange				
bromothymol blue				

Part B—pH ranges of indicators

TABLE 2 Indicator pH ranges

Indicator	Initial pH	pH at start of colour change	pH at definite colour change
beetroot			
litmus			
phenolphthalein			
methyl orange			
bromothymol blue			

DISCUSSION

1   Is beetroot juice suitable as an indicator to identify:

   a   acidic substances?

   b   basic solutions?

   Give reasons for your answers.

2 Use your results to state the pH range over which the beetroot indicator changes colour.

____

____

3 From your experimental observations, or from secondary sources, which of the following indicators—beetroot juice, phenolphthalein, blue litmus, methyl orange and bromothymol blue—would be effective in distinguishing between:

a NaCl and HCl solutions? ____________________

b NaCl and NaOH solutions? ____________________

4 From your observations, or from secondary sources, find out the pH range and colour change for the following indicators:

a phenolphthalein ____________________

b methyl orange ____________________

c bromothymol blue ____________________

CONCLUSION

5 Describe two everyday uses for indicators and identify the indicator used in each case.

____

____

____

____

RATING MY LEARNING	My understanding improved	Not confident ◯ ◯ ◯ ◯ ◯ Very confident	I answered questions without help	Not confident ◯ ◯ ◯ ◯ ◯ Very confident	I corrected my errors without help	Not confident ◯ ◯ ◯ ◯ ◯ Very confident

Determination of the ethanoic acid concentration of vinegar

Suggested duration: 40 minutes

INTRODUCTION

The sharp, acidic taste of vinegar is due to the presence of ethanoic acid, CH_3COOH. Ethanoic acid is a weak acid that is only partially ionised in water:

$$CH_3COOH(aq) + H_2O(l) \rightleftharpoons CH_3COO^-(aq) + H_3O^+(aq)$$

The ethanoic acid concentration in vinegar can be determined by performing an acid–base volumetric titration using a standard solution of sodium hydroxide as the base. This exercise enables you to practise performing calculations involving the dilution of a sample prior to titration.

PURPOSE

To determine the concentration of ethanoic acid in white vinegar.

MATERIALS
• 25 mL white vinegar
• 100 mL standard sodium hydroxide solution, NaOH (approximately 0.1 mol L^{-1})
• phenolphthalein indicator
• 250 mL deionised water
• 3 × 100 mL conical flasks
• 250 mL standard flask
• 20 mL pipette
• 25 mL pipette
• burette and stand
• small funnel
• white tile

PRE-LAB SAFETY INFORMATION		
Material used	**Hazard**	**Control**
0.1 mol L^{-1} sodium hydroxide solution	irritating to skin and eyes	Wear a laboratory coat and safety glasses.
phenolphthalein indicator	may cause irritation to skin and eyes	Wear a laboratory coat and safety glasses.
vinegar	may irritate eyes	Wear safety glasses.

Waste disposal: After each titration, organic wastes should be disposed of in an organic waste container in a fumehood.

Please indicate that you have understood the information in the safety table.

Name (print): _____

I understand the safety information (signature): _____

PROCEDURE

1   Record the brand name of the vinegar you are to analyse and the concentration of the sodium hydroxide solution you will use in the analysis in Table 1.

2   Dilute the vinegar by pipetting 25.00 mL into a 250 mL standard flask. Half-fill the flask with deionised water and shake it well to mix the solution. Add more water until the bottom of the meniscus is level with the calibration line of the flask. Mix thoroughly.

3   Fill a burette with standard sodium hydroxide solution. Record the initial burette reading to two decimal places in Table 2.

4   Place a 20.00 mL aliquot of the diluted vinegar into a 100 mL flask. Add three drops of phenolphthalein.

5   Place the conical flask containing diluted vinegar on a white tile beneath the burette and titrate until the moment when the solution just becomes permanently pink.

6   Record the final burette reading.

7   Repeat the titration (steps 4–6) until three concordant results have been obtained.

8   When cleaning up, thoroughly rinse the burette with water, followed by a small volume of diluted vinegar, then more water. Traces of sodium hydroxide solution left in the burette may cause taps to become 'frozen' in place.

RESULTS

TABLE 1 Vinegar information

Brand name of vinegar	
Concentration of NaOH (mol L^{-1})	

TABLE 2 Titration results

Titration number	Initial burette reading (mL)	Final burette reading (mL)	Titre (mL)
1			
2			
3			
4			

DISCUSSION

1   Write an equation for the reaction between ethanoic acid and sodium hydroxide solution.

2   Calculate the average titre of the sodium hydroxide solution used during the titrations.

3   Calculate the amount of sodium hydroxide, in mol, present in the average titre of sodium hydroxide solution.

4   Determine the amount of ethanoic acid present in each 20.00 mL aliquot of diluted vinegar.

5   Calculate the concentration of ethanoic acid (in mol L^{-1}) in the undiluted sample of vinegar.

6   Explain what is meant by a 'standard solution' of sodium hydroxide.

7 Winemaking companies may also produce vinegar. What is the connection between wine and vinegar?

_____

_____

_____

8 Complete the following table to show what liquids should be used to rinse each piece of apparatus in this experiment.

Equipment	Rinse with ...
standard flask	
burette	
pipette used to transfer the concentrated vinegar into the standard flask	
pipette used to transfer the diluted vinegar into the conical flask	
conical flasks	

CONCLUSION

9 State the ethanoic acid concentration of the vinegar you analysed. What possible source of error exists in this experiment? Comment on the accuracy and reliability of your results.

_____

_____

_____

RATING MY LEARNING	My understanding improved	Not confident ← → Very confident ○ ○ ○ ○ ○	I answered questions without help	Not confident ← → Very confident ○ ○ ○ ○ ○	I corrected my errors without help	Not confident ← → Very confident ○ ○ ○ ○ ○

Determination of two acid dissociation constants

Suggested duration: 15 minutes

INTRODUCTION

Ethanoic acid, CH_3COOH, and ammonium ions, NH_4^+, behave as weak acids in water. For example, ethanoic acid is ionised to produce hydrogen ions and ethanoate ions according to the equation:

$$CH_3COOH(aq) + H_2O(l) \rightleftharpoons H_3O^+(aq) + CH_3COO^-(aq)$$

The acid dissociation constant, or acidity constant, for this reaction is given by the expression:

$$K_a = \frac{[H_3O^+][CH_3COO^-]}{[CH_3COOH]}$$

The value of K_a provides a measure of the extent to which the acid ionises in water.

PURPOSE

To determine the value of the equilibrium constant for the ionisation of ethanoic acid and for the ionisation of the ammonium ion.

PRE-LAB SAFETY INFORMATION		
Material used	**Hazard**	**Control**
indicator solutions	may cause skin and eye irritation avoid contact	Wear safety glasses and lab coat.

Please indicate that you have understood the information in the safety table.

Name (print): _____

I understand the safety information (signature): _____

MATERIALS

- 20 mL 0.010 mol L^{-1} ethanoic acid, CH_3COOH
- 20 mL 0.10 mol L^{-1} ammonium chloride solution, NH_4Cl
- 2 × 100 mL beakers
- pH meter (and data collection system if available) or 4 cm strips of narrow range pH papers and
- colour charts
- wash bottle containing deionised water

PROCEDURE

Complete *either* Part A *or* Part B.

Part A—Using a pH meter

1   Calibrate the pH meter using the written instructions that accompany the instrument.

2   Insert the probe of the pH meter into a beaker containing about 20 mL of 0.010 mol L^{-1} ethanoic acid and allow it to stand for about 30 seconds before recording its pH in the Results table.

3   After rinsing the probe with deionised water, find the pH of 0.10 mol L^{-1} ammonium chloride solution in a similar way.

4   When you are finished, rinse the probe with deionised water and return it to the storage solution.

Part B—Using pH paper

1   Place a 2 cm length of pH paper in a beaker containing about 20 mL of 0.010 mol L^{-1} ethanoic acid. Estimate and record the pH of the solution in the Results table by matching the colour of the paper with the colour chart.

2   Repeat this procedure for 0.10 mol L^{-1} ammonium chloride solution.

RESULTS

Solution	pH
0.010 mol L^{-1} ethanoic acid	
0.10 mol L^{-1} ammonium chloride solution	

DISCUSSION: DATA ANALYSIS

1   Use the value you obtained for the pH of the ethanoic acid to calculate the concentration of H_3O^+ ions in the solution.

2   What is the concentration of CH_3COO^- ions in the solution?

3   The initial concentration of ethanoic acid molecules in the solution was 0.010 mol L^{-1}. What is the concentration after the ionisation reaction has occurred? Comment on the extent of this reaction.

4   Calculate a value for the acidity constant, K_a, of ethanoic acid.

5   Write an equation for the dissociation of ammonium ions in water and hence write an expression for its acidity constant, K_a.

6   Calculate the acidity constant of the ammonium ion.

CONCLUSION

Summarise your results and comment on the extent of hydrolysis of ethanoic acid and ammonium chloride solution. How reliable and accurate do you think your results are?

Buffers

Suggested duration: 20 minutes

INTRODUCTION

A buffer is a solution that resists change in pH when acid or base is added to the solution. This ability to restrict a pH change is most important in biological systems. In particular, it is most important in the blood and in gastric juices.

A buffer is made from a weak acid and its weak conjugate base. The acid and base are in equilibrium. For example, the equilibrium in a buffer made from ethanoic acid and ethanoate ions can be represented as:

$$CH_3COOH(aq) + H_2O(l) \rightleftharpoons H_3O^+(aq) + CH_3COO^-(aq)$$

When an acid or a base is added to a buffer solution, the position of the equilibrium adjusts and minimises the large pH changes that would otherwise occur.

PURPOSE

To prepare a buffer solution and to investigate the properties of a buffer solution.

PRE-LAB SAFETY INFORMATION		
Material used	**Hazard**	**Control**
universal indicator solution	may cause skin and eye irritation avoid contact	Wear safety glasses and lab coat.

Please indicate that you have understood the information in the safety table.

Name (print): _____

I understand the safety information (signature): _____

MATERIALS

- 5 mL × 0.01 mol L^{-1} hydrochloric acid, HCl
- 5 mL × 0.01 mol L^{-1} sodium hydroxide, NaOH
- 10 mL × 0.1 mol L^{-1} ethanoic acid, CH$_3$COOH
- 10 mL × 0.1 mol L^{-1} sodium ethanoate, NaCH$_3$COO
- universal indicator and colour chart
- pH meter and data collection system (optional)
- deionised water
- 8 semi-micro test-tubes
- 2 small test-tubes
- semi-micro test-tube rack
- test-tube rack
- 4 dropping pipettes

PROCEDURE

1   Put two drops of universal indicator in each of four semi-micro test-tubes and half-fill each tube with deionised water.

2   Add one drop of deionised water to the first test-tube, one drop of HCl to the second, one drop of NaOH solution to the third tube and one drop of ethanoic acid to the fourth.

3   Measure the pH of each solution. Record your results in Table 1 in the 'pH without buffer' column. (Alternatively, a pH meter can be used to more accurately measure the pH.)

Preparing a buffer solution

4   Pour about 10 mL of NaCH$_3$COO solution into a 100 mL beaker and add four drops of universal indicator.

5   Add CH$_3$COOH drop by drop to the solution in the beaker until the colour of the indicator matches the colour of the indicator in deionised water.

6   Half-fill another four semi-micro test-tubes with this buffer solution and repeat Step 2 using these tubes. Measure the pH of each solution and record your results in the 'pH with buffer' column of Table 1.

Effect of CO$_2$

7   Put four drops of universal indicator into each of two small test-tubes (not semi-micro test-tubes). Fill one tube to a depth of about 2 cm with deionised water and the other to a depth of about 2 cm with buffer solution. Note the pH of the liquid in Table 2.

8   Use a straw to blow carbon dioxide gas into each solution and note the pH. Record all results in Table 2.

RESULTS

TABLE 1 pH with and without the buffer solution

Solution	pH without buffer	pH with buffer
Deionised water		
With HCl		
With NaOH		
With CH_3COOH		

TABLE 2 Effect of CO_2 on pH of water and buffer solutions

pH without buffer		pH with buffer	
No CO_2 gas	With CO_2 gas	No CO_2 gas	With CO_2 gas

DISCUSSION

1   Compare the pH changes that occur when water and solutions of HCl, NaOH and CH_3COOH are added to water and to a buffer solution. What is the effect of the presence of a buffer?

2   CO_2 gas reacts with water to form a weak acid, carbonic acid, H_2CO_3. Write an equation for this reaction.

3   Explain the effect of blowing CO_2 gas into solutions that did and did not contain buffers.

CONCLUSION

4   Summarise the effect the buffer has on solutions and explain how a buffer solution minimises the change in pH when an acid or base is added to it.

DEPTH STUDY 6.1

Practical investigation—focus on acids and bases

Suggested duration: 4 hours 15 minutes (including writing time and preparation of poster)

INTRODUCTION

This depth study requires you to design and conduct a quantitative or qualitative practical investigation about acids and bases. You will develop a question about some aspect of acids and bases and propose a hypothesis. Then you will collect and process data and draw conclusions based on your evidence. You will communicate your results in a scientific poster. The Toolkit also provides advice on conducting a practical investigation. GO TO ➤ Chemistry toolkit page ix

PLANNING YOUR INVESTIGATION

This practical investigation will allow you to understand a little of how the ideas of chemistry have been discovered and refined. You will work in a scientific manner and develop skills used by research chemists. To start your investigation:

- formulate a question about some aspect of acids and bases that is of interest to you and approved by your teacher
- write an aim which describes what you will investigate
- develop a hypothesis that predicts the result of the investigation (the hypothesis should connect the variables in a cause-and-effect relationship)
- identify the variables in your investigation.

You will then carefully design and plan your investigation with the assistance of your teacher, and consider ethical and safety issues. You will discuss the reliability, validity, accuracy and precision of your method and results, and describe your results and observations to answer the question you initially proposed.

Research scientists constantly use logbooks where they record information, findings, equipment, ideas and concepts related to their investigations. You should set up a logbook, either in electronic form or in a notebook.

If your investigation is quantitative, it is important to consider the variables involved. The table below summarises different types of variables.

Independent variable	Dependent variable	Controlled variables
The variable changed by the researcher	The variable that the researcher measures. This may change as the independent variable changes.	All variables that are kept constant during the investigation

Some suggested questions for your investigation are listed below. Alternatively, you can modify a question or design your own.

1 How are solutions of acids and bases analysed?

2 How does pH indicate the difference between the strength of acids and base?

3 How can models and animations be used to show the differences between strong, weak, diluted and concentrated acids and bases?

4 Can insect stings be neutralised using native plants instead of synthetic ointments?

5 How much vitamin C is present in native Australian fruits compared to oranges and lemons grown in Australia?

6 Can flowers be used to determine soil acidity or alkalinity?

7 How does pH change when fruit ripens, and how does this affect the taste of the fruit?

8 How are neutralisation processes used in industry?

9 What is the role of water in solutions of acids and bases?

10 How is the buffer system in the ocean being affected by global warming?

QUESTIONING AND PREDICTING

Consider your chosen question.

- What data do you need to answer your question?
- What further questions arise that you will need to research and investigate?

....

DEPTH STUDY 6.1

- Predict an answer to your question.

CONDUCTING YOUR INVESTIGATION

For each source that you access during this investigation, you should fill in a summary table such as the one below. Make as many copies of this table as you need.

Bibliographic information	
Summary of content (be concise and coherent) and tables of data	
Relevant findings and evidence	
Limitations, bias or flaws within the article	
Reliability of the conclusions you are drawing from the articles	
Useful quotations	
Additional notes	

ANALYSING DATA AND INFORMATION

After you have completed your research summaries and are satisfied you have collected sufficient information, plan the presentation of your results. You should consider questions such as:

- What variables are being considered?
- What background chemistry concepts need to be included?
- Which chemical terms need to be defined?
- What will you include in the introduction?
- What sub-headings will you need to use?
- What images, graphs and tables are relevant and helpful and should be included?
- What errors should be considered?
- How reliable are your conclusions?
- What will you include on the poster?

COMMUNICATING RESULTS

Your poster should contain no more than 1000 words to illustrate the process you followed and the conclusions you drew from your results. Your presentation should include:

- your question, prediction and aim
- the information you needed to answer the question
- tables of data that you analysed, and calculations/graphs produced to answer the question.
- images that assisted in communicating your answer to the question
- a bibliography.

Multiple choice

1 Which one of the following best defines an acid according to the Brønsted–Lowry theory?

   A A substance that donates H^+ ions.

   B A substance that reacts to produce OH^- ions.

   C A substance that produces H^+ ions in water

   D A substance that contains protons.

2 Which one of the following is the conjugate base of $H_2PO_3^-$?

   A H_3PO_3

   B HPO_3^{2-}

   C PO_3^{3-}

   D H_3PO_4

3 If solution A has a pH of 1 and solution B has a pH of 2, the ratio of the concentration of hydrogen ion in solution A to that in solution B is:

   A 1:2

   B 2:1

   C 1:10

   D 10:1

4 The concentrations of ions in four different solutions are listed below at 25°C. Which one is acidic?

   A solution I, $[H^+] = 10^{-7} \, mol \, L^{-1}$

   B solution II, $[OH^-] = 10^{-5} \, mol \, L^{-1}$

   C solution III, $[H^+] = 10^{-9} \, mol \, L^{-1}$

   D solution IV, $[OH^-] = 10^{-8} \, mol \, L^{-1}$

5 Which one of the following best describes the end point in an acid–base titration?

   A It is the point at which the pH of the solution is equal to 7.

   B It is the point at which equal moles of acid and base have been mixed.

   C It is the point at which the indicator changes colour.

   D It is the point at which the reactants have been mixed in an equal stoichiometric ratio.

6 Equal volumes of the following $0.1 \, mol \, L^{-1}$ solutions were mixed. Which one would be least effective as a buffer?

   A $CH_3COOH(aq)$ and $NaCH_3COO(aq)$

   B $H_2SO_4(aq)$ and $NaHSO_4(aq)$

   C $NH_4^+(aq)$ and $NH_3(aq)$

   D $CO_2(aq)$ and $NaHCO_3(aq)$

Short answer

7 10.0 mL of a $0.200 \, mol \, L^{-1}$ nitric acid solution is added to 16.0 mL of a $0.100 \, mol \, L^{-1}$ sodium hydroxide solution.

   a Write an ionic equation for the reaction that occurs.

   b Calculate the number of moles of excess reactant in the final solution.

   c Calculate the pH of the final solution.

   d Calculate the pOH of the final solution.

8 Citric acid, $H_6C_8O_7$, is a weak dioprotic acid that is found in lemon juice. It can be used to make a buffer to control the acidity in foods.

   a Explain, using equations, the meaning of the term 'diprotic'.

   b Write the formula of a chemical that can be added to a solution of citric acid to make a buffer.

   c Explain, using an equation, how this buffer solution resists a pH change if acid is added.

9 A 0.100 mol L^{-1} solution of hypochlorous acid, HOCl, has a pH of 4.26.

a Write an equation for the ionisation of hypochlorous acid.

_____

b Identify the conjugate acid–base pairs in the equation you wrote for part **a**.

_____

c Hypochlorous acid is classified as a weak acid. Explain.

_____

_____

d Write an expression for K_a for hypochlorous acid.

_____

e Calculate the concentration of H$_3$O$^+$ in the solution.

_____

_____

_____

f Calculate K_a for hypochlorous acid.

_____

_____

_____

_____

_____

10 A solution of a weak base, ammonia, is used in an industrial process. A chemist analyses the solution by titration with a solution of standard hydrochloric acid. Before performing the titration, the chemist first accurately dilutes the ammonia solution.

a Describe how the ammonia solution can be accurately diluted.

_____

_____

_____

b Write an equation for the reaction that occurs during the titration.

_____

c A 25.00 mL sample of the ammonia solution was accurately diluted to 250.0 mL. A 25.00 mL aliquot of the diluted ammonia solution was placed in a conical flask. Indicator was then added and the solution was titrated with 0.208 mol L^{-1} hydrochloric acid. The indicator changed colour permanently when 19.64 mL of the acid had been added. Calculate the concentration of ammonia in the original solution.

_____

_____

_____

_____

d Instead of using an indicator in this titration, the chemist could have identified the equivalence point of the reaction using either a pH meter or conductivity meter. Sketch and label the graphs the chemist would obtain for this titration using these instruments.

e Explain how each graph in part **d** can be used to detect the equivalence point.

_____

_____

_____

Outcomes

By the end of this module you will be able to:

- analyse and evaluate primary and secondary data and information CH12-5
- solve scientific problems using primary and secondary data, critical thinking skills and scientific processes CH12-6
- communicate scientific understanding using suitable language and terminology for a specific audience or purpose CH12-7
- analyse the structure of, and predict reactions involving, carbon compounds CH12-14

Content

NOMENCLATURE

INQUIRY QUESTION | How do we systematically name organic chemical compounds?

By the end of this module you will be able to:

- investigate the nomenclature of organic chemicals, up to C8, using IUPAC conventions, including simple methyl and ethyl branched chains, including: (ACSCH127) ICT
  - alkanes
  - alkenes
  - alkynes
  - alcohols (primary, secondary and tertiary)
  - aldehydes and ketones
  - carboxylic acids
  - amines and amides
  - halogenated organic compounds
- explore and distinguish the different types of structural isomers, including saturated and unsaturated hydrocarbons, including: (ACSCH035) ICT
  - chain isomers
  - position isomers
  - functional group isomers

HYDROCARBONS

INQUIRY QUESTION | How can hydrocarbons be classified based on their structure and reactivity?

By the end of this module you will be able to:

- construct models, identify the functional group, and write structural and molecular formulae for homologous series of organic chemical compounds, up to C8 (ACSCH035): ICT
  - alkanes
  - alkenes
  - alkynes

Module 7 • Organic chemistry

- conduct an investigation to compare the properties of organic chemical compounds within a homologous series, and explain these differences in terms of bonding (ACSCH035)
- analyse the shape of molecules formed between carbon atoms when a single, double or triple bond is formed between them
- explain the properties within and between the homologous series of alkanes with reference to the intermolecular and intramolecular bonding present ICT
- describe the procedures required to safely handle and dispose of organic substances (ACSCH075) ICT
- examine the environmental, economic and sociocultural implications of obtaining and using hydrocarbons from the Earth

PRODUCTS OF REACTIONS INVOLVING HYDROCARBONS

INQUIRY QUESTION **What are the products of reactions of hydrocarbons and how do they react?**

By the end of this module you will be able to:
- investigate, write equations and construct models to represent the reactions of unsaturated hydrocarbons when added to a range of chemicals, including but not limited to:
  - hydrogen (H_2)
  - halogens (X_2)
  - hydrogen halides (HX)
  - water (H_2O) (ACSCH136) ICT
- investigate, write equations and construct models to represent the reactions of saturated hydrocarbons when substituted with halogens

ALCOHOLS

INQUIRY QUESTION **How can alcohols be produced and what are their properties?**

By the end of this module you will be able to:
- investigate the structural formulae, properties and functional group including:
  - primary
  - secondary
  - tertiary alcohols ICT
- explain the properties within and between the homologous series of alcohols with reference to the intermolecular and intramolecular bonding present ICT
- conduct a practical investigation to measure and reliably compare the enthalpy of combustion for a range of alcohols ICT N
- write equations, state conditions and predict products to represent the reactions of alcohols, including but not limited to (ACSCH128, ACSCH136):
  - combustion
  - dehydration
  - substitution with HX
  - oxidation

- investigate the production of alcohols, including:
  - substitution reactions of halogenated organic compounds
  - fermentation
- investigate the products of the oxidation of primary and secondary alcohols
- compare and contrast fuels from organic sources to biofuels, including ethanol ICT

REACTIONS OF ORGANIC ACIDS AND BASES

INQUIRY QUESTION | What are the properties of organic acids and bases?

By the end of this module you will be able to:
- investigate the structural formulae, properties and functional group including:
  - primary, secondary and tertiary alcohols ICT
  - aldehydes and ketones (ACSCH127) ICT
  - amines and amides
  - carboxylic acids
- explain the properties within and between the homologous series of carboxylic acids, amines and amides with reference to the intermolecular and intramolecular bonding present ICT
- investigate the production, in a school laboratory, of simple esters
- investigate the differences between an organic acid and organic base
- investigate the structure and action of soaps and detergents
- draft and construct flow charts to show reaction pathways for chemical synthesis, including those that involve more than one step ICT

POLYMERS

INQUIRY QUESTION | What are the properties and uses of polymers?

By the end of this module you will be able to:
- model and compare the structure, properties and uses of addition polymers of ethylene and related monomers, for example:
  - polyethylene (PE) ICT
  - polyvinyl chloride (PVC) ICT
  - polystyrene (PS) ICT
  - polytetrafluoroethylene (PTFE) (ACSCH136) ICT
- model and compare the structure, properties and uses of condensation polymers, for example:
  - nylon
  - polyesters

Key knowledge

Structure and nomenclature of organic compounds

Carbon is a unique element. It has the unusual property of bonding strongly to itself, by covalent bonds, to form long chains or rings of carbon atoms. It also bonds covalently to other non-metals such as hydrogen, nitrogen, oxygen, sulfur and the halogens. As a consequence, millions of carbon-containing compounds are known. The study of these compounds and their properties and reactions is called organic chemistry.

DIVERSITY OF CARBON COMPOUNDS

Molecular shape

Carbon atoms form four covalent bonds to complete their outer shell. These bonds can be either single bonds or multiple bonds. Due to electron pair repulsion, the arrangement of four single bonds in space around a carbon atom is in the shape of a tetrahedron. The **valence shell electron pair repulsion (VSEPR) theory** indicates that these electron pairs repel each other so the bonds are as far apart as possible, at an angle to each other of nearly 109.5°.

As shown in Figure 7.1, when a carbon atom forms a double bond, the electron pair arrangement around the atom is trigonal planar because there are three sets of electron pairs determining the shape (double and triple bonds affect shape in a similar way as a single bond). A linear electron pair arrangement around each carbon atom occurs when there is a triple bond present, because the two sets of electron pairs repel each other.

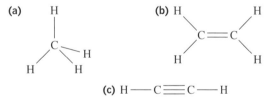

FIGURE 7.1 Molecular shape is dependent on electron pair repulsion. Tetrahedral (a), trigonal planar (b) and linear (c) shaped molecules

Covalent bonds involving carbon have different bond strengths. Carbon–carbon triple bonds are stronger, shorter and more stable than carbon–carbon double bonds, which are stronger, shorter and more stable than carbon–carbon single bonds (Figure 7.2).

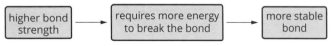

FIGURE 7.2 The relationship between bond strength and bond stability.

Saturated hydrocarbons

Saturated hydrocarbons are compounds of carbon and hydrogen that have only carbon–carbon single bonds. They belong to a **homologous series** called the **alkanes**, with a general chemical formula of C_nH_{2n+2}. A homologous series is a group of organic compounds whose members differ by one CH_2 unit. The simplest saturated hydrocarbon is methane, CH_4. The first eight alkanes are listed in Table 7.1.

Branches on a chain formed from alkanes have the formula C_nH_{2n+1}, and are called **alkyl groups** (Table 7.1). Alkyl groups (alkanes with one hydrogen atom removed) are often found in organic molecules. They are named according to the parent alkane, but with a -yl suffix.

TABLE 7.1 Homologous series of alkanes and alkyl groups

Alkane	Formula	Alkyl group	Formula
methane	CH_4	methyl	$-CH_3$
ethane	CH_3CH_3	ethyl	$-CH_2CH_3$
propane	$CH_3CH_2CH_3$	propyl	$-(CH_2)_2CH_3$
butane	$CH_3(CH_2)_2CH_3$	butyl	$-(CH_2)_3CH_3$
pentane	$CH_3(CH_2)_3CH_3$	pentyl	$-(CH_2)_4CH_3$
hexane	$CH_3(CH_2)_4CH_3$	hexyl	$-(CH_2)_5CH_3$
heptane	$CH_3(CH_2)_5CH_3$	heptyl	$-(CH_2)_6CH_3$
octane	$CH_3(CH_2)_6CH_3$	octyl	$-(CH_2)_7CH_3$

Unsaturated hydrocarbons

Unsaturated hydrocarbons are compounds of carbon and hydrogen that contain at least one carbon–carbon double bond or a carbon–carbon triple bond. Hydrocarbons with one double bond belong to a homologous series called the **alkenes** (general formula C_nH_{2n}). Hydrocarbons with one triple bond belong to the **alkynes** (formula C_nH_{2n-2}). Table 7.2 lists the first seven members of the alkenes and alkynes.

TABLE 7.2 Homologous series of alkenes and alkynes

Alkene	Formula	Alkyne	Formula
ethene	C_2H_4	ethyne	C_2H_2
propene	C_3H_6	propyne	C_3H_4
butene	C_4H_8	butyne	C_4H_6
pentene	C_5H_{10}	pentyne	C_5H_8
hexene	C_6H_{12}	hexyne	C_6H_{10}
heptene	C_7H_{14}	heptyne	C_7H_{12}
octene	C_8H_{16}	octyne	C_8H_{14}

Representing organic molecules

You are familiar with **molecular formulae** such as $C_6H_{12}O_6$ for glucose. Molecular formulae do not show how the atoms are arranged.

A **structural formula** shows the arrangement of atoms in space and all the bonds between atoms. **Condensed structural (or semi-structural) formulae** show the atoms that are connected to each carbon atom but do not show the bonds. The differences between a molecular formula, a condensed structural formula and a structural formula are shown in Table 7.3.

Isomers

Isomers are compounds that have the same molecular formula (same number of each type of atom) but differ in the way the atoms are arranged.

Structural isomers are isomers that differ in the way the atoms are bonded to each other. They may have similar, but not identical, properties. Figure 7.3(a) shows two isomers of butane, butane ($CH_3CH_2CH_2CH_3$) and 2-methylpropane ($(CH_3)_3CH$), that have the same molecular formula (C_4H_{10}) but have their carbon chains arranged differently. They are called **chain isomers**.

The two isomers of butene in Figure 7.6(b) have a different position of the functional group (the carbon–carbon double bond) and different molecular shapes, and are called **position isomers**.

TABLE 7.3 Formulae of some organic compounds, showing types of formulae

Name	Molecular formula	Condensed structural formula	Structural formula
propan-1-ol	C_3H_8O	$CH_3CH_2CH_2OH$	
propan-2-ol	C_3H_8O	$CH_3CH(OH)CH_3$	
but-2-ene	C_4H_8	$CH_3CHCHCH_3$	

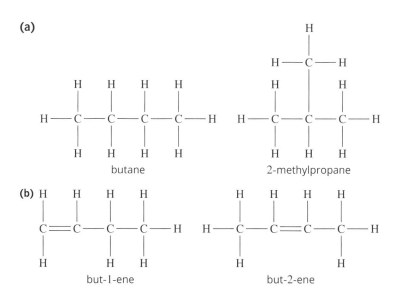

(a)

butane   2-methylpropane

(b)

but-1-ene   but-2-ene

FIGURE 7.3 (a) Structural chain isomers of butane and (b) structural position isomers of butene

There is third group of structural isomers, called **functional group isomers**, which have the same molecular formula but different functional groups. The three types of structural isomers are summarised in Table 7.4.

TABLE 7.4 Types of structural isomers

Type	Definition	Example
Chain isomer	The arrangement of carbon atoms in the carbon chain differs.	\n\n$CH_3CH_2CH_2CH(CH_3)_2$ $CH_3CH_2CH(CH_3)CH_2CH_3$ $(CH_3)_3CCH_2CH_3$
Position isomers	The position of one or more functional groups differs.	
Functional group isomers	The molecules have different functional groups and therefore belong to different homologous series.	

NOMENCLATURE OF HYDROCARBONS

In order to name organic compounds unambiguously, the International Union of Pure and Applied Chemistry (IUPAC) has developed a set of rules. Some of these rules for naming hydrocarbons are listed in Table 7.5.

TABLE 7.5 IUPAC rules for naming hydrocarbons

Rule		Example	Name
1	Choose the longest carbon chain and name according to the alkane with the same number of carbon atoms. This chain should contain a C=C or C≡C bond, if one is present.	$CH_3CH_2CH_2CH_2CH_2CH_3$	hexane
2	If there is a C=C, replace -ane with -ene and number from the end that gives the smallest number for the first carbon atom involved in the bond.	$CH_3CH=CHCH_2CH_2CH_3$	hex-2-ene (not hex-4-ene)
3	If there is a C≡C bond, replace -ane with -yne and number from the end that gives the smallest number for the first carbon atom involved in the bond.	$CH_3C≡CCH_2CH_3$	pent-2-yne (not pent-3-yne)
4	When there is a branch and numbers have not already been established (such as by a double bond), number from the end that gives the smallest number to the branch.	$CH_3CH_2CH(CH_3)CH_3$	2-methylbutane (not 3-methylbutane)
5	Number all branches. Use prefixes such as di-, tri- and tetra- if branches are identical.	$CH_3CH(CH_3)CH(CH_3)CH_3$	2,3-dimethylbutane
6	If different alkyl branches are present, write them in alphabetical order.	$CH_3CH(CH_3)CH(CH_2CH_3)CH_2CH_3$	3-ethyl-2-methylpentane

FUNCTIONAL GROUPS

A **functional group** is an atom or group of atoms that determines the properties of a molecule. They change the way the molecule reacts and behaves.

Table 7.6 lists common functional groups. The systematic naming of compounds with functional groups follows the same general rules for hydrocarbons. The presence of a functional group is indicated using specific prefixes or suffixes. The rules for naming compounds containing functional groups are listed in Table 7.7.

TABLE 7.6 Common functional groups

Functional group	Homologous series to which they belong	Structure	Prefix or suffix used
double bond	alkenes	C=C	-ene
triple bond	alkynes	–C≡C–	-yne
hydroxyl	alcohols	–OH	-ol
carboxyl	carboxylic acids	–COOH	-oic acid (The carbon atom in this group is always numbered as carbon 1 and never given in the name because it is understood.)
halo	halohydrocarbons	–F, –Cl, –Br, –I	fluoro–, chloro-, bromo-, iodo-
amino	amines	–NH$_2$	-amine
amide	amides (also present in proteins, where they are called peptides)	–CONH–	-amide
carbonyl	aldehydes (If the carbonyl group, C=O, is bonded to a hydrogen atom; the carbonyl group in aldehydes is at the end of the carbon chain.)	–CO A carbonyl group in an aldehyde	-al
carbonyl	ketones (if the carbonyl group is in the middle of the chain)	–CO A carbonyl group in a ketone	-one
ester	esters	–COOC–	The name has two parts: the part singly bonded to oxygen is written in front of the parent name and ends in -yl, and the parent name ends in -oate.

TABLE 7.7 Rules for naming organic compounds with functional groups

Rule		Example	Name
1	For alcohols, replace the -e of the hydrocarbon with -ol at the end of the hydrocarbon name. Indicate the position of the hydroxyl group with a number before the –ol ending.	$CH_3CH_2CH_2OH$ $CH_3CH_2(OH)CH_3$	propan-1-ol propan-2-ol
2	For amines, replace the -e of the hydrocarbon with -amine at the end of the hydrocarbon name. Indicate the position of the amino group with a number before the -amine ending.	$NH_2CH_2CH_2CH_3$ $CH_3CH(NH_2)CH_3$	propan-1-amine propan-2-amine
3	For haloalkanes, insert fluoro-, chloro-, bromo- or iodo- at the front of the hydrocarbon name. Indicate the position of the group with a number before the halo name.	$CH_3CH_2CH_2Cl$ $CH_3CHBrCH_3$	1-chloropropane 2-bromopropane
4	For carboxylic acids, replace -e with -oic acid. Remember, the carbon atom doubly bonded to oxygen is always counted as carbon 1.	CH_3CH_2COOH	propanoic acid
5	Esters can be regarded as being made from an alcohol and a carboxylic acid. To name an ester, the first part of the name comes from the alcohol, replacing -anol with -yl , and the second part of the name comes from the carboxylic acid, replacing -oic acid with -oate. Remember, the carbon atom doubly bonded to oxygen is always counted as carbon 1.	$CH_3CH_2COOCH_2CH_2CH_2CH_3$	butyl propanoate

IUPAC NOMENCLATURE FOR FUNCTIONAL GROUPS

When there are two functional groups in a molecule, **IUPAC nomenclature** indicates an order of priority (Table 7.8).

- The functional group with the higher priority determines the parent name of the molecule.
- The presence of a functional group with the lower priority is shown by a prefix in front of the parent name; a number indicates its position in a molecule.

TABLE 7.8 IUPAC table of priority for functional groups

Functional group priority order	Parent name
carboxyl	-oic acid
hydroxyl	-ol
amine	-amine
alkene	-ene
alkyne	-yne
halo	halo- (prefix)

For example, the name of $CH_3CH(OH)CH_2COOH$ is 3-hydroxybutanoic acid and $CH_3CHClCH(OH)CH_3$ is 3-chlorobutan-2-ol.

Note that the highest priority is a carboxyl functional group.

Properties of hydrocarbons and haloalkanes

Hydrocarbons are commonly found in petroleum deposits in the form of crude oil and natural gas. They were formed millions of years ago from the decomposition of marine plants and animals. When burnt for use as fuels, fossil fuels produce greenhouse gases (CO_2 and H_2O) and are non-renewable. The components of crude oil are separated by fractional distillation before being used.

BOILING POINTS, MELTING POINTS AND SOLUBILITIES OF ORGANIC COMPOUNDS

Alkanes, alkenes and alkynes have similar physical properties as a consequence of their non-polar nature, molecular shape and the strength of the intermolecular forces between the molecules. Some of the properties and features of the different types of hydrocarbons are compared in Table 7.9.

TABLE 7.9 Comparison of alkanes and alkenes

Property or feature	Alkanes	Alkenes	Alkynes
Type of bond between molecules	dispersion forces	dispersion forces	dispersion forces
Polarity of molecules	non-polar	non-polar	non-polar
Solubility in water	insoluble	insoluble	insoluble
General formula	C_nH_{2n+2}	C_nH_{2n}	C_nH_{2n-2}
Saturated or unsaturated	saturated	unsaturated	unsaturated
Main reaction type	substitution	addition	addition

The only intermolecular forces between hydrocarbon molecules are dispersion forces. As the number of carbon atoms in the molecules increases, the strength of the dispersion forces increases and their melting and boiling points therefore increase. Table 7.10 shows the trend in boiling points for the alkanes, alkenes and alkynes.

TABLE 7.10 Comparison of boiling points of alkanes, alkenes and alkynes

Alkane			Alkene			Alkyne		
Name	Molecular formula	Boiling point (°C)	Name	Molecular formula	Boiling point (°C)	Name	Molecular formula	Boiling point (°C)
methane	CH_4	−162	—	—	—	—	—	—
ethane	C_2H_6	−89	ethene	C_2H_4	−103.7	ethyne	C_2H_2	−84
propane	C_3H_8	−45	propene	C_3H_6	−47.6	propyne	C_3H_4	−23.4
butane	C_4H_{10}	−1	but-1-ene	C_4H_8	−6.3	but-1-yne	C_4H_6	8.1
pentane	C_5H_{12}	36	pent-1-ene	C_5H_{10}	30.2	pent-1-yne	C_5H_8	40.2
hexane	C_6H_{14}	69	hex-1-ene	C_6H_{12}		hex-1-yne	C_6H_{10}	71

Branched molecules have weaker dispersion forces between the molecules because they do not pack as closely, so their boiling points are lower than straight-chain hydrocarbons with the same molecular formula (Figure 7.4).

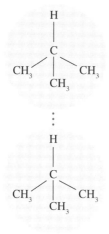

butane
- unbranched molecule
- molecules are closer
- boiling point −0.5°C

2-methylpropane
- branched molecule
- molecules are further apart
- boiling point −11.7°C

FIGURE 7.4 The molecular shape affects the boiling point. Both butane and 2-methylpropane have the formula C_4H_{10}. Stronger dispersion forces exist between butane molecules than between 2-methylpropane molecules because butane molecules pack more closely.

The nature of the bonds between hydrocarbon molecules also determines their solubility. As Table 7.9 indicates, all hydrocarbons are insoluble in water. Strong hydrogen bonds exist between water molecules. The weak dispersion forces that are present between non-polar hydrocarbon molecules and between hydrocarbon molecules and water are not strong enough to break the hydrogen bonds in water. As a result, when a liquid hydrocarbon is mixed with water they do not dissolve in each other, and two layers are formed; the liquids are said to be **immiscible**.

The existence of multiple bonds in alkenes and alkynes changes their chemical properties and reactivity compared with those of the alkanes (covered below).

IMPACTS OF USES OF ORGANIC SUBSTANCES

Alkanes in crude oil are separated by **fractional distillation**. Since the boiling points of the alkanes depend on the strength of the dispersion forces between molecules, fractional distillation of crude oil results in the separation of molecules of different molecular mass.

Although some of the hydrocarbon fractions obtained from the fractional distillation of crude oil are used as raw materials for manufacturing other chemicals, their main use is as fuels to provide energy for electricity production and transport. Some of the implications of the mining and processing of crude oil and the use of its products as fuels are listed in Table 7.11.

TABLE 7.11 Environmental, economic and sociocultural implications of obtaining and using hydrocarbons

Environmental implications	Economic implications	Social implications
• air pollution • acid rain • thermal pollution of waterways near power stations • global warming emissions, resulting in climate change, increasing ocean acidity and consequences for marine food chains	• widely available • cheap to produce • readily used for electricity production, heating and cooking, transport fuel • modern society is dependent on the use of fossil fuels	• non-renewable • mining causes destruction of land and can have harmful effects on local communities • can pollute water ways • global warming emissions, resulting in negative effects on coastal communities, food supplies, and tourism

The safe handling, transport and disposal of organic compounds generally requires careful consideration of the health and safety issues involved. In the laboratory, only the minimum amounts of chemicals required should be used to reduce waste and pollution of the environment. The Safety Data Sheets (SDS) for each chemical provides information about their hazards as well as instructions for their use and disposal. In general, organic compounds should not be poured down the sink or drain. Instead they should be collected and disposed of appropriately to prevent a fire or explosion, and to minimise exposure in order to avoid health issues.

Products of reactions involving hydrocarbons

Key reactions of alkanes and alkenes are shown in Table 7.12. Alkanes undergo **substitution reactions**, whereas alkenes undergo **addition reactions**. Both alkanes and alkenes undergo **combustion reactions** with oxygen.

Alcohols

PHYSICAL AND CHEMICAL PROPERTIES OF ALCOHOLS

Types of alcohols

The term **alcohol** is used for a hydrocarbon containing a hydroxyl (–OH) group. There are three types of alcohols, depending on the position of the –OH group (Figure 7.5):

- A **primary alcohol**, such as butan-1-ol, is one in which the carbon atom bonded to the –OH group is bonded to no more than one other carbon.
- A **secondary alcohol**, such as butan-2-ol, is one in which the carbon atom bonded to the –OH group is bonded to two other carbons.
- A **tertiary alcohol**, such as 2-methylpropan-2-ol, is one in which the carbon atom bonded to the –OH group is bonded to three other carbons.

TABLE 7.12 Reactions of hydrocarbons

Type of reaction	Description	Examples
substitution	Replacement of an atom or group of atoms by another atom or group of atoms. At least two new products are formed.	$CH_3CH_3(g) + Cl_2(g) \xrightarrow{\text{light or heat}} CH_3CH_2Cl(g) + HCl(g)$ (A H atom is replaced by a Cl atom.) $CH_3Cl(g) + NH_3(g) \rightarrow CH_3NH_2(g) + HCl(g)$ (The Cl atom is replaced by the NH_2 group.)
addition	Addition to both ends of a C=C bond. One product is formed (so there are no by-products).	 $CH_2 = CH_2 + Br_2 \longrightarrow CH_2Br\text{–}CH_2CH_2Br$ 1, 2 -dibromoethane $CH_2 = CH_2 + H_2O \xrightarrow[300°C]{\substack{H_3PO_4 \\ \text{catalyst}}} CH_3CH_2OH$ ethanol $CH_2=CH_2 + H_2 \xrightarrow{\text{nickel catalyst}} CH_3CH_3$ $CH_2=CH_2 + HCl \rightarrow CH_3CH_2Cl$
combustion	A type of oxidation reaction involving oxygen.	Complete combustion: $CH_4(g) + 2O_2(g) \rightarrow CO_2(g) + 2H_2O(l)$ Incomplete combustion: e.g. $2CH_4(g) + 3O_2(g) \rightarrow 2CO(g) + 4H_2O(l)$

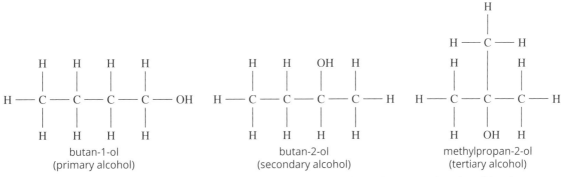

FIGURE 7.5 Three types of alcohols. They have the same molecular formula and are structural position isomers.

Structure and physical properties of alcohols

As you can see in Figure 7.5, primary, secondary and tertiary alcohols can be classified as structural position isomers because the position of the functional group (–OH) differs.

Strictly speaking, primary, secondary and tertiary alcohols belong to three different homologous series, although in a casual sense, they are often described as members of a general homologous series of alcohols. The physical properties of alcohols can be understood in terms of their intermolecular bonding.

Boiling point

The presence of an –OH group in alcohols causes hydrogen bonding between molecules. This relatively strong form of intermolecular bonding gives an alcohol a higher boiling point than the alkane of the same parent name. As the chain length increases, the dispersion forces increase, and this increases the boiling point further.

The degree of branching around the position of the –OH group also affects the boiling points. In primary alcohols there is no branching on the C atom attached to the –OH group, so the hydrogen bonds are strong and the boiling points are relatively high.

In secondary alcohols the –OH group is attached to the middle of the chain, so the boiling point decreases because the molecules cannot pack as closely to each other.

In tertiary alcohols, three alkyl groups are bonded to the carbon atom attached to the –OH group, so the packing of the molecules is further reduced and the strength of the forces between molecules is weaker, causing the boiling points to be lower. The boiling points of the position isomers of the alcohol butanol are shown in Table 7.13.

TABLE 7.13 Boiling points of primary, secondary and tertiary alcohols with the formula C_4H_9OH

Alcohol	Type of alcohol	Boiling points (°C)
butan-1-ol	primary	118
butan-2-ol	secondary	100
2-methylpropan-2-ol	tertiary	82

Solubility

Small alcohols dissolve well in water because they can form hydrogen bonds with water molecules (Figure 7.6). As the hydrocarbon chain increases in length, the solubility decreases because of the disruption of hydrogen bonding between water molecules by the long non-polar hydrocarbon chains, which can only form dispersion forces. Alcohols do not dissociate to any significant extent in water, and their solutions can be regarded as neutral.

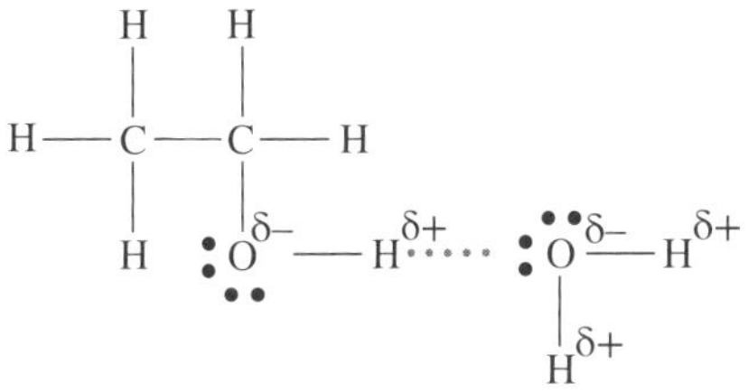

FIGURE 7.6 Hydrogen bonds between molecules of ethanol and water are shown as dotted lines.

Production of alcohols

Alcohols can be produced in different ways, including by a substitution reaction of haloalkanes and by **fermentation**. These two reactions are shown in Table 7.14.

TABLE 7.14 Reactions to produce alcohols

Substitution	Fermentation
Replacement of a halogen by an –OH group, by reaction with an aqueous solution of NaOH Equation: $CH_3CH_2Cl(aq) + OH^-(aq) \rightarrow CH_3CH_2OH(aq) + H_2O(l)$	An anaerobic process involving glucose and enzymes in yeast. Equation: $C_6H_{12}O_6(aq) \rightarrow 2CH_3CH_2OH(aq) + 2CO_2(g)$

When ethanol is produced by fermentation it is often called **bioethanol**, and is the most commonly used biofuel.

Chemical reactions of alcohols

Alcohols undergo a variety of reactions, including combustion, **dehydration**, substitution, **oxidation** and **condensation** (Table 7.15).

TABLE 7.15 Reactions of alcohols

Reaction	Description	Example
combustion	a type of oxidation reaction involving oxygen	$CH_3CH_2OH(l) + 3O_2(g) \rightarrow 2CO_2(g) + 3H_2O(l)$
dehydration	a type of **elimination reaction** where a C=C double bond is formed by removal of H_2O	$CH_3CH_2OH(g) \xrightarrow{H_2SO_4 \text{ and heat}} CH_2{=}CH_2(g) + H_2O(g)$
substitution	replacement of OH group	$CH_3CH_2OH(aq) + HCl(aq) \rightarrow CH_3CH_2Cl(aq) + H_2O(l)$ $CH_3CH_2OH(aq) + NH_3(aq) \rightarrow CH_3CH_2NH_2(aq) + H_2O(l)$
oxidation	involves a change in oxidation number (in organic reactions this often involves an increase in the number of C–O bonds and a simultaneous decrease in the number of C–H bonds)	1 Primary (1°) alcohols $CH_3CH_2OH(aq) \xrightarrow{Cr_2O_7^{2-} \text{(or } MnO_4^-\text{)}, H^+ (aq)} CH_3CHO(aq) \xrightarrow{Cr_2O_7^{2-} \text{(or } MnO_4^-\text{)}, H^+ (aq)} CH_3COOH(aq)$ 1° alcohol $\longrightarrow$ aldehyde $\longrightarrow$ carboxylic acid 2 Secondary (2°) alcohols $CH_3CH(OH)CH_3 \xrightarrow{Cr_2O_7^{2-} \text{(or } MnO_4^-\text{)}, H^+ (aq)} CH_3COCH_3$ 2° alcohol $\longrightarrow$ ketone 3 Tertiary (3°) alcohols do not undergo oxidation reactions readily.
condensation	a reaction between an alcohol and a carboxylic acid in the presence of a catalyst, concentrated H_2SO_4, to form an ester	$CH_3COOH(l) + CH_3CH_2OH(l) \xrightarrow{\text{conc. } H_2SO_4} CH_3COOCH_2CH_3(l) + H_2O(l)$

FOSSIL FUELS AND BIOFUELS

Fuels contain chemical energy that is relatively easily released as a useful source of energy. Energy sources can be classified in terms of their renewability.

- **Non-renewable** resources are resources that are used at a rate faster than they can be replaced. Examples are fossil fuels, which include coal, crude oil, petroleum gas and coal seam gas.
- **Renewable** resources are resources that can be continually replaced, or which do not involve the consumption of the resource. Examples are wind, water, tides, biomass and solar energy. **Biofuels**, such as bioethanol, biogas and biodiesel, are fuels obtained from living systems. Biofuels are renewable but not necessarily **sustainable**. Sustainable sources of energy are those that are not expected to be depleted within the lifetime of the human race. The use of sustainable energy sources causes no long-term damage to the environment.

Non-renewable fuels

Fuels such as coal, oil and natural gas have been formed over millions of years from plant and animal matter and so are referred to as fossil fuels (Table 7.16). The chemical energy contained in **fossil fuels** initially came from solar energy. The use of fossil fuels has significant environmental disadvantages such as:

- enhancing the greenhouse effect, as greenhouse gases (CO_2 and H_2O) are emitted when the fuels are burnt
- producing SO_2 gas, which forms acid rain
- producing nitrogen oxides, which increase air pollution.

TABLE 7.16 Comparison of some non-renewable energy sources

Fossil fuel	Description	Reasons for use	Energy content and main uses
coal	• mixture of organic molecules with molar masses as high as 3000 • found as black coal, brown coal and peat, with decreasing percentage carbon content	• cheap to mine • large deposits worldwide	• high energy content • as the percentage of carbon increases, energy content and efficiency of energy production increase while environmental impact decreases • produces more pollutants than other fossil fuels • used in electricity production
crude oil	• mixture of alkanes • needs to be fractionally distilled and then cracked to obtain useful fuels such as petrol	• relatively cheap and easy to mine, but known deposits may only last decades	• high energy content • transport fuel
petroleum gas	• may be found trapped between rock layers (called shale gas) • a component of crude oil	• relatively cheap • widely available • readily transported	• high energy content • transport fuel
natural gas, including coal seam gas	• natural gas adsorbed onto coal surface is called coal seam gas • usually contains water	• more efficient in energy production compared to coal • moderate cost • when burnt, produces less particulate matter in emissions than coal	• high energy content • electricity production; heating; cooking; transport fuel

Renewable fuels

Living organisms obtain energy from the Sun, either directly or indirectly, by the process of **photosynthesis**. The equation for this process can be written as:

$$6CO_2(g) + 6H_2O(l) \xrightarrow{\text{sunlight}} C_6H_{12}O_6(aq) + 6O_2(g)$$
$$\text{glucose}$$

Plants convert solar energy to chemical energy in glucose, which then undergoes polymerisation to form starch and cellulose. Starch is stored in plants, then hydrolysed to glucose for the controlled release of energy in the process of respiration. Starch, cellulose and other plant material can be converted to biofuels such as bioethanol, **biogas** and **biodiesel** for transport and industrial and domestic uses (Table 7.17).

Biofuels are renewable fuels made from plants such as sugar cane, grains, vegetable waste or oils. Although carbon dioxide is produced when biofuels burn, the plants also absorb it as they grow. The use of biofuels, rather than fossil fuels, has the potential for an overall reduction in the levels of carbon dioxide emitted. However, energy is needed in growing and harvesting the plants and in the manufacture of the biofuel. This energy production produces greenhouse gases, so the production of biofuels is not strictly carbon-neutral.

One question that arises with respect to biofuel production is whether it is appropriate to use farmland to produce biofuels instead of food crops.

TABLE 7.17 Comparison of some renewable energy sources

Biofuel and how it is produced	Energy content and use
bioethanol • produced by fermentation of glucose—an anaerobic process involving yeast: $C_6H_{12}O_6(aq) \rightarrow 2CH_3CH_2OH(aq) + 2CO_2(g)$	• less energy available per litre than petrol • transport fuel, but may cause greater engine wear than petrol
biogas • mainly a gaseous mixture of CO_2 and CH_4 • generated when organic waste matter is digested anaerobically by the action of microorganisms 	• low energy content • for heating and to power homes and farms
biodiesel • composed of a mixture of esters • produced by reaction between vegetable oils (esters) and an alcohol, commonly methanol	• more energy available per litre than petrol • transport fuel

Reactions of organic acids and bases

STRUCTURE AND PHYSICAL PROPERTIES OF CARBOXYLIC ACIDS, AMINES AND AMIDES

The molecular structures of carboxylic acids, amines and amides are shown in Table 7.18. Their physical properties are a consequence of the hydrogen bonds that exist between the molecules.

Boiling point

The presence of hydrogen bonds between molecules causes higher boiling points for carboxylic acids, amines and amides compared to alkanes of the same parent name. As the chain length increases, dispersion forces increase, and this increases the boiling points as well.

The presence of the C=O in –COOH and –CONH$_2$ groups cause carboxylic acids and amides to form dimers (Figure 7.7). Hydrogen bonding holds the dimers together. The increase in molecular size of the dimer increases the dispersion forces significantly, resulting in higher boiling points. Hence the boiling points of carboxylic acids and amides are much higher than for amines of similar size.

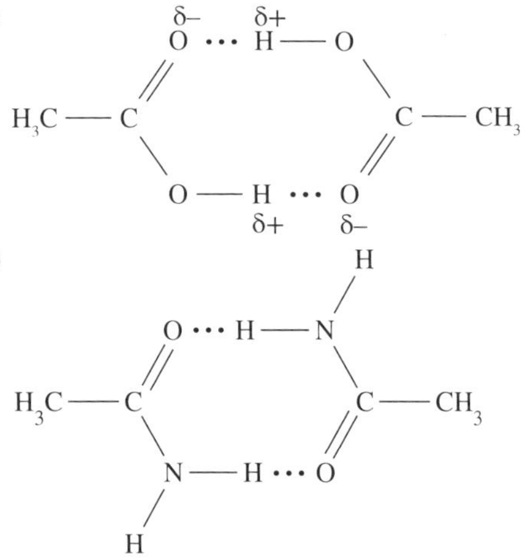

FIGURE 7.7 (a) Hydrogen bonds between two ethanoic acid molecules results in the formation of a dimer. (b) Two ethanamide molecules can also form a dimer.

Amides tend to have higher boiling points than similar sized carboxylic acids. This is explained by the presence of two H atoms bonded to nitrogen in a primary amide whereas there is only one H atom bonded to oxygen in a carboxylic acid. This means there are two locations where hydrogen bonding can occur on primary amide molecules. In amides, a dimer can hydrogen bond through this second hydrogen atom to other amide dimers, increasing the boiling point significantly above the boiling points of carboxylic acids of similar size (Table 7.19).

TABLE 7.19 Comparison of boiling points

Homologous series	Condensed structural formula	Molar mass (g mol^{-1})	Boiling point (°C)
alkane	$CH_3CH_2CH_2CH_3$	58	–1
carboxylic acid	CH_3CH_2COOH	74	141
amine	$CH_3CH_2CH_2NH_2$	59	48.6
amide	$CH_3CH_2CONH_2$	73	213

Solubility

Small carboxylic acids, amines and amides are soluble because they can form hydrogen bonds with water molecules. As the chain length increases the solubility decreases.

STRUCTURE AND PHYSICAL PROPERTIES OF ALDEHYDES AND KETONES

Aldehydes and ketones contain the carbonyl functional group, C=O. The location of the carbonyl functional group in a molecule determines whether the molecule is an aldehyde or ketone. When the C=O is at the end of the chain it becomes a CHO group, and the molecule is an aldehyde. When the the C=O is in the middle of the chain, the molecule is a ketone (Table 7.6).

Aldehydes and ketones with the same parent name are functional group structural isomers.

TABLE 7.18 Structure and bonding of carboxylic acids, amines and amides

Structure and property	Carboxylic acids	Amines (primary)	Amides (primary)
Molecular structure	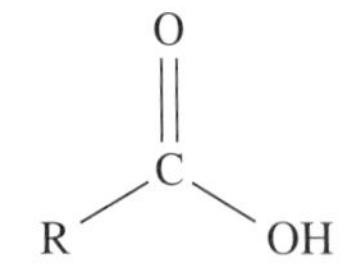 The structure of a carboxylic acid. The carboxyl functional group (-COOH) contains a hydroxyl functional group bonded to a carbonyl functional group.	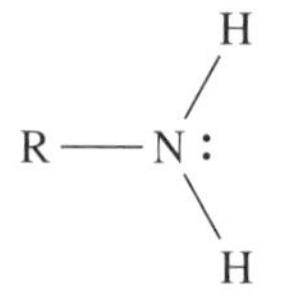 The structure of an amine.	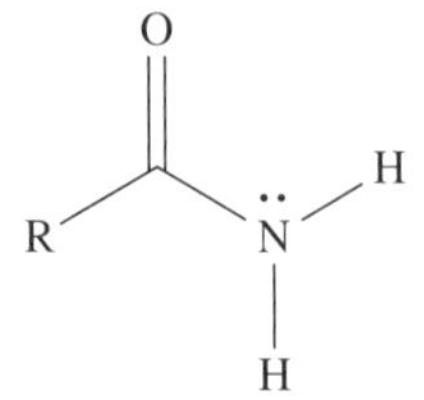 The structure of an amide. The functional group of a primary amide (-CONH$_2$) contains an amino functional group bonded to a carbonyl functional group.
Intermolecular forces	Hydrogen bonding (because hydrogen is covalently bonded to O).	Hydrogen bonding (because hydrogen is covalently bonded to N within the molecule).	

The physical properties of aldehydes and ketones are determined largely by the intermolecular bonds between molecules. The C=O bond is polar, and dipole–dipole forces exist between the molecules (Figure 7.8). Because hydrogen is not covalently bonded directly to N, O or F in these molecules, aldehydes and ketones do not form hydrogen bonds.

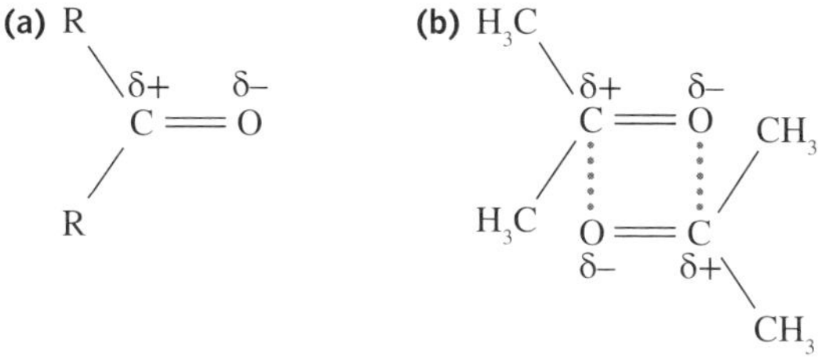

(a) R
$\delta+$ $\delta-$
C ══ O
R

(b) H_3C
$\delta+$ $\delta-$
C ══ O CH_3
H_3C O ══ C
$\delta-$ $\delta+$
CH_3

FIGURE 7.8 (a) A carbonyl bond is polar. (b) Dipole–dipole attractions occur between ketone molecules.

Boiling points

Because dipole–dipole forces are stronger than dispersion forces, aldehydes and ketones have higher boiling points than alkanes of the same parent name. As the chain length of aldehydes and ketone molecules increases, the dispersion forces increase, so the boiling point also increases.

Solubility

Small-chain aldehydes and ketones dissolve well in water because water can form hydrogen bonds with these polar molecules. They form neutral solutions. As the hydrocarbon chain increases in length, the solubility decreases because of the disruption of hydrogen bonding between water molecules by the non-polar hydrocarbon chains, which can only form dispersion forces.

CHEMICAL PROPERTIES OF ORGANIC ACIDS AND BASES

Reactions of carboxylic acids

Carboxylic acids react with alcohols in a condensation reaction to form esters. For example:

$CH_3COOH(aq) + CH_3CH_2OH(aq) \rightarrow CH_3COOCH_2CH_3(aq) + H_2O(l)$

Amides are formed when carboxylic acids react with amines. For example:

$CH_3COOH(aq) + CH_3NH_2(aq) \rightarrow CH_3CONHCH_3(aq) + H_2O(l)$

Acid–base properties

The acid–base properties of these compounds are summarised in Table 7.20.

TABLE 7.20 Acid–base properties of carboxylic acids, amines and amides

Property	Carboxylic acids	Amines (primary)	Amides (primary)
Acid–base strength	• weak acids	• weak bases	• very weak base
Dissociation and ionisation in water	• $CH_3COOH(aq) + H_2O(l) \rightleftharpoons$ $CH_3COO^-(aq) + H_3O^+(aq)$	• $CH_3NH_2(aq) + H_2O(l) \rightleftharpoons$ $CH_3NH_3^+(aq) + OH^-(aq)$	• do not readily dissociate because the lone pair of electrons on the nitrogen atom is drawn towards the C=O part of the molecule, making the molecule less reactive.
Acid–base properties	• partially dissociate in water • turn litmus red • react with carbonates to form CO_2 gas • undergo neutralisation reactions with strong bases: $CH_3COOH(aq) + OH^-(aq) \rightleftharpoons$ $CH_3COO^-(aq) + H_2O(l)$	• partially dissociate in water • turn litmus blue • undergo neutralisation reactions with strong acids: $CH_3NH_2(aq) + H^+(aq) \rightleftharpoons$ $CH_3NH_3^+(aq)$	• do not dissociate readily in water • not usually considered to have acid–base properties

SOAPS AND DETERGENTS

Fats and oils are called triglycerides. A triglyceride molecule contains three ester functional groups and three long hydrocarbon chains.

Soap is produced by a **hydrolysis reaction** between a triglyceride and sodium hydroxide in a process known as **saponification** (Figure 7.9).

In soap-making the three ester links in the triglyceride are hydrolysed, producing glycerol and three particles of soap, such as the sodium stearate shown in Figure 7.9. The soap particle contains a charged hydrophilic ('water-loving') carboxylate end and a non-polar hydrophobic ('water-hating') hydrocarbon tail.

Cleaning action of soap

When a solution of soap in water comes into contact with grease, as in Figure 7.10, the long non-polar, hydrocarbon chains of the soap particles form dispersion forces with the grease and the charged ionic carboxylate ends bond with water by ion-dipole forces. Gradually, with agitation, the non-polar grease becomes surrounded by the hydrophilic carboxylate ends of the soap molecule. As a result, the grease becomes soluble in water and is easily washed away (Figure 7.11).

Detergents

Detergents are now used more widely than soaps because they do not form a scum (precipitate) with soluble ionic salts in water, such as calcium and magnesium salts. They have a similar structure to soap (Figure 7.12) and behave in a similar way, but are made from petroleum products.

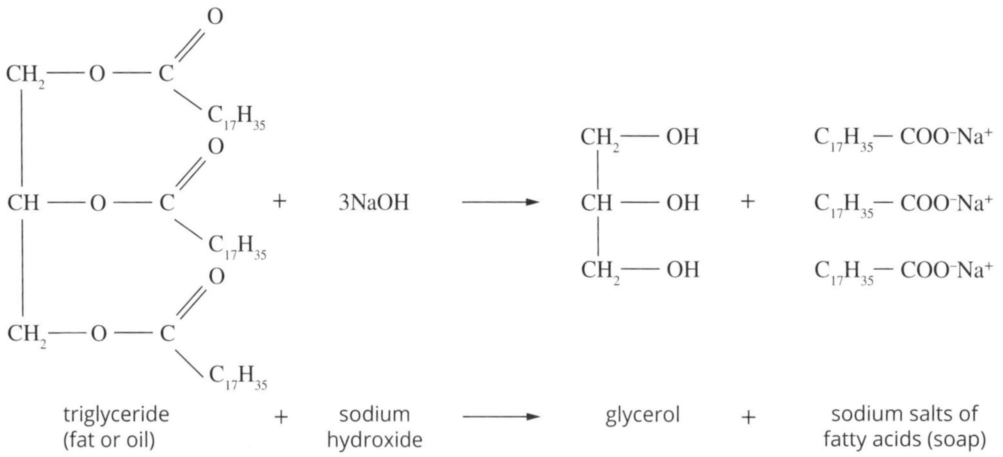

FIGURE 7.9 The formation of soap

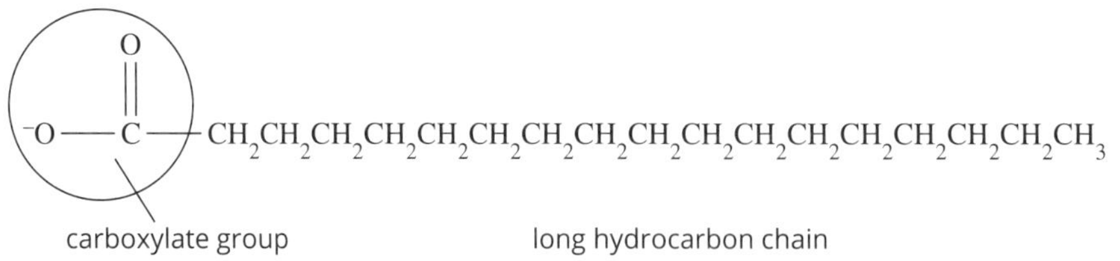

FIGURE 7.10 The structure of sodium stearate, a soap. A soap can be described as the salt of a long-chain carboxylic acid.

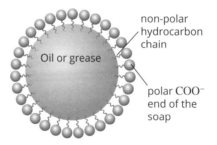

FIGURE 7.11 Soap particles attach to a grease droplet to form a hydrophilic surface. This makes the droplet soluble in water, allowing it to be washed away.

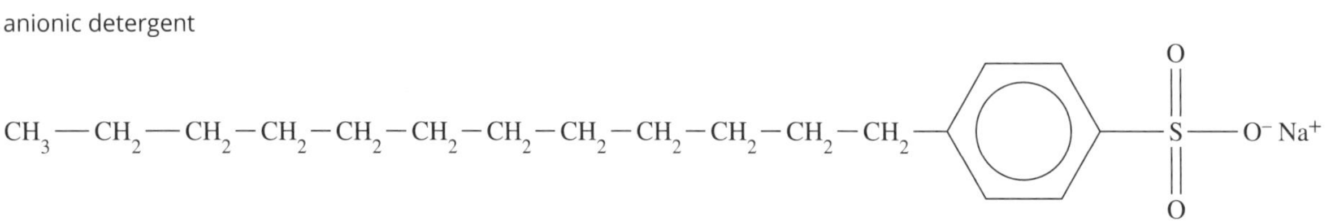

anionic detergent

FIGURE 7.12 Structure of a detergent made from crude oil

ORGANIC REACTION PATHWAYS

Organic chemicals are often made using a sequence of reactions, rather than in a single step from reactants to products. For example, an ester can be produced from an alkane or an alkene using the reaction pathway shown in Figure 7.13.

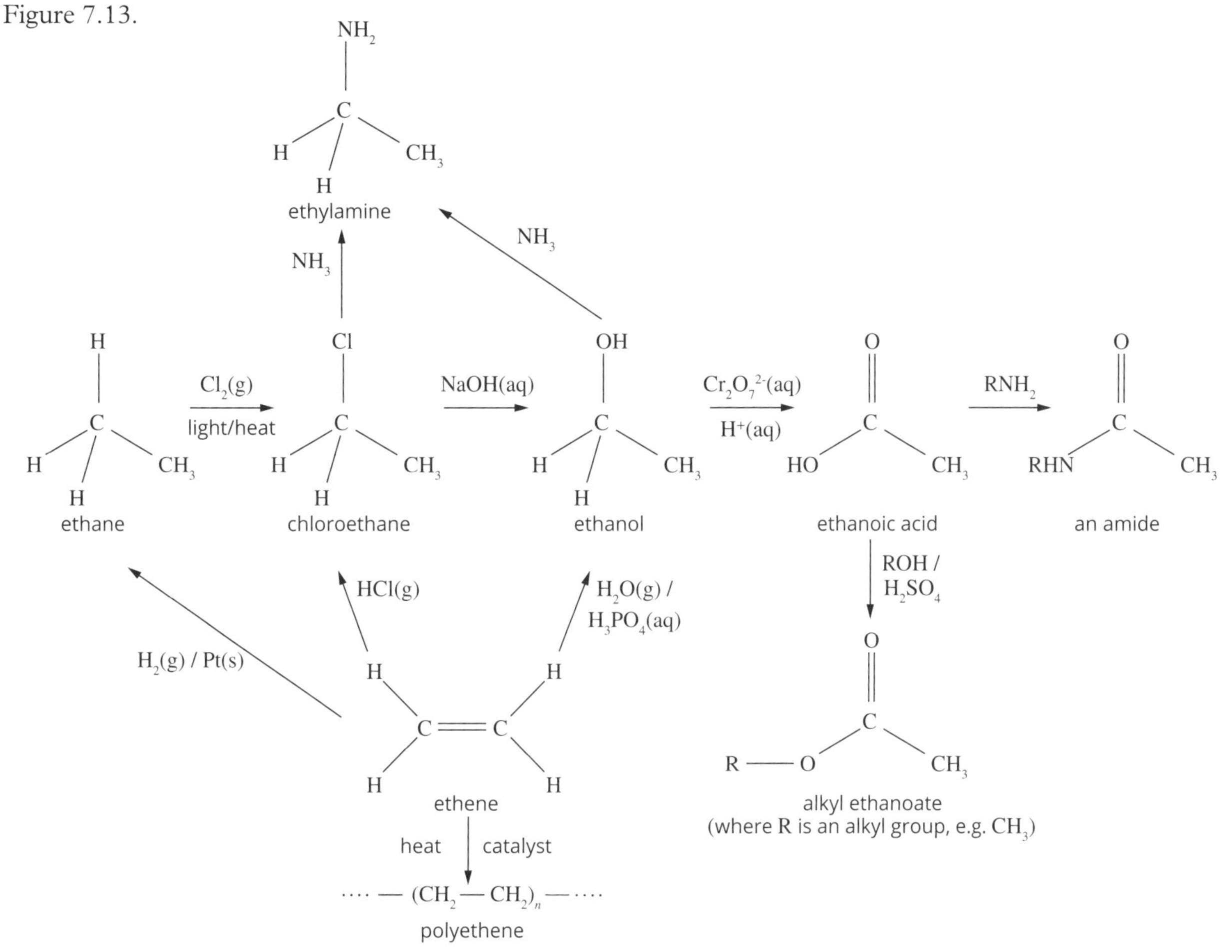

FIGURE 7.13 Simple organic reaction pathways involving ethane

Polymers

Polymers are substances that:
- consist of small molecules, called monomers, linked together
- contain thousands of atoms
- are produced by a process called **polymerisation**.

Polymers can be classified as **thermoplastic**, **thermosetting** or **elastomers**. Table 7.21 describes the structure, properties and applications of these different types of polymers. Thermoplastic polymers are usually formed in a single stage reaction, whereas the manufacture of thermosetting polymers and elastomers often involves a second stage of production in which strong covalent bonds called **cross-links** are formed between different chains. This is usually achieved by:
- heating the material after the polymer chains have been formed
- adding another substance that reacts with the atoms on the chains, joining the chains together.

TABLE 7.21 Types of polymers

Type of polymer	Structure	Properties	Examples of applications
thermoplastic	• linear • strong covalent bonds within chains • weak forces between different chains	• flexible • soften on heating, so able to be remoulded/recyclable	• items produced by moulding, e.g. laundry baskets, milk bottles, toys
thermosetting	• strong covalent bonds within chains • cross-links between different chains	• do not melt, but char when heated so cannot be remoulded • rigid • not recyclable	• laminates
elastomer	• strong covalent bonds within chains • small number of cross-links between different chains	• elastic, i.e. can be pulled out of shape but will regain original shape when force is removed	• rubber

ADDITION POLYMERISATION

Addition polymerisation is a process that produces linear polymers. The monomers are small unsaturated molecules that contain a carbon–carbon double bond which is broken during the polymerisation process. The monomers are covalently bonded together to form long-chain polymer molecules (Figure 7.14).

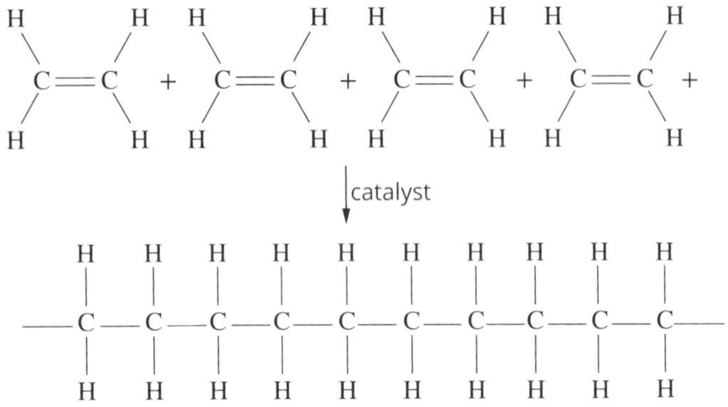

FIGURE 7.14 Formation of polyethene (PE) by the addition polymerisation of ethene

Many different monomers that contain a carbon–carbon double bond can undergo addition polymerisation. Some of these reactions are shown in Figure 7.15.

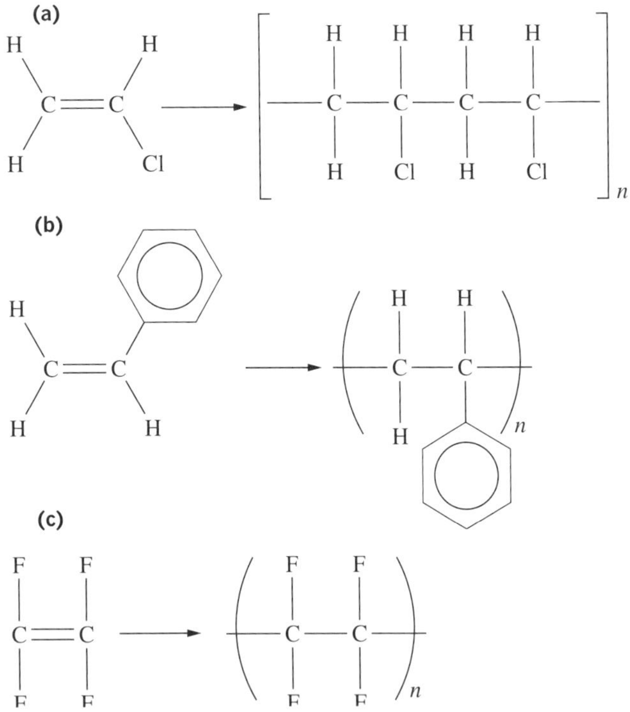

FIGURE 7.15 Addition polymerisation reactions that form some common materials: (a) polyvinyl chloride (PVC), (b) polystyrene (PS), and (c) polytetrafluoroethene (PTFE)

Factors affecting polymer properties

Several factors determine the properties of polymers, including:

- the length of the chain, which is determined by the number of monomer units. The longer the chain, the greater the dispersion forces and the higher the melting point.
- functional groups on the monomer that affect the intermolecular bonding between polymer chains. The stronger these forces, the higher the melting point and the more rigid the polymer.
- the alignment of the polymer chains that produce different regions in the polymer. When lined up in an orderly fashion the polymer chains can pack closer together and bond more strongly. These **crystalline regions** are stronger and more rigid, whereas the disordered (**amorphous**) sections are softer.
- the inclusion of additives that can improve the properties to make the polymer less flammable, more stable in sunlight and even coloured
- the degree of branching that occurs as the polymer forms. This is controlled by altering the reaction conditions (Table 7.22).

CONDENSATION POLYMERISATION

Some monomers that have functional groups at both ends of their molecules can undergo condensation reactions to produce a polymer. Unlike addition polymerisation, in which all of the monomer becomes part of the polymer, a small molecule (usually H_2O or HCl) is released during **condensation polymerisation**.

Nylon and polyester are examples of condensation polymers (Figures 7.16 and 7.17). The properties and uses of nylon and polyester are summarised in Table 7.23. Many large biological molecules, such as proteins and polysaccharides (cellulose and starch), are also produced in condensation polymerisation reactions.

TABLE 7.22 Properties and uses of polyethene

Name	Branching	Production pressure	Properties	Examples of uses
high-density polyethene (HDPE)	small amount	atmospheric pressure	stronger, less flexible	pipes, buckets, toys
low-density polyethene (LDPE)	highly branched	high pressure	weaker, more flexible	plastic wraps, garbage bags

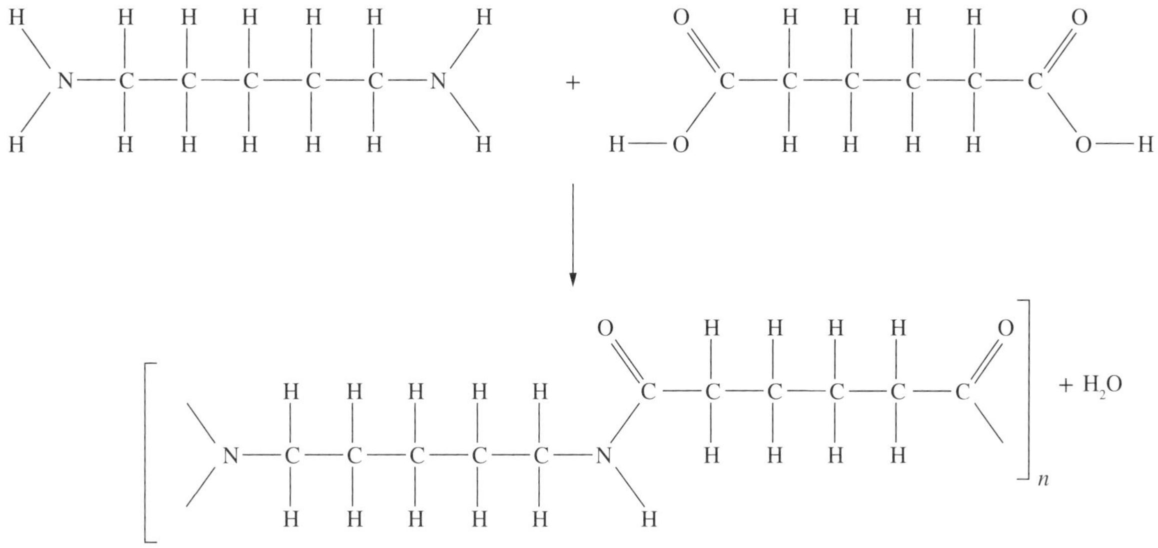

FIGURE 7.16 Nylon is produced by a condensation polymerisation reaction between hexamethylene diamine and hexandioic acid. The reaction also produces water.

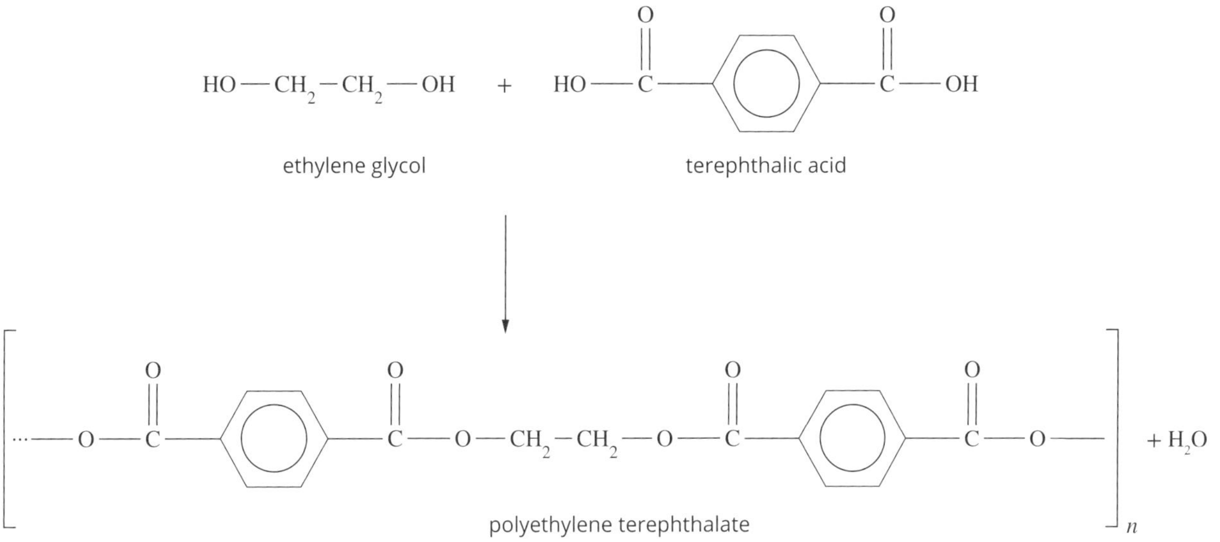

ethylene glycol   terephthalic acid

polyethylene terephthalate

FIGURE 7.17 Polyester is an extremely versatile polymer. It is made from an alcohol and a carboxylic acid by condensation polymerisation. Water is also formed in the reaction.

TABLE 7.23 Properties and uses of nylon and polyesters

Polymer	Properties	Examples of uses
nylon	• strong • elastic • easy to clean • dries quickly and retains shape • resistant to heat, UV rays and chemicals • hydrogen bonds between chains, producing a more rigid polymer	• fabric for clothing • rope • luggage • umbrellas
polyester	• strong fibre • withstands repetitive movements • highly crystalline • good heat and chemical resistance • dipole–dipole forces between chains, producing a softer polymer	• textiles • packaging • bottles of beverages because of low oxygen permeability • upholstery • carpets and rugs • homewares

Knowledge review—molecular shape and intermolecular forces

1 Complete the crossword by writing the term that matches each definition. This will help you check your knowledge and understanding of the key ideas and processes involved in determining molecular shape and intermolecular forces, in preparation for your study of organic chemistry.

Across

5 Pair of outer shell electrons not involved in bonding (4, 4)

6 Force of attraction between dipoles (6–6)

9 Molecules that have two oppositely charged ends

10 Molecular shape when the angles between the electron pairs are 120°

11 Shape of a methane molecule

12 Strong dipole–dipole attraction that exists between molecules in which a hydrogen atom is covalently bonded to an oxygen, nitrogen or fluorine atom (8, 7)

13 Electron-attracting power of an atom

14 Molecular shape of a water molecule

Down

1 Discrete particle containing two or more atoms held together by covalent bonds

2 Type of bond involving the sharing of electrons by two non-metallic atoms

3 Type of dipole that exists in non-polar molecules

4 Shape of a carbon dioxide molecule

7 Weakest type of intermolecular attraction (10, 6)

8 Type of dipole that exists in polar molecules

2 Indicate whether the following statements are true or false, and write the corrected statement where necessary.

a There are 4 electron pairs around the oxygen atom in water, and a linear shape is predicted using the VSEPR theory.

TRUE / FALSE _____

b In methane the electron pair arrangement forms a tetrahedral shape and so the molecular shape is tetrahedral.

TRUE / FALSE _____

c A polar molecule must have polar bonds and be symmetrical.

TRUE / FALSE _____

d The bigger the difference in electronegativity between the elements forming a covalent bond, the less polar the bond.

TRUE / FALSE _____

e Electrostatic attraction between the oppositely charged ends of polar molecules holds the molecules together in the solid and liquid states.

TRUE / FALSE _____

f Hydrogen bonding is stronger than other forms of dipole–dipole bonds and stronger than covalent bonds.

TRUE / FALSE _____

g Dispersion forces are always present between atoms, due to the attraction between electrons and protons.

TRUE / FALSE _____

h The forces between molecules determine the melting points of molecular substances.

TRUE / FALSE _____

WORKSHEET 7.2

Families of hydrocarbons—alkanes, alkenes and alkynes

Crude oil deposits contain hydrocarbons formed millions of years ago from the decomposition of plants and animals. Alkanes are separated from the crude oil by fractional distillation. This process separates alkane fractions on the basis of their boiling points, which depend on the strength of intermolecular forces. Different fractions have many different uses, such as fuels, sources of raw materials for synthesising organic compounds, and road construction materials.

1   The environmental, economic and social aspects of obtaining and using crude oil and other fossil fuels are important issues for society.

a   Explain how the use of hydrocarbons as fuels is damaging to the environment, using air pollution and acid rain as examples.

b   Modern society depends on the use of fossil fuels. Discuss two economic reasons for this dependence.

c   The mining and use of fossil fuels can have significant social consequences. Briefly describe how global climate change and land destruction may affect individuals and communities.

2 The structural formulae of 15 hydrocarbon compounds are shown below.

A 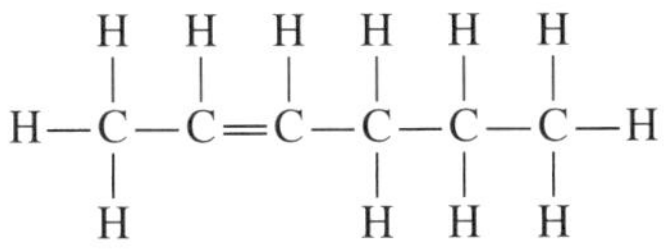 H—C—C=C—C—C—C—H (with H substituents)	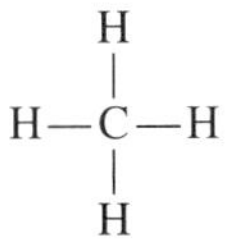 B H—C—H (with H top and bottom)	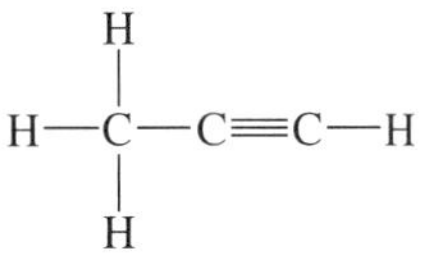 C H—C—C≡C—H (with H substituents)
D branched structure with H—C—H groups	E C=C (ethene structure)	F H—C≡C—H
G H—C—C—C—C—H (with H substituents)	H H—C—C≡C—C— (with H substituents)	I branched structure with H—C—H groups
J H—C—C—C—H with H—C—H branch	K H—C—C—C—C—C—C—H (with H substituents)	L H—C—C—C=C—C—C—C—(with H substituents)
M C=C—C—C—C—C—H (with H substituents)	N branched structure with H—C—H groups	O H—C—C—C—C—C—C—C—C—H (with H substituents)

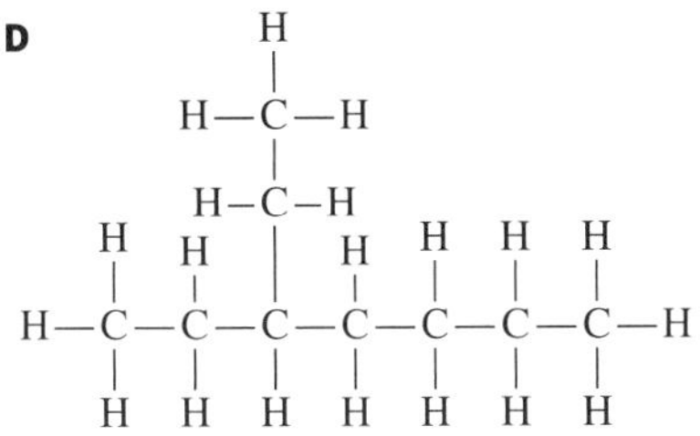

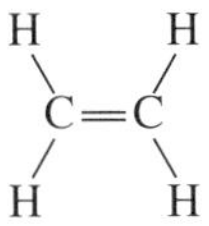

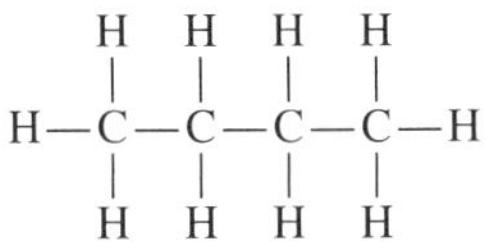

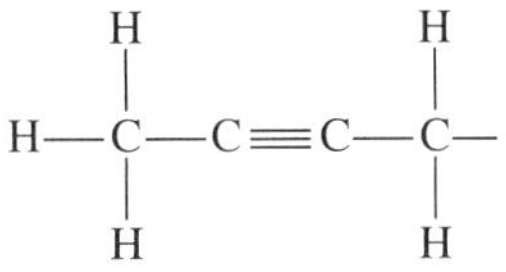

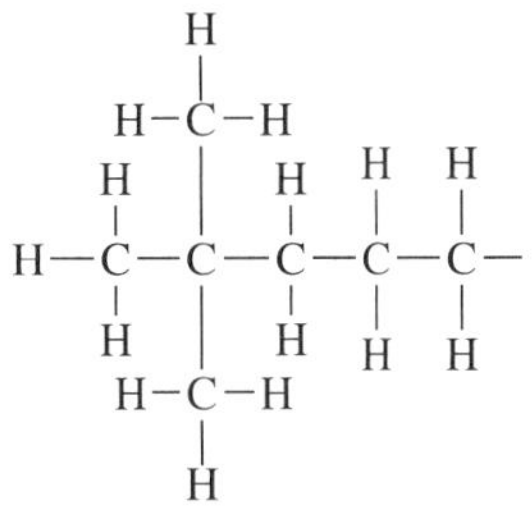

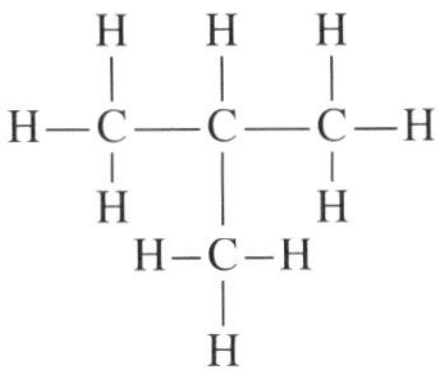

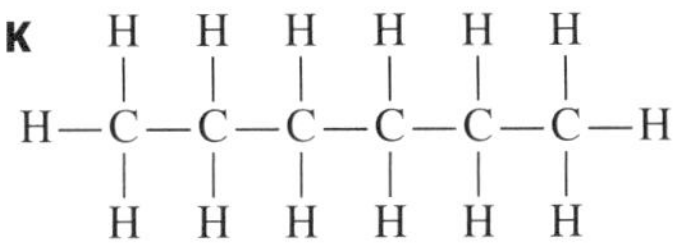

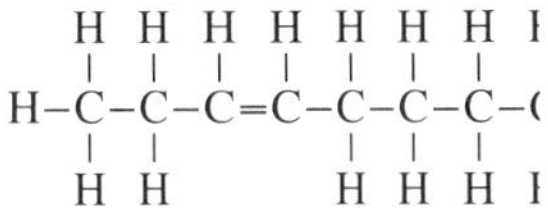

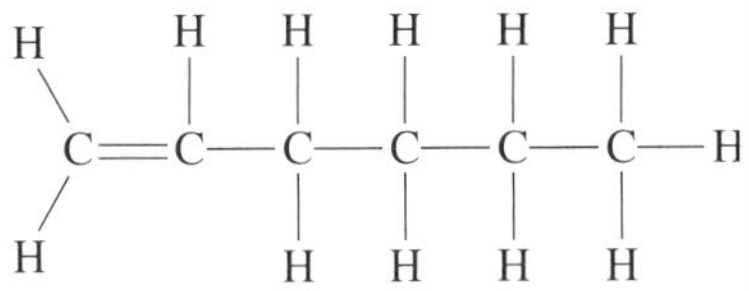

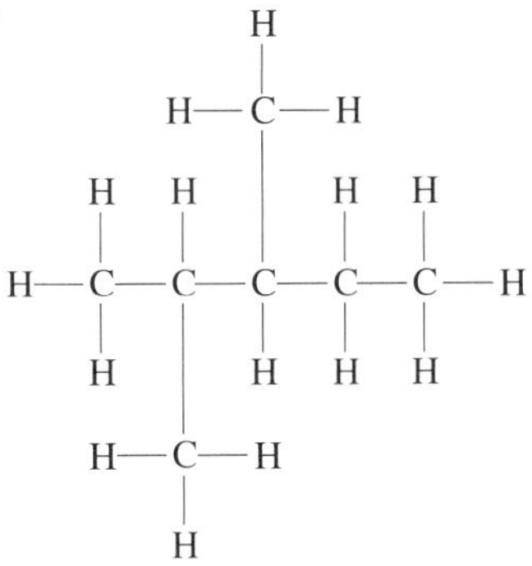

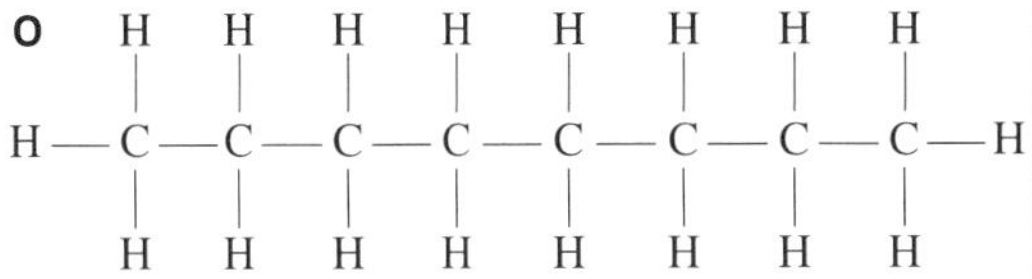

a List the letters of all compounds that are unbranched alkanes.

b List the letters of all compounds that are branched alkanes.

c List the letters of all the compounds that are alkenes.

d List the letters of all the compounds that are alkynes.

e i Define the term *homologous series*.

    ii Write the condensed structural formulae of the next two members of the same homologous series that follow the molecule with the condensed formula CH_3CH_2OH.

_____

_____

f List the letters of all the compounds that are unsaturated.

_____

g List the letters of all the compounds that are saturated.

_____

h Summarise the meaning of the terms *saturated* and *unsaturated*.

_____

_____

i Identify the compound you would expect to have the lowest boiling point, and explain your answer.

_____

_____

j Identify the compounds you would expect to decolourise bromine, and explain your answer.

_____

_____

k Identify two chain isomers from the compounds shown above.

_____

l Identify two position isomers from the compounds shown above.

_____

m Summarise the difference between chain and position structural isomers.

_____

_____

n Give the systematic name of each compound.

A _____	I _____
B _____	J _____
C _____	K _____
D _____	L _____
E _____	M _____
F _____	N _____
G _____	O _____
H _____	

RATING MY LEARNING	My understanding improved	Not confident ○ ○ ○ ○ ○ Very confident	I answered questions without help	Not confident ○ ○ ○ ○ ○ Very confident	I corrected my errors without help	Not confident ○ ○ ○ ○ ○ Very confident

Families examined—properties and structure

Complete each cell of the following table. State whether each statement is true or false in the last column.

Name of molecule	Condensed structural formula	Structural formula	Statement	True or false?
ethanol			Is soluble in water and dissolves by forming hydrogen bonds.	
			Has the general formula C_nH_{2n}.	
			Formed by a substitution reaction between NaOH and chloroethane.	
			Undergoes dehydration to form an alkene.	
hexan-2-one			Contains a C=C bond.	
			Is the product of oxidation of hexan-2-ol.	
			Contains a carbonyl group.	
			Is a functional group isomer of hexanal.	
butanamide			Is insoluble in water.	
			Does not have significant acid–base properties.	
			Can form hydrogen bonds.	
	$CH_3CH_2CH(OH)CH_3$		Is a primary alcohol.	
			Does not form hydrogen bonds.	
			Is a saturated alcohol.	
	$CH_3CH_2CH_2COOH$		Is soluble in water.	
			Partially dissociates in water to form H_3O^+.	
			Is a member of the homologous series of alcohols.	
			Has only dispersion forces between molecules.	

Name of molecule	Condensed structural formula	Structural formula	Statement	True or false?
	$CH_3CH_2COOCH_3$		Is a polar molecule.	
			Forms dipole–dipole forces between molecules.	
			Is formed by reaction of methanoic acid with propan-1-ol in the presence of sulfuric acid.	
2-chloropentane			Is an isomer of 2-chloro-2-methylbutane.	
			Undergoes substitution reactions.	
			Is the chain isomer of 1-chloropentane.	
	$CH_3CHC(CH_3)$ CH_2CH_3		Undergoes addition reactions.	
			Belongs to the homologous series of alkanes.	
			Dissolves in water by forming hydrogen bonds.	
	$CH_3CH_2CH_2NH_2$		Is unsaturated.	
			Is a position isomer of $CH_3CH(NH_2)$ CH_3.	
			Acts as a base in water.	
			Dissolves in water by forming hydrogen bonds.	
			The final oxidation product would be a carboxylic acid.	
			Is a saturated compound.	
			Is a polar molecule.	
			Is soluble in water.	
	CH_3CH_2CHO		Will oxidise to form propanoic acid.	
			Forms hydrogen bonds between molecules.	
			Is soluble in water.	
			The boiling point is lower than the alkane of the same parent name.	

RATING MY LEARNING | My understanding improved — Not confident ○ ○ ○ ○ ○ Very confident | I answered questions without help — Not confident ○ ○ ○ ○ ○ Very confident | I corrected my errors without help — Not confident ○ ○ ○ ○ ○ Very confident

124   Pearson Chemistry 12 NSW | Skills and Assessment | Module 7   ISBN 978 1 4886 1934 2

Observing organics—properties of functional groups

The following table shows the results of several small experiments testing the properties of samples of each of the following types of organic chemicals: saturated and unsaturated hydrocarbons, alcohols, carboxylic acids and esters.

Compound	Observations
A	• liquid with a fruity smell • slightly soluble in water
B	• white powder • soluble in water • reacted with $NaHCO_3$(aq) to produce a gas that was shown to be carbon dioxide
C	• clear liquid • soluble in water • flammable • reacted with compound B to produce a sweet-smelling liquid similar to A • reacted with a mixture of orange $K_2Cr_2O_7$(aq) and H_2SO_4(aq) to produce a green solution
D	• clear liquid • insoluble in water • flammable • changed colour immediately when bromine solution was added
E	• clear liquid • insoluble in water • flammable • did not change colour when bromine solution was added

1   Using the information given, state the type of organic compound to which compound B belongs. Explain your answer.

_____

2   Write a general equation for the reaction of compound B with $NaHCO_3$ solution.

_____

3   Using the information given, state the type of organic compound to which compound C belongs. Explain your reasoning.

_____

4   Write a general equation for the reaction of B and C to produce a compound similar to A.

_____

5   Which type of compound is A? _____

6   Write a general equation for the reaction involving $K_2Cr_2O_7$(aq), H_2SO_4(aq) and compound C. Show only the organic reactant and product.

_____

7   Has compound C been oxidised, or has it been reduced? _____

8   To which group of organic compounds do compounds D and E belong?

_____

9   Write an appropriate safety statement for a student performing these experiments, including the safe disposal of the organic materials.

_____

| RATING MY LEARNING | My understanding improved | Not confident ◄————► Very confident ○ ○ ○ ○ ○ | I answered questions without help | Not confident ◄————► Very confident ○ ○ ○ ○ ○ | I corrected my errors without help | Not confident ◄————► Very confident ○ ○ ○ ○ ○ |

ISBN 978 1 4886 1934 2   Pearson Chemistry 12 NSW | Skills and Assessment | Module 7   **125**

WORKSHEET 7.5

Converting chemicals—organic reaction pathways

Use the terms and formulae below to help you complete this worksheet. (Terms can be used more than once and some might not be used.)

UV light	ethanoic acid	$Cr_2O_7{}^{2-}$ / H^+	Cl_2 / UV light	ethene
ethyl ethanoate	1,2-dibromoethane	polyethene	concentrated H_2SO_4	H_2O / H_3PO_4
HCl(g)	catalyst	CO_2(g)	O_2(g)	H_2O(g)
NaOH(aq)	Br_2(g)	H_2(g)	ethyne	hydrolysis
combustion	esterification	oxidation	reduction	hydrogenation
substitution	polymerisation	addition	subtraction	condensation

1   Complete the flow chart below, using ethane as the starting material and the terms in the box. Draw the structural formulae in the boxes above the chemical names in the flow chart where required. Give the chemical required in the boxes beside the arrows.

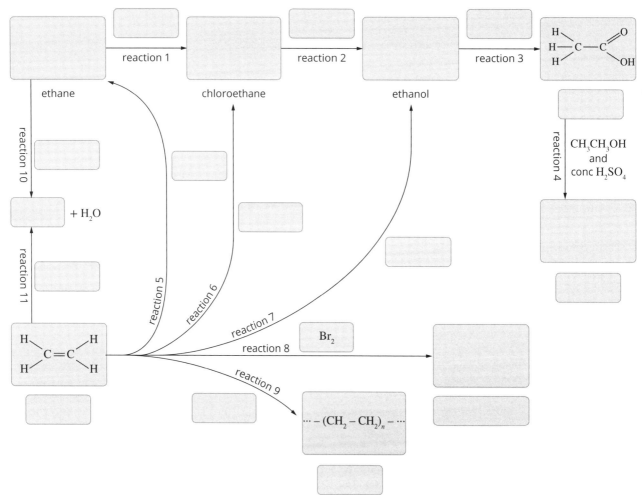

2 In the table below, classify the numbered reactions in the flow chart in question **1** using the terms in the box. (There may be more than one classification for a particular reaction.)

Reaction number	Classification
1	
2	
3	
4	
5	
6	
7	
8	
9	
10	
11	

WORKSHEET 7.6

Focus on functional groups—effect on chemical reactions

Functional groups in the molecules of organic compounds determine their properties and, therefore, their reactivity. The presence of polar groups in a hydrocarbon chain makes the compound more polar, more soluble in water and often more reactive than the corresponding hydrocarbon.

1   Alcohols contain the hydroxyl functional group. The position of a hydroxyl group in an alcohol molecule affects its reactivity and the products formed in the presence of oxidising agents.

Draw the structural formulae of the organic reactant and product molecules (where appropriate) for the following reactions. If there is more than one step in the reaction, draw all products.

   a   Butan-1-ol and dichromate ions are mixed in acidic conditions.

   b   3-methylpentan-3-ol and permanganate ions are mixed in acidic conditions.

   c   Hexan-2-ol and dichromate ions are mixed in acidic conditions.

2   Considering your answers to question **1** and, using the terms in the box, complete the following summary of the oxidation of alcohols.

                        ketones   aldehydes   carboxylic acids

Primary alcohols can be oxidised to _____ and then to _____.

Secondary alcohols can be oxidised to _____.

Tertiary alcohols cannot be oxidised under normal conditions.

3 Esters and amides are often called derivatives of carboxylic acids because they are produced by reactions with carboxylic acids.

Draw the structural formulae for the organic reactant and product molecules for the following reactions, which involve esters and amides.

a Propan-1-ol and butanoic acid are mixed with concentrated sulfuric acid.

b Methanamine reacts with propanoic acid.

4 Using structural formulae, write equations for the following substitution and addition reactions of alkanes and alkenes:

a the reaction of propene with hydrogen

b the reaction of HCl and ethene.

....

WORKSHEET 7.6

   c the reaction of but-2-ene and steam

5   **a** Draw structural formulae for the organic reactants and products in the production of an amide.

     i Start with the reaction of chloroethane with ammonia.

     ii React the organic product in part **i** with butanoic acid.

  b Draw structural formulae for the organic reactants and products in the production of butyl butanoate (which is an ester) from a series of reactions involving butan-1-ol, acidified potassium permanganate solution and concentrated sulfuric acid.

RATING MY LEARNING	My understanding improved	Not confident ← → Very confident ○ ○ ○ ○ ○	I answered questions without help	Not confident ← → Very confident ○ ○ ○ ○ ○	I corrected my errors without help	Not confident ← → Very confident ○ ○ ○ ○ ○

Biofuels—biogas, bioethanol and biodiesel

Biogas, bioethanol and biodiesel are renewable fuels that are derived from plant material. They are sometimes described as being carbon neutral. In the process of photosynthesis, carbon dioxide is removed from the air and is converted into plant material that is used to make biofuels. When the fuel derived from the plants undergoes combustion, carbon dioxide is produced that can then be recycled as more plants grow.

However, energy is needed for the production of these fuels, and the greenhouse gases that are emitted as a consequence prevent the fuels from being completely carbon neutral. Nevertheless, the production of biogas, especially in villages, is very close to carbon neutral.

Use the terms below to answer questions **1** and **2**. (Some terms may be used more than once, and others might not be used.)

methanol	anaerobic	aerobic	ethanol
methane	hydrogen	biodiesel	microorganisms
photosynthesis	biogas	glucose	efficiency
fermentation	fossil fuels	yeast	plant
+	$\rightarrow$	2	6
$C_6H_{12}O_6(aq)$	$CO_2(g)$	$O_2(g)$	$H_2O(l)$
$H_2(g)$	$HCl(aq)$	$CH_3COOH(aq)$	$CH_3CH_2OH(aq)$

1 Complete the summary statements about biofuels.

As the world's population grows and the demand for energy increases, governments are examining ways of improving the _____ of energy generation, as well as reducing the use of _____. Alternative fuels that may replace fossil fuels in the future are biogas, bioethanol and biodiesel. Biofuels derived from renewable sources such as _____ matter can be blended or used pure.

In villages and on farms, collection of agricultural waste and the use of a digester enable _____ to be generated under _____ conditions and in the presence of _____. Biogas is mainly _____ and carbon dioxide.

Fermentation of sugars, such as _____, in sugar cane or sugar beet involves the use of _____ and produces bioethanol. Bioethanol can be produced from a wide variety of _____ matter.

Biodiesel is produced by an esterification reaction between a vegetable oil, or a triglyceride, and an alcohol, usually _____.

2 Complete the diagram below, writing appropriate equations where necessary.

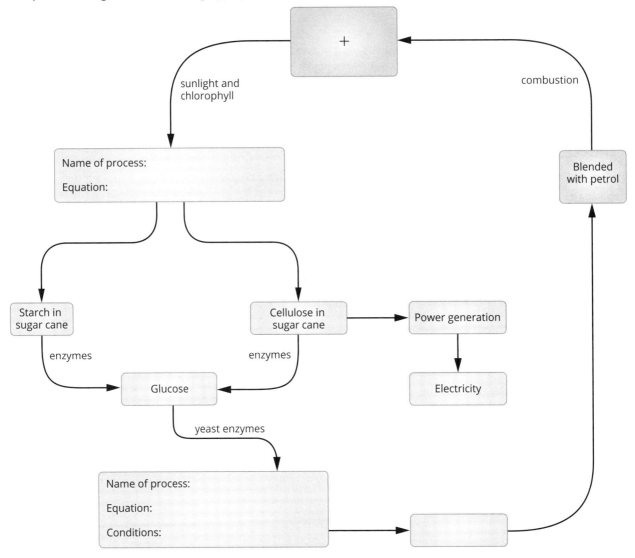

3 Explain why the use of biofuels produced from crops may be limited.

_____

_____

_____

4 A student made biodiesel in the laboratory by reacting vegetable oil and methanol with a potassium hydroxide catalyst. The student then burnt the biodiesel in a burner below a container of water, as shown in the diagram on the following page.

The student measured the initial and final temperature of the water and the mass of biodiesel burnt. From this data, the student was able to calculate the energy content of the biodiesel.

Use this information to complete the calculations and questions below.

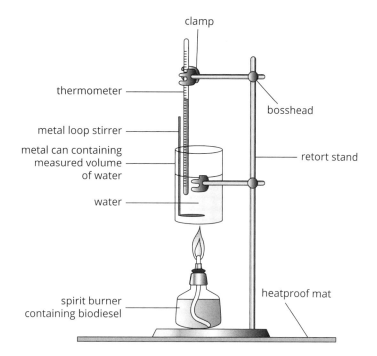

The student's results were:

Mass of biodiesel burnt: 2.00 g

Mass of water heated: 500 g

Temperature change of the water: 28.4°C

a Calculate the energy content, in $kJ\,g^{-1}$, of the biodiesel using the student's data. (The specific heat capacity of water is $4.18\,J\,g^{-1}\,°C^{-1}$.)

_____

_____

_____

_____

b The energy content of biodiesel is $-41\,kJ\,g^{-1}$. Compare this value with the value you calculated for biodiesel. Suggest a reason why the experimental value determined for biodiesel is different.

_____

_____

c Another form of diesel that is widely used as a transport fuel is petrodiesel. Petrodiesel is made from fossil fuels. Outline the difference in the environmental impacts of petrodiesel and biodiesel. (Consider their production as well as their combustion.)

_____

_____

_____

_____

Consumer products—polymers and soaps

1   Addition polymers are formed from unsaturated monomers. Complete the following table by naming and drawing the structural formulae of monomers or sections of the relevant addition polymer.

Monomer name and structure	Polymer name and structure
Monomer name:	Polymer name:
Monomer name:	Polymer name:
Monomer name: vinyl chloride	Polymer name:
Monomer name:	Polymer name:
Monomer name:	Polymer name:

2 a Starch is a polymer that is made by a condensation reaction that occurs in plants. Its structure is shown below. (Some carbon atoms have been omitted for clarity.) Draw the monomer of starch.

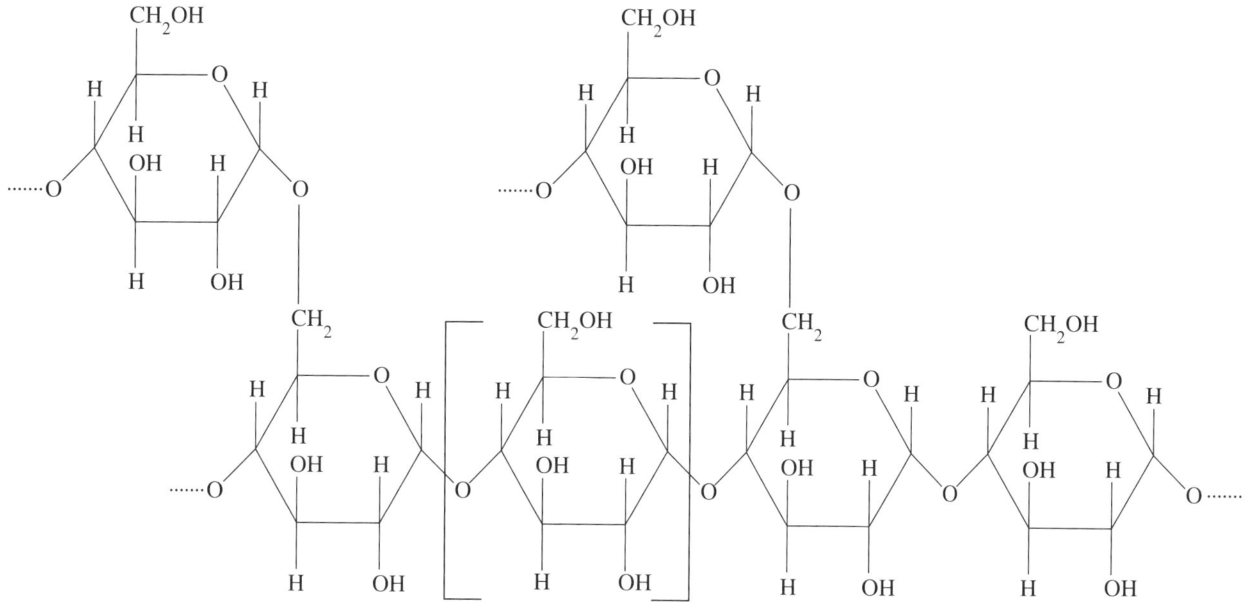

CH_2OH ... (starch polymer structure — two rows of linked glucose ring units with CH_2OH, H, OH groups and glycosidic O linkages)

b Proteins are condensation polymers formed from amino acids. Draw a small section of protein that could be made from the amino acids shown below.

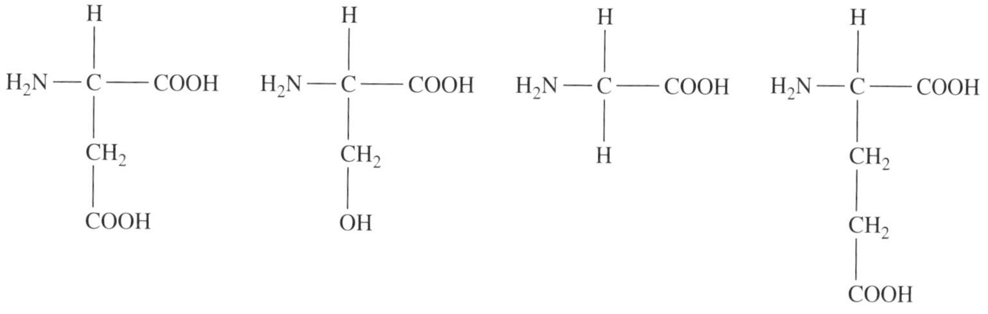

$$H_2N-\underset{\underset{\underset{COOH}{|}}{\underset{CH_2}{|}}{\overset{\overset{H}{|}}{C}}-COOH \qquad H_2N-\underset{\underset{\underset{OH}{|}}{\underset{CH_2}{|}}{\overset{\overset{H}{|}}{C}}-COOH \qquad H_2N-\underset{\underset{H}{|}}{\overset{\overset{H}{|}}{C}}-COOH \qquad H_2N-\underset{\underset{\underset{\underset{COOH}{|}}{\underset{CH_2}{|}}}{\underset{CH_2}{|}}{\overset{\overset{H}{|}}{C}}-COOH$$

c i Silk is a protein that is one of the strongest fibres known, but it loses up to 20% of its strength when wet. Examine the piece of silk protein drawn below and explain, in terms of the intermolecular bonding, why wetting silk reduces it tensile strength.

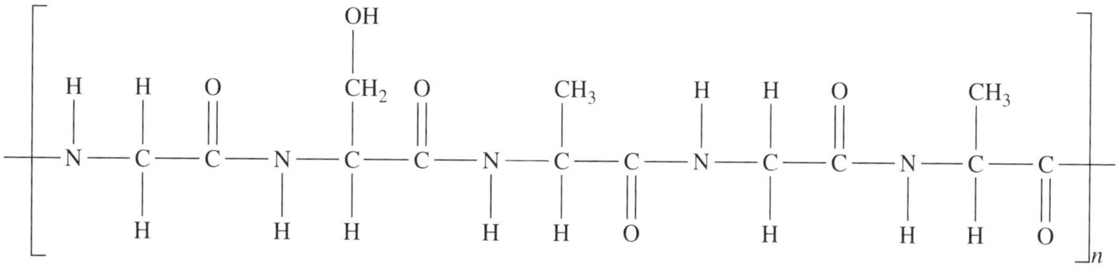

(silk protein structure: repeating peptide backbone with OH, CH_2, O, CH_3, H side groups, bracketed with subscript n)

ii Draw three amino acids from which the silk protein is made.

3 When soapy water comes into contact with grease on a surface, the processes that occur are illustrated below. From the terms in the box below, select the appropriate term to label the diagram in the spaces provided.

grease droplet forms   non-polar tails   hydrophilic surface   grease spot

water penetrating under grease spot   grease droplet in solution   charged polar head

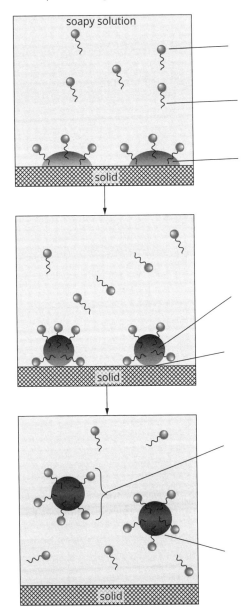

Literacy review—reviewing organic chemistry

1 Complete the following table to review your understanding of some of the terms in this module.

Statement	Term
Hydrocarbons which contain carbon–carbon single bonds	
Series of organic compounds with members differing by one CH_2 unit.	
Molecules with different arrangements of atoms but the same molecular formula.	
The type of reaction that forms an amide.	
A group of organic compounds that contain a hydroxyl group.	
Type of organic compound with a systematic name ending in -oate.	
Type of reaction involving a C=C bond.	
Atom or group of atoms whose properties determine the properties of organic compounds.	
Organic molecules with a carbonyl functional group at the end of the chain.	
Organic molecule that contains a –COOH group.	
Organic molecule that contains at least one carbon–carbon triple bond.	
A hydrolysis reaction between sodium hydroxide and a triglyceride to produce soap.	
A fuel that can be produced from plant matter.	
The regions of a polymer that are ordered and pack well together.	
A type of polymerisation reaction made using monomers with functional groups at both ends.	

2 **a** Explain to a classmate the differences in structure and products of oxidation between primary, secondary and tertiary alcohols.

b Explain to your chemistry teacher how an ester is made from ethanol and butanoic acid.

c In a group with two classmates, discuss some of the factors that determine the properties of polymers.

d The heat of combustion of an alcohol can be estimated by simply burning the alcohol in a spirit burner below a can containing a known volume of water. The mass of alcohol burnt and the temperature rise of the water are measured.

List some of the assumptions and practical errors associated with determining the heat of combustion of an alcohol by this method. Describe some modifications that could be made to improve the results.

_____

_____

_____

e Using the IUPAC rules of nomenclature for organic compounds, help a Year 11 Chemistry student to work out the name the compound shown in the following figure. You should do this by asking a series of relevant questions, and helping the student to complete the answer. Fill in the questions and answers in the table below.

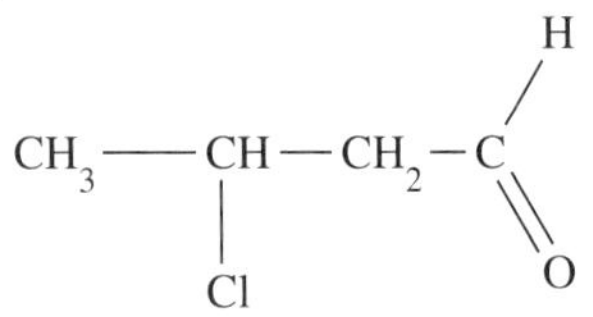

$$CH_3 - CH - CH_2 - C \overset{H}{\underset{O}{\diagdown}}$$
$$| \atop Cl$$

Question	Answer

Name of compound: _____

RATING MY LEARNING | My understanding improved — Not confident ◄——► Very confident ○ ○ ○ ○ ○ | I answered questions without help — Not confident ◄——► Very confident ○ ○ ○ ○ ○ | I corrected my errors without help — Not confident ◄——► Very confident ○ ○ ○ ○ ○

Thinking about my learning

On completion of Module 7: Organic chemistry, you should be able to describe, explain and apply the relevant scientific ideas. You should also be able to interpret, analyse and evaluate data.

1   The table lists the key knowledge covered in this module. Read each and reflect on how well you understand each concept. Rate your learning by shading the circle that corresponds to your level of understanding for each concept. It may be helpful to use colour as a visual representation. For example:

- green—very confident
- orange—in the middle
- red—starting to develop.

Concept focus	Rate my learning				
	Starting to develop ◄————————► Very confident				
Nomenclature	◯	◯	◯	◯	◯
Hydrocarbons	◯	◯	◯	◯	◯
Products of reactions Involving hydrocarbons	◯	◯	◯	◯	◯
Alcohols	◯	◯	◯	◯	◯
Reactions of organic acids and bases	◯	◯	◯	◯	◯
Polymers	◯	◯	◯	◯	◯

2   Consider points you have shaded from starting to develop to middle-level understanding. List specific ideas you can identify that were challenging.

_____

_____

_____

_____

_____

3   Write down two different strategies that you will apply to help further your understanding of these ideas.

_____

_____

_____

_____

PRACTICAL ACTIVITY 7.1

Investigating hydrocarbons

Suggested duration: 30 minutes

INTRODUCTION

Hydrocarbons are organic compounds composed only of carbon and hydrogen. Hydrocarbons are non-polar molecules and therefore are insoluble in polar solvents. When they undergo complete combustion, they react with oxygen to form carbon dioxide and water. If the combustion is incomplete, carbon (or carbon monoxide) and water form.

A saturated hydrocarbon has only single bonds between carbon atoms. If a hydrocarbon is unsaturated, it contains double or triple bonds between at least two carbon atoms in the hydrocarbon. If permanganate solution reacts with a hydrocarbon, the hydrocarbon must be unsaturated. The distinctive purple colour of the permanganate disappears as the double bond in the hydrocarbon breaks and an OH group is added to each of the carbon atoms that was originally involved in the double or triple bond. For example:

$$5CH_2 = CH_2 + 2H_2O + 2MnO_4^- + 6H^+ \rightarrow 5CH_2(OH)CH_2OH + 2Mn^{2+}$$

PURPOSE

To investigate the properties of hydrocarbons.

PRE-LAB SAFETY INFORMATION		
Material used	**Hazard**	**Control**
$1 \, mol \, L^{-1}$ sulfuric acid	corrosive to skin	Use eye and skin protection.
potassium permanganate solution	stains skin and clothes	Use eye and skin protection.
heptane or octane	highly flammable	Keep away from naked flame; use eye protection.
hex-1-ene or any other alkene	highly flammable	Keep away from naked flame; use eye protection.
cyclohexane	highly flammable	Keep away from naked flame; use eye protection.
cyclohexene	highly flammable	Keep away from naked flame; use eye protection.
methane (from Bunsen burner)	highly flammable	Keep away from naked flame; use eye protection.

Disposal of waste: Do not pour hydrocarbons down the sink. Place all organic waste in a waste bottle in the fume cupboard.

Please indicate that you have understood the information in the safety table.

Name (print): _____

I understand the safety information (signature): _____

PROCEDURE

Carry out the following tests in a fume cupboard.

Test A: Solubility of hydrocarbons in water

1   Mix 10 drops of each hydrocarbon to be tested with 10 drops of coloured water in small test-tubes. Record your observations about the solubility of each hydrocarbon in Results Table 1 below.

Test B: Saturation and unsaturation in hydrocarbons

2   Place 10 drops of each of the hydrocarbons to be tested into separate test-tubes. Add two drops of potassium permanganate solution dropwise to each test-tube and then add one drop of sulfuric acid. Note whether the distinctive purple colour of the permanganate solution remains or disappears.

3   Repeat the tests in parts A and B for each of the hydrocarbons. Record your observations in Results Table 1.

Test C: Combustion of hydrocarbons

4   Light a Bunsen burner. The major hydrocarbon present in natural gas is methane (CH_4). Keep the Bunsen flame yellow by closing the air hole of the burner. Using a test-tube holder or a pair of tongs, hold an empty test-tube in the flame for 10 seconds. Describe in Results Table 2 what happens to the bottom of the test-tube.

5   After a few minutes, open the air hole of the Bunsen burner and continue heating the test-tube in the blue flame. Describe in Results Table 2 what now happens to the outside of the test-tube.

RESULTS

TABLE 1 Solubility and reactivity

Hydrocarbon	Solubility in water	Observations of reaction with permanganate solution
heptane or octane		
hex-1-ene or any other alkene		
cyclohexane		
cyclohexene		

TABLE 2 Combustion of methane

Observations in yellow flame	Observations in blue flame

DISCUSSION

1   Explain your observations about the solubility of hydrocarbons in water in terms of the polarity of hydrocarbon molecules.

_____

_____

_____

_____

2   Write balanced chemical equations for the combustion of natural gas:

   a when the air hole of the Bunsen burner is closed (assume only carbon and water form)

   _____

   b when the air hole is open.

   _____

3   What evidence of these different combustion reactions did you observe?

   _____

   _____

4   In the past, bromine solution was used to test whether a hydrocarbon was saturated or unsaturated. Bromine is a reddish liquid at room temperature. (It is also highly toxic.) Write a chemical equation for the reaction that would occur between the unsaturated hydrocarbon(s) used in this experiment and bromine solution, $Br_2(aq)$.

   _____

   _____

   _____

5   Suggest why the experiment using bromine solution worked particularly well.

   _____

   _____

   _____

CONCLUSION

6   Summarise the similarities you observed in the different hydrocarbons with regard to their solubility in water.

   _____

   _____

7   Based on your observations in this practical activity, write a general chemical equation for the complete combustion of an unsaturated hydrocarbon with the general formula C_xH_y.

   _____

   _____

8   Classify each of the hydrocarbons you investigated in this practical activity as saturated or unsaturated.

   _____

   _____

   _____

RATING MY LEARNING	My understanding improved	Not confident ← → Very confident ○ ○ ○ ○ ○	I answered questions without help	Not confident ← → Very confident ○ ○ ○ ○ ○	I corrected my errors without help	Not confident ← → Very confident ○ ○ ○ ○ ○

PRACTICAL ACTIVITY 7.2

Modelling hydrocarbons, functional groups and organic reactions

Suggested duration: up to 90 minutes, depending on the number of molecules constructed

INTRODUCTION

This task will help you to identify and explain the role of functional groups, and discuss the effect that they have on the reactions and solubility of organic compounds.

PURPOSE

- To examine the bonding, shape and nomenclature of a number of organic molecules with common functional groups.
- To investigate the concept of structural isomers.
- To model reactions involving common functional groups.
- To write equations for organic reactions.

PROCEDURE

Part A—Functional groups

For each of the molecules in Part A of the materials list, or as directed by your teacher:

1   Write the condensed structural formula.

2   Draw the structural formula.

3   State the type(s) of bonding between molecules.

Complete your answers in Table 1.

Part B—Structural isomers

Draw the structural isomers and construct models of all isomers of the following molecules. Write the systematic name of each isomer where possible. Label as chain, position or functional group isomers where appropriate.

1   dichloroethene

2   pentane

3   butanol

4   propanone

Complete your answers in Table 2.

Part C—Reactions

Do the following for each of the pairs of reactants in the Part C materials list.

1   Construct a three-dimensional model of each organic reactant.

2   Rearrange the atoms in the reactants to form models of the products.

3   Complete your answers in Table 3 by writing equations for the organic reactions.

MATERIALS

This activity requires a molecular model building kit for constructing the following molecules.

Part A
- alkanes: methane, butane
- alkenes: ethene, propene, but-1-ene, but-2-ene
- chloroalkanes: 1,1-dichloroethane
- alcohols: ethanol, butan-2-ol
- carboxylic acids: methanoic acid, propanoic acid
- esters: ethyl propanoate
- amines: ethanamine
- amides: ethanamide
- aldehydes: ethanal
- ketones: propanone

Part B
- dichloroethene
- pentane
- butanol
- hydroxybutanoic acid
- pentan-2-one

Part C
- ethane and chlorine
- ethene and hydrogen chloride
- ethene and hydrogen
- ethene and chlorine
- ethene and water
- ethanol and ethanoic acid
- methanamine and ethanoic acid

RESULTS

TABLE 1 Functional groups

Name	Condensed structural formula	Structural formula	Strongest type of bonding between molecules
methane			
butane			
ethene			
propene			
but-1-ene			
but-2-ene			
1,1-dichloroethane			
ethanol			
butan-2-ol			
methanoic acid			
propanoic acid			
ethyl propanoate			
ethanamine			
ethanamide			
ethanal			
propanone			

ISBN 978 1 4886 1934 2

TABLE 2 Structural isomers

dichloroethane	
pentane	
butanol	
propanone	

TABLE 3 Equations for the reactions in Part C

DISCUSSION

1 What type of bonding is present within the molecules?

_____

2 Complete the table naming the functional groups present in the molecules constructed in Parts A and B.

Names of functional groups in Parts A and B

Homologous series	Functional group present	Homologous series	Functional group present
alkanes		esters	
alkenes		amines	
chloroalkanes		amides	
alcohols		aldehydes	
carboxylic acids		ketones	

3 Define the term 'structural isomers'. Explain the differences between chain, position and functional group isomers.

_____

_____

_____

4 Draw structural formulae to show the organic reactants and products for each reaction in Part C.

CONCLUSION

5 How do functional groups affect the bonding and solubility of organic compounds?

_____

_____

_____

RATING MY LEARNING	My understanding improved	Not confident ←———→ Very confident ○ ○ ○ ○ ○	I answered questions without help	Not confident ←———→ Very confident ○ ○ ○ ○ ○	I corrected my errors without help	Not confident ←———→ Very confident ○ ○ ○ ○ ○

PRACTICAL ACTIVITY 7.3

Determining the heat of combustion of alcohols

Suggested duration: 30 minutes

INTRODUCTION

Alcohols are useful fuels; both methanol and ethanol have been used as substitutes for petrol. In this experiment the energy released by burning an alcohol is used to heat water. Knowing that 4.18 J of energy is required to heat 1 g (1 mL) of water by 1°C, the quantity of energy released by combustion of the alcohol can be calculated using the formula:

$$q = m \times c \times \Delta T$$

where:

q is the energy transferred to the water in joules (J)

m is the mass of the water in grams (g) which is equal to the volume of water in mL

c is the specific heat capacity of water $4.18\,\mathrm{J\,g^{-1}\,K^{-1}}$.

In this experiment it is assumed that all the heat released by the alcohol is absorbed by the water. This will give only an estimate of the heat of combustion of the alcohols. Although your results will be reliable and therefore reproducible, they will not give an accurate value.

Refer to the worksheets for an image of an apparatus for measuring heat of combustion. GO TO ➤ Worksheet 7.7

PURPOSE

To measure and compare the heat of combustion of various alcohols.

MATERIALS

- spirit burner containing one of the following alcohols, selected by your teacher:
  - ethanol, CH_3CH_2OH
  - propan-1-ol, $CH_3CH_2CH_2OH$
  - butan-1-ol, $CH_3CH_2CH_2CH_2OH$
- 250 mL measuring cylinder
- steel can
- thermometer, −10°C to 110°C
- retort stand and clamp
- bench mat
- electronic balance
- metal loop stirrer

PRE-LAB SAFETY INFORMATION		
Material used	**Hazard**	**Control**
ethanol	causes skin and eye irritation; flammable	Wear gloves, safety glasses and a laboratory coat. Keep bottle firmly stoppered. Do not refill spirit burners anywhere near an open flame.
propan-1-ol	flammable liquid and vapor; risk of serious damage to eyes; vapors may cause dizziness; may cause skin and respiratory tract irritation	Wear gloves, safety glasses and a laboratory coat. Do not refill spirit burners anywhere near an open flame.
butan-1-ol	flammable liquid and vapour; risk of serious damage to eyes; vapours may cause dizziness; may cause skin and respiratory tract irritation	Wear gloves, safety glasses and a laboratory coat. Do not refill spirit burners anywhere near an open flame.
Disposal of waste: Do not pour alcohols down the sink. Place all organic waste in a waste bottle in the fume cupboard.		
Please indicate that you have understood the information in the safety table. Name (print): _____ I understand the safety information (signature): _____		

PROCEDURE

1   Using a retort stand and clamp, set up steel can 3–4 cm above the wick of a spirit burner.

2   Pour 200 mL of water into the can and record its temperature.

3   Weigh the spirit burner filled with alcohol. Record the mass and the name of the alcohol in the table below.

4   Light the burner and heat the water. Stir continuously.

5   Once the water temperature has increased by about 20°C, extinguish the burner and record the highest temperature reached by the water in the table.

6   Measure the mass of the burner and use this to deduce the mass of alcohol consumed. Record this mass.

Using electronic data collection equipment

A temperature probe can be used instead of a thermometer. Collect data for 10 minutes. Data collection should begin about 45 seconds before the burner is lit. Extinguish the burner once the temperature rises by about 20°C or after 7 minutes of data collection, whichever occurs first. Display each set of data as a graph of temperature versus time.

RESULTS

Name of alcohol	
Initial mass of alcohol + burner (g)	
Initial temperature of water (°C)	
Final temperature of water (°C)	
Final mass of alcohol + burner (g)	
Mass of alcohol burnt (g)	
Temperature change of water (°C)	

DISCUSSION

1   Write balanced equations for the combustion of the alcohol you used in the burner (ethanol, propanol and butan-1-ol).

2   For the alcohol you used, calculate the energy absorbed by the water in the can when the alcohol burned.

3   Calculate the energy released per gram of alcohol burnt.

4   Calculate the heat of combustion for the alcohol you used, in units of kilojoule per mole.

5 Compare the values obtained for heats of combustion of ethanol, propanol and butan-1-ol in $kJ\,g^{-1}$. (Share results with other students if you did not perform the experiment using each alcohol.)

    a Petrol has a heat of combustion of about $-48\,kJ\,g^{-1}$. On the basis of its heat of combustion, which alcohol would be the most suitable alternative fuel to petrol?

    b Why is a high-energy release per unit mass an important consideration in selecting a fuel for use in transport, particularly air transport?

CONCLUSION

6 The heats of combustion of methanol, ethanol and propanol are -725, -1364 and $-2016\,kJ\,mol^{-1}$ respectively.

    a How well do your class results agree with these values for ethanol and propanol?

    b Comment on the main sources of error in this experiment, and suggest how the experiment could be improved.

7 **a** Graph the theoretical heats of combustion for each alcohol as stated in question **6** against the number of carbon atoms in each alcohol.

    b Estimate the value of the heat of combustion of butan-1-ol.

    c Use a book of chemical data to see how close your estimate for butan-1-ol is to the accepted value.

PRACTICAL ACTIVITY 7.4

Preparing artificial fragrances and flavours

Suggested duration: 30 minutes

INTRODUCTION

Esters are commonly used as artificial flavourings in foods such as ice-cream and sweets. They are partially responsible for many familiar odours, including those of coffee, perfumes and fruit.

PURPOSE

To prepare several esters that are widely used as artificial fragrances and flavours.

PRE-LAB SAFETY INFORMATION		
Material used	**Hazard**	**Control**
concentrated sulfuric acid	causes serious skin burns and eye damage; caustic	Wear gloves, safety glasses and a laboratory coat.
glacial ethanoic acid	causes serious skin burns and eye damage; flammable liquid and vapour	Wear gloves, safety glasses and a laboratory coat. Keep away from open flames.
salicylic acid	causes serious eye irritation	Wear gloves, safety glasses and a laboratory coat.
decanoic acid	causes skin and eye irritation; may cause respiratory irritation	Wear gloves, safety glasses and a laboratory coat.
pentan-1-ol	causes skin irritation; may cause respiratory irritation; flammable liquid and vapour	Wear gloves, safety glasses and a laboratory coat. Keep away from open flames.
ethanol	causes serious eye irritation; flammable liquid and vapour	Wear gloves, safety glasses and a laboratory coat. Keep away from open flames.
esters	irritating to eyes, respiratory system and skin	smell esters produced for a very short time (1–2 seconds)

Disposal of waste: Do not pour organic chemicals down the sink. Place all organic waste in a waste bottle in the fume cupboard.

Complete and indicate that you have understood the information in the safety table.

Name (print): _____

I understand the safety information (signature): _____

PROCEDURE

1   Label two semi-micro test-tubes 'A' and 'B'. Place 10 drops of pentan-1-ol in each tube.

2   Wearing gloves, add 10 drops of glacial ethanoic acid to test-tube A and a similar volume of salicylic acid to test-tube B. Then add two drops of concentrated sulfuric acid to each tube.

3   Heat the mixtures for 10 minutes in a beaker of boiling water and then pour each one into a 250 mL beaker containing 200 mL of cold water.

4   Try to identify the odour of the esters produced by cautiously wafting the vapour from the ester towards you. Note the name of the carboxylic acid and alcohol used in this test and describe the smell of the ester in the Results table.

5   Wash out the beakers thoroughly and repeat steps 1–4 using clean semi-micro test-tubes and other combinations of alcohols and carboxylic acids. Record the results.

RESULTS

Combination	Alcohol	Carboxylic acid	Smell
1			
2			
3			
4			
5			

DISCUSSION

1   Salicylic acid has the formula $C_6H_4(OH)COOH$. Complete the following table by writing equations for each of the reactions you performed in this experiment and naming the esters formed. (Esters made from salicylic acid end with the name *salicylate*.)

Combination	Equation	Name of ester formed
1		
2		
3		
4		
5		

2   What is the role of the concentrated sulfuric acid in these reactions?

3   Write a general equation for the formation of an ester from an alcohol and a carboxylic acid.

PRACTICAL ACTIVITY 7.5

Modelling polymers

Suggested duration: 50 minutes

INTRODUCTION

The properties of a polymer are related to the strength of the forces between polymer molecules. These forces may be dispersion forces, hydrogen bonds or covalent bonds.

Remember that the atoms within polymer molecules are always held together by covalent bonds.

PURPOSE

- To model ethene and different derivatives of ethene and the polymers formed from these monomers.
- To model the formation of a condensation polymer.
- To demonstrate the effect on the properties of a polymer of the degree of branching of polymer chains.

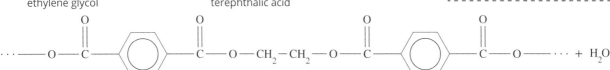

ethylene glycol   terephthalic acid

polyethylene terephthalate

PROCEDURE, RESULTS AND DISCUSSION

1 From the chemicals in the Materials list, select a monomer that will make an addition polymer. Make models of three molecules of this monomer, then make the polymer from these models.

2 Draw these molecules and label the bonds between the atoms in the monomer and between the atoms in the polymer section.

3 What type of intermolecular forces would exist between your polymer molecules? Explain your answer.

_____

_____

4 What is a possible use of your polymer?

_____

5 Repeat steps 1–5 by selecting monomers that will make a condensation polymer.

6 Select a polymer with molecules held together by dispersion forces. Make models of three or four molecules of your chosen polymer. Your models should have at least eight carbon atoms in the backbone or main chain. One pair of students should model unbranched chains and a second pair should model chains with some branching.

Sketch your models.

7 Pack the chains together as they might be packed within a polymer. Consider the effect branching has on the closeness of the polymer chains. How easily can chains move past each other?

_____

_____

8 Predict how the two polymers will behave when heated.

_____

_____

CONCLUSION

9 Summarise:

- the properties of monomers that form addition and condensation polymers
- the effects of branching and cross-linking on the properties of a polymer.

_____

_____

_____

_____

| RATING MY LEARNING | My understanding improved | Not confident ←———→ Very confident ○ ○ ○ ○ ○ | I answered questions without help | Not confident ←———→ Very confident ○ ○ ○ ○ ○ | I corrected my errors without help | Not confident ←———→ Very confident ○ ○ ○ ○ ○ |

What is the importance of organic chemistry to society?

Suggested duration: 4 hours 30 minutes

INTRODUCTION

This depth study requires you to conduct an investigation into a question you develop about the importance of organic chemistry to society. This is a general topic and you can select or develop a question that discusses the properties and uses of organic compounds, the structure and bonding of organic compounds, or the different reactions that can be used to produce more environmentally friendly chemicals for particular uses. You will investigate secondary-sourced data, and process and analyse the information. If your question requires you to discuss molecular structure, you can use molecular model kits to model the molecules and explore the reasons for their reactivity. You must communicate your findings in a presentation, which could include photographs of the molecular models you have made.

The questions below are a guide to how you might proceed in the development and completion of this depth study. Your teacher may provide you with additional guidelines for your study and presentation. The toolkit also provides advice on conducting a secondary-sourced investigation. | GO TO ➤ | Chemistry toolkit page xii

MATERIALS
- molecular modelling kit
- a camera or phone

QUESTIONING AND PREDICTING

Choose one research question from the list below or, alternatively, develop your own question in consultation with your teacher.

1 Will biofuels replace fossil fuels in the future?

2 Should the use of plastics be banned?

3 Is biodiesel superior to bioethanol as a transport fuel?

4 Is bioethanol superior to petrol as a fuel for cars?

5 Does the use of fuels such as biodiesel and ethanol reduce global warming?

6 Are synthetic detergents superior in all respects to soap?

7 What factors affect the production of alcohol by fermentation?

8 In terms of structure and energy production, how do fuels from organic sources, such as petrol or diesel, differ from biofuels, such as bioethanol or biodiesel?

Consider your chosen question.
- What data do you need to answer your question?
- What further questions arise that you will need to research and investigate?
- Predict an answer to your question.

CONDUCTING YOUR INVESTIGATION

For each source that you access during this investigation, you should fill in a summary table such as the one below. Make as many copies of this table as you need.

Bibliographic information	
Summary of content (be concise and coherent) and tables of data	
Relevant findings and evidence	
Limitations, biases or flaws within the article	
Useful quotations	
Additional notes	

ANALYSING DATA AND INFORMATION

After you have completed your research summaries and are satisfied that you have collected sufficient information, plan the presentation of your results in your notebook. You should consider questions such as the following.

- What background chemistry concepts need to be included?
- Which chemical terms need to be defined?
- What will you include in the introduction?
- What subheadings will you need to use?
- What images, graphs, tables are relevant and helpful and should be included?
- How will you model the molecules and how will you illustrate the relationship between properties, structure and reactions?
- What photographs should you take of your modelled molecules and reactions?

COMMUNICATING RESULTS

Your teacher may ask you to present your investigation in a particular way that includes the use of photographs, or you might be able to choose another format. For example:
- a poster
- an oral presentation, perhaps using presentation software such as Microsoft PowerPoint
- a written report
- a web page.

In order to choose the best format, you should consider your audience.

Whichever format you choose, remember to use suitable language and terminology. Your final report should contain no more than 1000 words, with photographs to illustrate the models you have made. Your presentation should include:
- your question, prediction and aim
- the information you needed to answer the question
- tables of data that you analysed, and any calculations and graphs that you produced to answer the question
- images that will assist in communicating your conclusion
- a bibliography.

Multiple choice

1 What is the name for the molecule shown below?

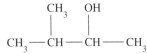

- **A** pentan-3-ol
- **B** pentan-2-ol
- **C** 2-methylbutan-3-ol
- **D** 3-methylbutan-2-ol

2 Which one of the following compounds is an isomer of CH_3CH_2COOH?

- **A** $HOOCCH_2CH_3$
- **B** $CH_3CH_2CH_2COOH$
- **C** CH_3COOCH_3
- **D** $CH_3CH_2CO_2H$

3 Which of the following compounds would melt at the highest temperature?

- **A** $CH_3CH_2CH_2CH_3$
- **B** $CH_3CH_2CH_2OH$
- **C** $CH_3CH_2CH_2CH_2NH_2$
- **D** CH_3CH_2COOH

4 Oxidation of butan-2-ol with an acidified solution of potassium dichromate can result in the formation of:

- **A** butanone
- **B** butanal
- **C** butanoic acid
- **D** butyl butanoate

5 Which one of the following pairs of compounds is most likely to react to form the compound shown below?

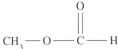

- **A** ethanoic acid and methanol
- **B** methanoic acid and methanol
- **C** ethanoic acid and potassium dichromate
- **D** ethanoic acid and ethanol

6 Which one of the following statements is correct about a polymer made from a monomer by condensation polymerisation?

- **A** The product contains many long branches.
- **B** The empirical formula of the polymer is the same as the formula of the monomer.
- **C** The polymer is made from a monomer that contains double or triple bonds.
- **D** The mass of product formed is less than the total mass of the monomer reacting.

Short answer

7 For each of the following reactions, write the formulae of the carbon-containing products.

- **a** $CH_3CH(OH)CH_3 \xrightarrow{Cr_2O_7^{2-}/H^+}$
- **b** $CH_3CH{=}CHCH_3 \xrightarrow{H_2O}$
- **c** $C_6H_{12}O_6 \xrightarrow{yeast}$
- **d** $CH_3CH_2OH + CH_3CH_2COOH \xrightarrow{H^+}$
- **e** $CH_3CH_2OH \xrightarrow{Cr_2O_7^{2-}/H^+}$
- **f** $CH_2{=}CH_2 \xrightarrow{HCl} \qquad \xrightarrow{NH_3}$

8 Soaps, detergents and polymers are organic compounds of industrial importance.

- **a** Explain the distinction between soaps and synthetic detergents in terms of their origin and structure.

_____

_____

_____

- **b** Describe how the behavior of the particles in soap and detergent assist the washing process.

_____

_____

_____

- **c** A section of a polymer chain in a polyester is shown below.

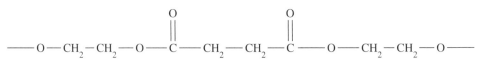

- **i** Write the formulae of the two different monomers from which the polymer is made.

_____

_____

ii Name the other compound that is produced when the two monomers react.

_____

iii What is the name given to this type of polymerisation reaction?

_____

d A section of a polymer chain is shown below.

i Write the formulae of the monomer from which the polymer is made.

_____

_____

ii What is the name given to this type of polymerisation reaction?

_____

9 Crude oil is composed of a complex mixture of hydrocarbons. The hydrocarbons in oil are of varying lengths but most belong to the homologous series of alkanes.

a Explain the meaning of the term 'homologous series'.

_____

_____

b Draw the structural formulae and write the names of all the isomers of an alkane with five carbon atoms.

_____

c What is the name the main type of bonding present within an alkane molecule?

_____

d Explain the following observations.

i Butane boils at a lower temperature than pentane.

_____

_____

_____

ii 2-Methylpropane boils at a lower temperature than butane, but both compounds have the same molecular formula.

_____

_____

_____

e Describe the procedures required to safely handle and dispose of organic compounds in the laboratory.

_____

_____

_____

10 A chloroalkane, A, has a molar mass of $78.5\,g\,mol^{-1}$. One sample of this compound was allowed to react with potassium hydroxide solution. The product of this reaction, compound B, was heated with acidified potassium dichromate solution to form an acidic compound, C.

A second sample was allowed to react with ammonia to form a basic compound, D.

a Draw and name the structural formulae of compounds A, B, C and D.

Compound A   Compound B   Compound C   Compound D

Name: _____   Name: _____   Name: _____   Name: _____

b Give the name or formula of a suitable laboratory oxidising agent for the conversion of compound B into compound C.

_____

Applying chemical ideas

Outcomes

By the end of this module you will be able to:

- develop and evaluate questions and hypotheses for scientific investigation CH12-1
- design and evaluate investigations in order to obtain primary and secondary data and information CH12-2
- conduct investigations to collect valid and reliable primary and secondary data and information CH12-3
- select and process appropriate qualitative and quantitative data and information using a range of appropriate media CH12-4
- communicate scientific understanding using suitable language and terminology for a specific audience or purpose CH12-7
- describe and evaluate chemical systems used to design and analyse chemical processes CH12-15

Content

ANALYSIS OF INORGANIC SUBSTANCES

INQUIRY QUESTION   How are the ions present in the environment identified and measured?

By the end of this module you will be able to:

- analyse the need for monitoring the environment S EU ICT
- conduct qualitative investigations—using flame tests, precipitation and complexation reactions as appropriate—to test for the presence in aqueous solution of the following ions: ICT N
    - cations: barium (Ba^{2+}), calcium (Ca^{2+}), magnesium (Mg^{2+}), lead(II) (Pb^{2+}), silver ion (Ag^+), copper(II) (Cu^{2+}), iron(II) (Fe^{2+}), iron(III) (Fe^{3+})
    - anions: chloride (Cl^-), bromide (Br^-), iodide (I^-), hydroxide (OH^-), acetate (CH_3COO^-), carbonate (CO_3^{2-}), sulfate (SO_4^{2-}), phosphate (PO_4^{3-})
- conduct investigations and/or process data involving:
    - gravimetric analysis
    - precipitation titrations
- conduct investigations and/or process data to determine the concentration of coloured species and/or metal ions in aqueous solution, including but not limited to, the use of:
    - colorimetry
    - ultraviolet–visible spectrophotometry
    - atomic absorption spectroscopy

ANALYSIS OF ORGANIC SUBSTANCES

INQUIRY QUESTION | How is information about the reactivity and structure
of organic compounds obtained?

By the end of this module you will be able to:

- conduct qualitative investigations to test for the presence in organic molecules of the following functional groups:
  - carbon–carbon double bonds
  - hydroxyl groups
  - carboxylic acids (ACSCH130)
- investigate the processes used to analyse the structure of simple organic compounds addressed in the course, including but not limited to:
  - proton and carbon-13 NMR
  - mass spectroscopy (ACSCH19)
  - infrared spectroscopy (ACSCH130)

CHEMICAL SYNTHESIS AND DESIGN

INQUIRY QUESTION | What are the implications for society of chemical synthesis
and design?

By the end of this module you will be able to:

- evaluate the factors that need to be considered when designing a chemical synthesis process, including but not limited to:
  - availability of reagents
  - reaction conditions (ACSCH133)
  - yield and purity (ACSCH134)
  - industrial uses (e.g. pharmaceutical, cosmetics, cleaning products, fuels) (ACSCH131)
  - environmental, social and economic issues

Chemistry Stage 6 Syllabus © NSW Education Standards Authority
for and on behalf of the Crown in right of the State of NSW, 2017.

Key knowledge

Analysis of inorganic substances

Chemical analysis is used for many purposes, including:
- production of high quality drinking water
- production of healthy food
- maintenance of air quality
- maintenance of water quality of lakes, streams and oceans
- monitoring global warming in order to determine appropriate actions.

Many different analysis methods are available to chemists. They include tests for ions in aqueous solutions, techniques for determining the presence and structure of organic compounds, and methods for measuring the concentrations of metal ions and toxic contaminants.

THE SOURCE OF SALTS IN THE ENVIRONMENT

Chemical analysis is widely used to determine the concentration of salts in soil and water samples. In this context, 'salt' refers to any ionic compounds present. Salts that are found in soil and water samples can come from dissolved mineral deposits and pollution.

QUALITATIVE TECHNIQUES FOR DETECTING SALTS

Techniques for the analysis of ions in aqueous solutions include flame tests, precipitation and complexation. Each of these techniques is described on page 161. Table 8.1 summarises the tests used to analyse for different ions.

TABLE 8.1 Tests used to analyse for different ions

Ion	Technique and result for flame tests, precipitation and complexation
Cation	
barium (Ba^{2+})	Produces pale green flame; precipitates as white $BaSO_4$ with SO_4^{2-} ions.
calcium (Ca^{2+})	Produces yellow-red flame; produces white precipitate with OH^- ions.
magnesium (Mg^{2+})	Precipitates as white gelatinous $Mg(OH)_2$ with OH^- ions.
lead(II) (Pb^{2+})	Precipitates as white $PbCl_2$ with Cl^- ions; precipitates as white $Pb(OH)_2$ with dilute ammonia.
silver ion (Ag^+)	Precipitates as white $AgCl$ with Cl^- ions; complexes with ammonia to form colourless solution of $Ag(NH_3)_2^+$.
copper(II) (Cu^{2+})	Produces green-blue flame; precipitates as blue $Cu(OH)_2$ with OH^- ions or NH_3; complexes with excess ammonia to form purple–blue $Cu(NH_3)_4^{2+}$ solution.
iron(II) (Fe^{2+})	Precipitates as green $Fe(OH)_2$ with OH^- ions or NH_3.
iron(III) (Fe^{3+})	Precipitates as brown $Fe(OH)_3$ with OH^- ions or NH_3; complexes with SCN^- to form red $FeSCN^{2+}$.
sodium (Na^+)	Produces yellow flame; no precipitate.
potassium (K^+)	Produces lilac flame; no precipitate.
Anion	
chloride (Cl^-)	Precipitates as white $AgCl$ with Ag^+ ions.
bromide (Br^-)	Precipitates as pale cream $AgBr$ with Ag^+ ions.
iodide (I^-)	Precipitates as pale yellow AgI with Ag^+ ions; precipitates as bright yellow PbI_2 with Pb^{2+} ions.
hydroxide (OH^-)	Precipitates as white $Pb(OH)_2$ with Pb^{2+} ions which dissolves in excess OH^- forming colourless $Pb(OH)_4^{2-}$.
carbonate (CO_3^{2-})	Reacts with acid to form bubbles of CO_2 gas. If the gas is passed through limewater, $Ca(OH)_2$ (aq), a white, milky precipitate of $CaCO_3$ forms.
sulfate (SO_4^{2-})	Precipitates as white $BaSO_4$ with Ba^{2+} ions.
phosphate (PO_4^{3-})	Precipitates as white $Ba_3(PO_4)_2$ with Ba^{2+} ions.

Flame tests

You will recall that the electrons in an atom are arranged in energy levels, called shells. The lowest energy shells are closest to the nucleus and electrons fill these shells before they fill the higher shells. When atoms are heated, outer shell electrons can absorb energy and become **excited**, moving to higher energy levels. When this happens the atoms are unstable and the electrons quickly move back to a lower energy state, emitting energy as light of a specific wavelength and colour (Figure 8.1).

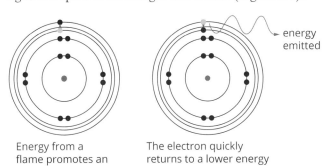

Energy from a flame promotes an electron to a higher energy level.

The electron quickly returns to a lower energy level, emitting light of a particular colour.

energy emitted

FIGURE 8.1 During a flame test, electrons 'jump down' from a higher to a lower energy level and lose energy (equal to the difference in energy levels) by emitting light of a specific colour.

When some metals or metal ions are placed in a Bunsen burner flame, the heat of the flame can be sufficient to excite their electrons, which then return to the lower energy state, emitting light. If the wavelength of the emitted light is in the visible region, the flame appears a characteristic colour. Sodium, for example, produces a yellow flame and potassium produces a purple flame. This process can be used to identify some metals and is called a **flame test**. Flame tests can only identify a few metals unambiguously, because many flame colours are similar or are masked by colours of other metals that may be present in a sample.

Precipitation

As you saw in Module 5, some ionic compounds are quite insoluble. The presence of particular ions in a sample can be determined by adding a solution of another ionic compound and observing the colour of any **precipitate** that is formed. For example, some cations can be identified by their precipitates with NaOH solution. You can refer to solubility products, K_{sp}, to determine the solubility of ionic compounds.

Complexation

Complexation reactions are those that form a **complex ion**, usually involving transition metals. A complex ion consists of a central metal cation surrounded by between 1 and 6 bound polar molecules or anions. These molecules or anions are called **ligands**. A type of covalent bond exists between the metal cation and the ligands. Many complexes are brightly coloured and their formation can be used to identify metal ions. For example, a test for Fe^{3+} in solution is to add SCN^- ions and see if red-coloured $FeSCN^{2+}$ is formed:

$$Fe^{3+}(aq) + SCN^-(aq) \rightarrow FeSCN^{2+}(aq)$$
(red)

GRAVIMETRIC ANALYSIS OF A SALT

Gravimetric analysis can be used to determine the percentage by mass of a specific element or ion present in a sample. It requires the formation of a precipitate and the use of mass–mass stoichiometry. Ions that can be analysed using gravimetric analysis because they form precipitates, include:

* silver ions
* calcium ions
* lead ions.

Figure 8.2 shows the steps in a gravimetric analysis.

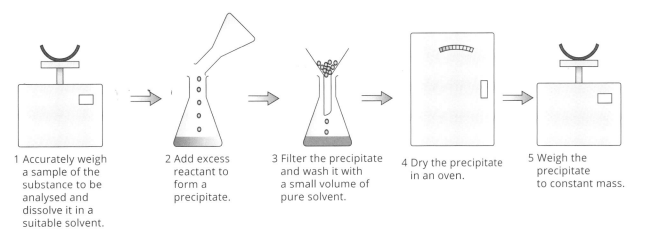

1 Accurately weigh a sample of the substance to be analysed and dissolve it in a suitable solvent.

2 Add excess reactant to form a precipitate.

3 Filter the precipitate and wash it with a small volume of pure solvent.

4 Dry the precipitate in an oven.

5 Weigh the precipitate to constant mass.

FIGURE 8.2 Steps in a gravimetric analysis

Precipitation titrations

Precipitation titrations can be used to determine the concentration of an ion in a sample. The technique involves forming a precipitate which contains the specific ion. For example, the concentration of Cl^- ions in a water sample can be determined by a titration with a silver nitrate solution.

$$Ag^+(aq) + Cl^-(aq) \rightarrow AgCl(s)$$

The **equivalence point** of the reaction is determined by adding another anion to the sample which forms a coloured precipitate with Ag^+ and is less soluble (has a smaller K_{sp}) than AgCl. This precipitate only forms when all the Cl^- ions have been precipitated and its appearance indicates the equivalence point.

An alternative way of judging the equivalence point of a precipitation titration is to monitor the electrical conductance of the solutions involved. This is called **conductometric titration**.

DETERMINING SALT CONCENTRATION BY COLORIMETRY AND UV-VISIBLE SPECTROSCOPY

The electromagnetic spectrum covers a continuous range of energy and wavelengths of electromagnetic radiation, from radio waves at the low-energy (high wavelength) end to gamma rays at the high-energy (low wavelength) end. Energy from different parts of the spectrum can be used for different spectroscopic techniques, for both qualitative and quantitative analysis.

Atoms and molecules absorb energies of different wavelengths. When a sample is exposed to energy of different wavelengths, the absorbed radiation may cause:

- electrons to jump to higher energy levels (the basis for **atomic absorption spectroscopy, colorimetry** and **ultraviolet–visible spectroscopy**)
- bonds to stretch or bend more vigorously (the basis for **infrared spectroscopy**)
- nuclei with magnetic properties to flip when in a magnetic field (the basis for **nuclear magnetic resonance spectroscopy**)

Details of some of these spectroscopic techniques are described below.

Colorimetry and UV-visible spectroscopy

Colorimetry and UV–visible spectroscopy (also known as UV–visible spectrophotometry) are spectroscopic techniques that are used to determine the concentration of a coloured species (often called a 'component') in a water sample. The UV and visible light used in these techniques causes electrons in the component to jump from a lower energy level to a higher one. The amount of light energy absorbed is directly proportional to the concentration of the component.

Soluble salts in water that can be analysed by colorimetry or UV–visible spectroscopy include:

- iron(II) ions, Fe^{2+}, particularly if oxidised to Fe^{3+} ions and mixed with potassium thiocyanate solution to form the red complex $FeSCN^{2+}$

- cobalt ions, Co^{2+}, in the form of a complex ion with phosphate ions, PO_4^{3-}.

The absorbance of the coloured solution is measured and the concentration of the component is determined by reference to a **calibration curve**. The wavelength used for absorbance measurements must be one at which the sample will absorb well. For colorimetry, the light chosen is the **complementary colour** of the component being analysed. Figure 8.3 shows the complementary colours, which are two colours that mix together to produce white or black. For UV–visible spectroscopy, a specific wavelength is used rather than a range of colours, which gives better sensitivity and precision than colorimetry.

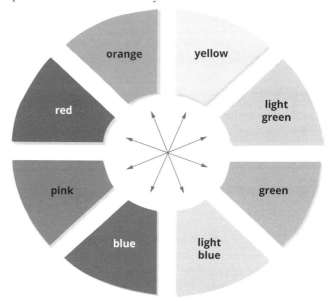

FIGURE 8.3 Complementary colours are opposite each other on a colour wheel. Light of the complementary colour to the component being analysed is used in a colorimeter. For example, blue light is used to analyse a yellow-coloured component.

The components of a UV–visible spectrophotometer are shown in Figure 8.4.

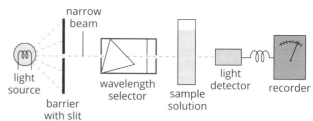

FIGURE 8.4 Basic components of a UV–visible spectrometer. A colorimeter has a similar construction, but uses a less accurate wavelength selector (coloured glass can be used) and is less expensive.

The steps involved in colorimetry or UV–visible spectroscopy for the construction of a calibration curve and determination of the concentration of a component in a sample are listed below.

1. **Standard solutions** of the component being analysed in the sample are prepared.
2. A wavelength is selected at which the component absorbs light strongly. (A colour range is selected for a colorimeter.)

3. The absorbance of the standard solutions at that wavelength is measured.
4. A calibration curve is plotted (absorbance versus concentration) using the results obtained for the standard solutions (Figure 8.5).
5. The absorbance of the sample is measured.
6. The sample's concentration is determined using the calibration curve.

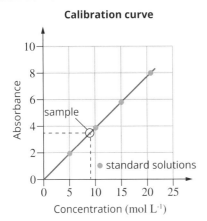

FIGURE 8.5 Calibration curve of concentration versus absorbance

Atomic absorption spectroscopy

Atomic absorption spectroscopy (AAS) is another spectroscopic technique that is used to detect the presence of metals and determine their concentration. The basis of the technique is that the electrons in atoms can absorb light energy of specific wavelengths, which causes the electrons to jump to higher energy levels.

The sample is atomised in a flame and a hollow cathode lamp containing the metal to be analysed is used to produce light with the specific wavelengths that the metal atoms in the sample can absorb. The amount of light absorbed by the element is proportional to the quantity of the element present. The exact concentration is determined by constructing a calibration curve. The components of an AAS instrument are shown in Figure 8.6.

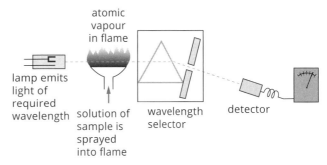

FIGURE 8.6 Basic components of an AAS instrument

Analysis of organic substances

We are surrounded by organic substances. They form the basis of life and are used in numerous applications, including foods, pharmaceuticals, fuels, and construction. While organic chemicals may be enormously beneficial, some become pollutants in river systems, oceans, the atmosphere and food supplies. Chemical analysis allows us to detect the presence and identity of organic compounds in samples. This can assist in many ways, including:

- design of new materials for specific applications
- treatment of disease and other medical conditions
- cleaning of chemical spills
- understanding and improving the reactivity of chemicals
- determining the harmful effects on living things and the environment.

Chemical tests and spectroscopy enable us to determine the functional groups present in an organic compound and find its structure.

CHEMICAL TESTS FOR FUNCTIONAL GROUPS

The tests for three important functional groups are listed in Table 8.2. You learnt about some of these in Module 7.

TABLE 8.2 Tests for functional groups

Functional group	Test	Explanation
carbon–carbon double bonds	bromine test	 $CH_2 = CH_2 + Br_2 \longrightarrow CH_2Br–CH_2Br$ 1, 2 -dibromoethane Only C=C double bonds react instantly with the Br_2 molecule, causing a colour change from orange to colourless. (I_2 can be used instead of Br_2.)
hydroxyl group	• sodium metal test • ester test	• Produces H_2 gas with sodium metal: $2CH_3OH + 2Na \rightarrow 2CH_3O^-Na^+ + H_2$ • Produces an ester when reacting with carboxylic acid. Esters are sweet-smelling. $CH_3COOH(l) + CH_3CH_2OH(l) \xrightarrow{\text{conc. } H_2SO_4} CH_3COOCH_2CH_3(l) + H_2O(l)$
carboxyl group	tests for acids	• Turns litmus red. • Produces CO_2 with carbonates: $2CH_3COOH(aq) + Na_2CO_3(aq) \rightarrow 2Na^+CH_3COO^-(aq) + CO_2(g) + H_2O(l)$ • Produces an ester when reacting with alcohol (see test for hydroxyl groups above). Esters smell fruity.

DETERMINING MOLECULAR STRUCTURE USING SPECTROSCOPY

The structure of organic molecules can be determined with the aid of elemental analysis and three types of spectroscopy: **mass spectroscopy** (also known as **mass spectrometry**), infrared (IR) spectroscopy and nuclear magnetic resonance (NMR) spectroscopy. There are two main types of NMR spectroscopy: proton (^{1}H) and carbon-13 (^{13}C) NMR. The steps involved in determining a structural formula are shown in Figure 8.7.

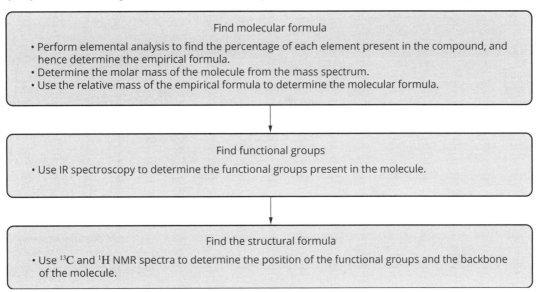

FIGURE 8.7 Finding a structural formula using spectroscopic techniques

Tables 8.3, 8.4 and 8.5 give details of the spectroscopic techniques used to analyse organic compounds.

TABLE 8.3 Mass spectrometry

Description	Basis of technique	Major uses	Interpretation of data
Interaction of gaseous sample with high energy electron beam to form positive ions. These cations are accelerated by an electric field and then deflected by a magnetic field.	The electron beam removes electrons, creating cations. As a result of the presence of electric and magnetic fields, the cations move in curved paths dependent on their mass/charge (*m/z*) ratio. The cation formed when a molecule loses an electron can be unstable. Some of them can break up into smaller fragments, where one fragment is a cation and the other is an uncharged free radical (atom or group of atoms with unpaired electrons).	Used qualitatively to: • determine the molecular mass (found by finding the mass of the **molecular ion** (or parent ion) which is the ion produced when an electron is lost from a molecule) • identify the isotopes of an element • assist in identifying structures of molecules.	The peak with the highest *m/z* ratio is usually due to the molecular (or parent) ion. Characteristic **fragmentation patterns** result from the break-up of the unstable parent ion, and are useful in determining the structure of molecules. The mass spectrometry of a compound can be complex, due to the occurrence of: • different isotopes • fragmentation of the molecule.

TABLE 8.4 Infrared (IR) spectroscopy

Description	Basis of technique	Major uses	Interpretation of data
Interaction of polar bonds in molecules with IR light. The energy absorbed depends on nature of bond: • single bonds absorb lower energy than a double bond between the same atoms • single bonds between heavy atoms absorb lower energy than those between lighter atoms.	Causes bonds in molecules to stretch (change distance between atoms) and bend (change angle between bonds), as shown in the diagram below.	Used qualitatively to identify types of bonds and functional groups present, e.g.: • C–O absorbs at $1000–1300\,cm^{-1}$ • O–H (acids) absorbs at $2500–3000\,cm^{-1}$ (usually very broadly) • C=O absorbs at $1680–1750\,cm^{-1}$.	The IR spectrum shows the the energies absorbed by the molecule. These are compared to those listed in databases to identify functional groups and multiple bonds. The IR spectrum shown below is for gaseous ethanol. Note that in IR spectra, by convention, **wavenumber** (unit of cm^{-1}) is used to represent energy on the horizontal axis, and the vertical axis measures transmittance (so peaks are inverted).

TABLE 8.5 ^{1}H and ^{13}C nuclear magnetic resonance spectroscopy (NMR)

Description	Basis of technique	Major uses	Interpretation of data
Interaction of nuclei of atoms in a strong magnetic field with radio wave energy.	Energy is absorbed by nuclei with an odd number of protons or neutrons such as ^{13}C. When this occurs, the nuclei are said to be in resonance. Atoms in the same chemical environment are said to be **equivalent**. Equivalent atoms form one signal in the NMR spectrum. Atoms in different chemical environments absorb different amounts of energy. The **chemical shift** (δ) of a signal in a spectrum indicates how far the signal is from the signal of a reference compound and is measured in ppm. Tetramethylsilane (TMS) is widely used as the reference (δ 0 ppm).	Used qualitatively to provide information about the C–H backbone of organic compounds.	For a ^{1}H or ^{13}C NMR spectrum: • the number of signals indicates the number of different H or C chemical environments • the chemical shift for each signal allows identification of the type of chemical environments of each H or C atom. The area under each signal in a ^{1}H spectrum is proportional to the number of different H atoms. In a ^{1}H NMR spectrum, signals can show **splitting patterns** that can provide further information about the molecule's structure. The number of signals in the splitting pattern is ($n + 1$), where n is the number of non-equivalent hydrogen atoms on adjacent carbon atoms. For example, the spectrum of CH_3CHCl_2 would have two major signals due to the methyl protons and the proton in the –CH group. As a result of splitting the: • –CH_3 proton signal is a doublet • –CH proton signal is a quartet.

Chemical synthesis and design

The chemical industry employs thousands of people and produces the raw materials from which many consumer products are made. Chemical industries are interdependent and the products or wastes of one industry are often the raw materials of another. As a consequence, many industries are located near each other to reduce transport costs and allow them to share facilities.

When developing a process for synthesising a chemical for use in society, the aim is for a high yield of a pure product that is produced quickly and efficiently at a marketable price, while ensuring the health and safety of employees and minimising damage to the environment.

FACTORS TO BE CONSIDERED WHEN DESIGNING A CHEMICAL SYNTHESIS

Availability of reagents

Suitable raw materials need to be readily available. Their purity, price, and the cost and ease of transport are considered, together with the energy expenditure required to transport them to the chemical plant. Methods of transport and storage are assessed in order to protect the environment and the community.

Reaction conditions

Consideration is given to the use of energy and the factors that determine the rate of reaction and the reaction yield. Such factors include:

- temperature
- surface area
- concentration
- pressure
- the use of catalysts.

Yield and purity

The formation of an equilibrium can limit the yield of a chemical synthesis. The factors that shift an equilibrium in the forward direction to maximise the amount of product formed can be in conflict with the factors affecting the rate of reaction. Temperature, pressure and concentration need to be carefully selected, and it may be necessary to make compromises to ensure optimum yield.

For example, reaction rate increases with increasing temperature, but, for an exothermic reaction, as temperature increases the equilibrium position shifts in favour of the reverse reaction and less products. In such a reaction, it may be best to use a moderate temperature and employ a catalyst to increase the rate of the reaction.

Once the product is formed, it must be separated from any other by-products and unused reactants that may be present in the reaction mixture. Further purification steps are often necessary. Testing to ensure purity is essential.

Atom economy

Atom economy measures the mass of reactant atoms that are used to make the final product. Ideally, for environmental and financial reasons, all or almost all of the atoms from the reactants should be incorporated in the final product and there should be as few 'wasted' atoms as possible.

$$\text{atom economy} = \frac{\text{molar mass of desired product}}{\text{molar mass of all reactants}} \times 100\%$$

Percentage yield

Inevitably, during a synthesis, there will be some loss of reactants and products as they are transferred between reaction vessels and in separation and purification stages, resulting in less product being obtained than expected. The formation of equilibria can further reduce the amount of product obtained.

Percentage yield compares the **actual yield** to the **theoretical yield** and indicates the efficiency of the reaction.

$$\text{percentage yield} = \frac{\text{actual yield}}{\text{theoretical yield}} \times 100\%$$

The yield for each step in a multi-step reaction has an effect on the overall yield. The overall percentage yield helps scientists decide on the best pathway to use to produce a desired product with minimal waste. The overall yield is determined by multiplying the percentage yields for each step together, and expressing the answer as a percentage.

Location of the plant

The uses, markets, safe storage and transport of the chemical product are some of the factors that are considered when determining the location of a chemical plant. At times the product is the raw material for another synthesis, so close proximity to another chemical plant is desirable.

Environmental, social and economic issues

Waste management is important in the production of any chemical; potential effects of unwanted chemicals on the environment and the health and safety of the community must be considered with care. Wastes may exist as solids, liquids, solutions or gases; they may be pure or mixed with water, soil, air or other chemicals; they may be harmless, poisonous, explosive, radioactive or cause disease.

The aim is to develop chemical industries that minimise or eliminate hazardous processes or products. Reduction of the toxicity and volume of waste reduces the impact on living organisms and the environment. Safe handling of toxic materials and the use of extreme temperature and pressure are assessed in order to prevent a fire or explosion, as well as other hazards such as negative impacts on water supplies and the atmosphere, and on workers in the industry and the general community.

In Australia the need for occupational health and safety is underpinned by laws that require companies to follow a duty of care. Severe penalties are incurred if the law is not adhered to. These laws cover:

- community awareness
- safe manufacturing
- environmental protection
- safe storage and transport
- employee health and safety.

Chemicals are classified as either dangerous goods or hazardous chemicals. Dangerous goods pose an immediate danger to people, property or the environment. Hazardous chemicals may harm the health and safety of people who work with them. **Safety data sheets (SDS)** are provided by the manufacturers of such chemicals. Warning signs are required to be used at any site where dangerous or hazardous goods are used, stored or transported.

A risk assessment is a formal process of assessing the possible risks and potential harm that a chemical may have when used in a specific situation, such as an industrial site or even a classroom. A risk assessment should include:

- identification of the hazardous chemicals
- assessment of the risk using the SDS for hazardous chemicals, including properties and dangers
- control of the risk, including precautions and safe handling, health effects and first aid treatment
- a record of the risk assessment and its author.

Economic considerations underpin all aspects of a commercial chemical industry. They include the cost of raw materials and catalysts, cost of building the plant to create suitable reaction conditions (e.g. high temperature, high pressure), use of energy and water, technology and computers, and marketing and waste disposal.

Figure 8.8 is a representation of some of the stages in the operation of an industrial chemical synthesis.

CASE STUDY: THE HABER PROCESS

The Haber process for the production of ammonia (Figure 8.9) illustrates some of the factors that need to be considered when designing a chemical synthesis process.

Industrial uses

Uses of ammonia include the production of fertilisers, as a cleaning agent, and the production of other chemicals such as explosives and synthetic fibres.

Availability of reagents

H_2 is usually obtained from steam reforming of hydrocarbons, and N_2 is from air. Steam reforming involves a reaction between natural gas and steam.

Reaction conditions: rate and equilibrium factors

$$N_2(g) + 3H_2(g) \rightleftharpoons 2NH_3(g) \qquad \Delta H = -91\,\text{kJ mol}^{-1}$$

To increase the equilibrium yield:

- decrease T because ΔH is negative, so K_{eq} increases when T decreases
- increase P because equilibrium position moves forward in direction of the least number of molecules.

To increase the rate of reaction:

- increase T
- increase P
- use a catalyst: usually porous Fe/Fe_3O_4.

The reaction runs at a faster rate at higher temperatures, but the best equilibrium yield occurs at lower temperatures. As a compromise, the reaction is run at a moderate temperature of 350–500°C and pressure of 250 atm, and a porous Fe/Fe_3O_4 catalyst is used.

The gas is passed quickly over the catalyst beds several times. It is cooled between passes to keep the temperature close to 500°C.

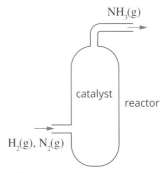

FIGURE 8.9 In the Haber process, hydrogen gas and nitrogen gas react at a moderate temperature under high pressure in the presence of a catalyst to produce a high yield of ammonia gas.

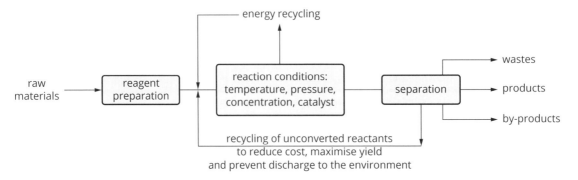

FIGURE 8.8 Sequence of operations in a chemical synthesis

Yield

NH_3 is liquefied for easy transport. Unreacted gases are recycled to achieve a 98% yield and reduce emissions.

Waste management

TABLE 8.6 Waste management issues for ammonia production

Waste issue	Treatment by...	Treatment causes a reduction in...
Sulfur in natural gas used in steam reforming to generate H_2 produces $SO_2(g)$	• desulfurisation and collection of $SO_2(g)$; sold as raw material for H_2SO_4 production	• emissions, minimising air pollution and acid rain • poisoning of catalysts
Flue gases (CO_2, NO_x, SO_2, CO) in steam reforming where $H_2(g)$ is produced	• liquefying $CO_2(g)$ and selling to food, beverage and fertiliser companies (some is released into air) • monitoring of CO(g) and $NO_x(g)$ emissions	• emissions, reducing enhanced greenhouse effect
Energy	• use of heat exchangers, allowing energy to be reused to preheat and generate steam during plant processes	• costs and inefficiency
Unreacted N_2 and H_2	• recycling	• waste of resources (process is more efficient)

Health and safety

Ammonia is a toxic gas that can be harmful by all means of exposure. Consequently, the industry maintains high standards of safety, operation and transport. Fire and explosions are other major hazards. As a consequence, industry workers wear protective clothing, gloves, face shields, rubber boots and aprons. Factories are well ventilated and breathing apparatus is available.

WORKSHEET 8.1

Knowledge review—atomic structure and stoichiometry

This worksheet will help you check your knowledge and understanding of atomic structure, precipitation reactions, stoichiometry and equilibrium.

1   Write electronic configurations for the following elements.

Potassium: _____

Sulfur: _____

2   The atomic number of fluorine is 9. Write the electronic configuration for:

   a   a ground state F atom: _____

   b   an excited state F atom: _____

   c   a fluoride ion, F⁻, in the ground state: _____

3   Write balanced ionic equations for the following reactions:

   a   Solutions of silver nitrate and sodium chloride react to form a precipitate of silver chloride and sodium nitrate solution.

   _____

   b   Solutions of iron(III) nitrate and potassium hydroxide react to form a precipitate of iron(III) hydroxide and potassium nitrate solution.

   _____

4   A sample of magnesium reacted completely with 20.00 mL of $1.00\,mol\,L^{-1}$ HCl, which was in excess. The reaction is represented by the equation:

$$Mg(s) + 2HCl(aq) \rightarrow MgCl_2(aq) + H_2(g)$$

The excess HCl was neutralised by reaction with 50.00 mL of $0.200\,mol\,L^{-1}$ NaOH. Given that the molar mass of magnesium is $24.3\,g\,mol^{-1}$, calculate the mass of the sample of magnesium.

5   One of the steps in the production of sulfuric acid in the contact process is:

$$2SO_2(g) + O_2(g) \rightleftharpoons 2SO_3(g) \qquad \Delta H = -197\,kJ\,mol^{-1}$$

   a   What would be the effect of increasing the temperature, at constant volume, on:

   i   the reaction rate? _____

   ii   the equilibrium constant? _____

   iii   the equilibrium yield? _____

   b   What would be the effect of increasing the pressure, at constant temperature, on:

   i   the reaction rate? _____

   ii   the equilibrium yield? _____

   iii   the equilibrium constant? _____

....

WORKSHEET 8.2

Puzzling about ions—testing techniques

1 Use Table 8.1 in the Key knowledge section (page 160) and your knowledge of flame test, precipitation and complexing to determine the labels on two bottles of solid compounds, A and B.

A and B are pure; there is only one cation and one anion present in each bottle. The following results were obtained from various tests.

a Compound A:

- produced a white precipitate when mixed with $BaCl_2$ solution
- dissolved in water to form a blue solution
- produced a green-blue flame
- produced a deep purple-blue solution with concentrated NH_3 solution.

Explain what information is obtained from each test, then determine the identity of Compound A.

_____

_____

_____

b Compound B:

- formed bubbles when added to hydrochloric acid
- produced a colourless solution when mixed with NH_3 solution
- produced a white precipitate when mixed with NaCl solution.

Explain what information is obtained from each test, then determine the identity of Compound B.

_____

_____

_____

2 Explain what happened within atoms to produce the green-blue flame colour when Compound A was heated.

_____

_____

3 It can be difficult to distinguish between the flame colours of some metal ions. For example, both copper and barium have green flame colours. Describe another test that can be used to distinguish between Cu^{2+} and Ba^{2+} ions.

_____

_____

4 Explain the following statement:

Complexation occurs when solution of copper(II) sulfate reacts with excess ammonia solution.

_____

_____

_____

RATING MY LEARNING	My understanding improved	Not confident ← → Very confident ○ ○ ○ ○ ○	I answered questions without help	Not confident ← → Very confident ○ ○ ○ ○ ○	I corrected my errors without help	Not confident ← → Very confident ○ ○ ○ ○ ○

WORKSHEET 8.3

Colorimetry and UV–visible spectroscopy

1 Choose from the terms listed to complete the summary statements outlining the key points about colorimetry and UV–visible spectroscopy. (Some terms are not used at all.)

concentration	mass	visible light	absorbance	ultraviolet and visible light
red light	blue light	absorbed	emitted	refraction

- Spectroscopic techniques usually involve the measurement of the _____ of electromagnetic radiation by a sample.
- In colorimetry, the type of electromagnetic radiation is _____. In UV–visible spectroscopy the type of electromagnetic radiation is _____.
- In both colorimetry and UV–visible spectroscopy, the amount of light _____ by a solution is directly related to the _____ of the substance being analysed in the solution.

2 The concentration of iron(II) ions in a sample of water is to be analysed using UV–visible spectroscopy. The ions are first converted to the metal complex $FeSCN^{2+}$, which is a blood-red colour. The absorption spectrum of $FeSCN^{2+}$ is shown in the figure below.

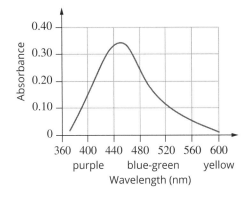

a i Which wavelength should be chosen for the analysis? Give a reason for your answer.

_____

_____

ii Give a reason why this wavelength might not actually be chosen.

_____

_____

b If the analysis were to be carried out by colorimetry and not UV–visible spectroscopy, what colour light would you choose for the analysis? Give a reason for your answer.

_____

_____

3 A calibration curve for analysis of $FeSCN^{2+}$ is shown below.

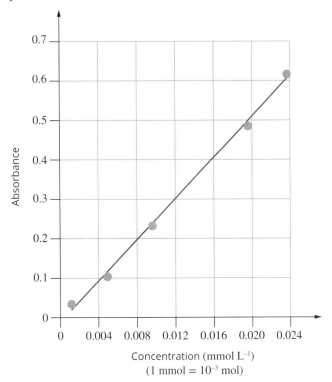

Concentration (mmol L^{-1})
(1 mmol = 10^{-3} mol)

a The absorbance of the sample of water is found to be 0.34. What is the concentration of Fe^{2+}, in mol L^{-1}?

_____

b Calculate the concentration of Fe^{2+} ions in the water sample in mg L^{-1}.

WORKSHEET 8.4

Atomic absorption spectroscopy

1 Briefly explain the principles underlying atomic absorption spectroscopy (AAS).

2 Explain why light of different and specific energies are absorbed by different elements.

3 The concentration of cadmium in a sample of polluted soil was measured using AAS. A mass of 1.20 g of the sample is heated with 10 mL of nitric acid and filtered.

To determine the concentration of cadmium, a cathode lamp for cadmium was fitted into the AAS instrument. Standard solutions of various concentrations of cadmium were prepared and the absorbance of each of these solutions was measured. The results are shown below.

a Graph these results on the grid provided at right.

Concentration (ppm)	Absorbance
5.0	2.1
10	3.9
15	5.9
20	8.1

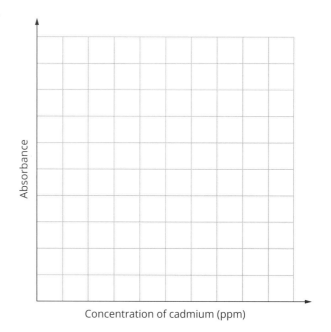

Concentration of cadmium (ppm)

b The measured absorbance of the solution from the soil sample was 3.5. Determine the concentration of cadmium, in ppm, in the 10 mL sample.

c Calculate the concentration of cadmium in the 1.20 g sample of soil in $\mu g\,g^{-1}$ ($1\,\mu g = 10^{-6}\,g$).

| RATING MY LEARNING | My understanding improved | Not confident ⟵———⟶ Very confident ○ ○ ○ ○ ○ | I answered questions without help | Not confident ⟵———⟶ Very confident ○ ○ ○ ○ ○ | I corrected my errors without help | Not confident ⟵———⟶ Very confident ○ ○ ○ ○ ○ |

WORKSHEET 8.5

Forensic testing—blood alcohol concentration

Small portable instruments are used by police to detect motorists driving under the influence of alcohol. Motorists blow into the instrument. If ethanol is present in the breath, it is oxidised to ethanoic acid and oxygen gas from air is reduced to water. A voltage is produced by this reaction and is converted to a measurement of the ethanol concentration in the breath.

1 Because the concentration of ethanol in the blood is related to the concentration of ethanol in the breath, the instrument gives an indication of the blood alcohol concentration (BAC).

   The BAC is measured in milligrams of ethanol per 100 mL of blood. The legal limit in New South Wales is 0.05 mg per 100 mL for most motorists with a full licence. Convert a BAC reading of 0.05 to mole per litre.

2 The roadside test is quick and reliable, but it is not used for evidence in court cases because a higher level of accuracy is required. If the reading is above 0.05, the driver is tested further at a testing station, where they must breathe continuously into an infrared (IR) spectrometer.

   Examine the IR spectrum of ethanol shown in the figure below. The intensity of the peak at 2950 cm^{-1} is measured for the driver's breath and compared with the intensity of ethanol standards to obtain an accurate measurement. The driver's breath also contains water vapour, which absorbs strongly at about 3800 cm^{-1}, 3600 cm^{-1}, 3200 cm^{-1} and 1600 cm^{-1}.

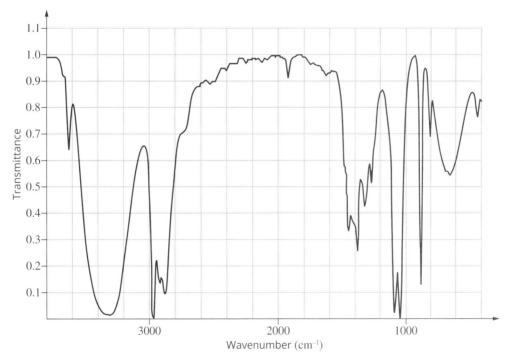

a Suggest why a wavenumber value of 2950 cm^{-1} is chosen for the detection of ethanol rather than, for example, 3650 cm^{-1}.

b Why do water and ethanol produce bands in the same region of the spectrum?

c Using the information in the following table, suggest which bond in ethanol is responsible for absorption at each of the following frequencies.

i 2950 cm^{-1} _____

ii 3350 cm^{-1} _____

iii 1050 cm^{-1} _____

Band	Location	Wavenumber and intensity
C=O	in carboxylic acids, esters, aldehydes and ketones	1680–1750 cm^{-1}, strong
C–O	in alcohols, ethers	1000–1300 cm^{-1}, strong
C–H	in alkanes, alkenes, alkynes	2850–3300 cm^{-1}, strong
O–H	in alcohols, phenols	3230–3550, strong, broad
O–H	in carboxylic acids	2500–3000, strong, broad

| RATING MY LEARNING | My understanding improved | Not confident ◄———► Very confident ○ ○ ○ ○ ○ | I answered questions without help | Not confident ◄———► Very confident ○ ○ ○ ○ ○ | I corrected my errors without help | Not confident ◄———► Very confident ○ ○ ○ ○ ○ |

176   Pearson Chemistry 12 NSW | Skills and Assessment | Module 8   ISBN 978 1 4886 1934 2

WORKSHEET 8.6

Nuclear magnetic resonance

Nuclear magnetic resonance (NMR) spectroscopy is widely used by analytical chemists. It provides detailed information about the nuclei of certain atoms, particularly hydrogen and carbon.

1 Briefly explain the principles of NMR spectroscopy.

2 Complete the following table.

Compound	No. of different types of carbon atoms	No. of different types of hydrogen atoms
3-methylpentane $CH_3CH_2CH(CH_3)CH_2CH_3$		
propanoic acid CH_3CH_2COOH		
methypropane $(CH_3)_3CH$		

3 Five ^1H NMR spectra and five ^{13}C NMR spectra are shown. Using the labels A–J, correctly match each chemical listed in the table with its corresponding spectrum. The ^1H NMR spectra shown are low-resolution spectra and do not show any splitting of the signals (signal splitting might be seen in high-resolution spectra). On the ^1H NMR spectra the numbers in circles indicate the number of hydrogen atoms with each chemical shift.

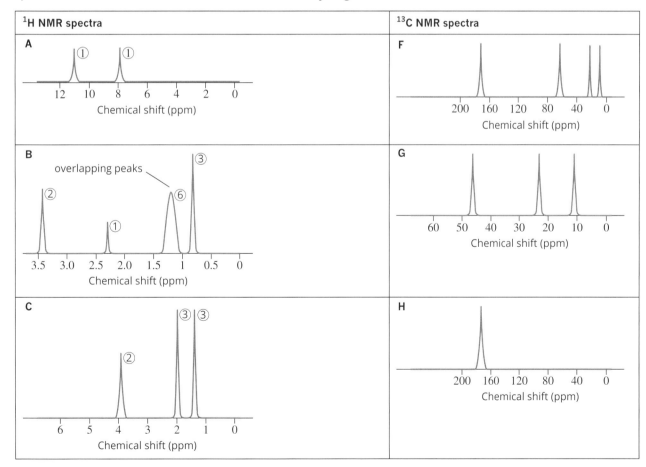

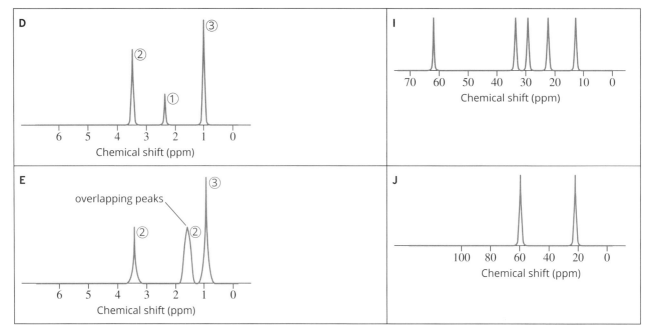

Chemical	Corresponding ^{1}H spectrum (A–E)	Corresponding ^{13}C spectrum (F–J)
CH_3CH_2OH		
$CH_3COOCH_2CH_3$		
HCOOH		
$CH_3CH_2CH_2Cl$		
$CH_3CH_2CH_2CH_2CH_2OH$		

Solving a chemical mystery using spectroscopy

It has been known from early times that the bark of willow trees contains a chemical that assists in the relief of pain. This chemical itself has no medicinal effect, but in the human body it is converted into an active chemical, salicylic acid. Chemists can use different spectroscopic techniques to discover the identity and structure of such compounds.

Identifying salicylic acid

1 Mass spectrometry can be used to confirm the identity of a sample of a white powder thought to be salicylic acid. The fragmentation pattern observed in a mass spectrum is characteristic of the compound being investigated. By analysing this pattern and comparing it with a database of known chemicals, a chemist can decide if a sample is salicylic acid.

a The mass spectrum of the sample of white powder is shown below. Label the parent ion (molecular ion) with an asterisk.

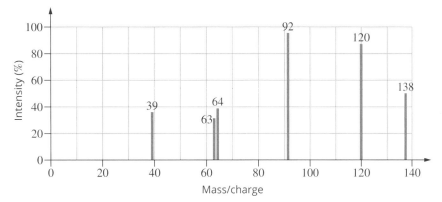

b Likely molar mass: _____ $g\,mol^{-1}$

c Knowing that the molecular formula of salicylic acid is $C_7H_6O_3$, is the white powder likely to be salicylic acid? Explain.

_____

_____

d What are possible formulae of the cations that have masses corresponding to peaks in the mass spectrum at:

92: _____

120: _____

The functional groups present in a molecule can often be determined by infrared (IR) spectroscopy. Table 1 shows the characteristic absorption bands of different functional groups. The IR spectrum of salicylic acid is shown on page 180. The peaks in the IR spectrum of salicylic acid between 1400 and $1600\,cm^{-1}$ are found in compounds called arenes, which are based on benzene. Benzene (C_6H_6) can be represented by the structure shown in Figure a below.

In arenes, a hydrogen atom bonded to a carbon atom in the benzene ring can be replaced by other groups. Phenol is an example of an arene (Figure b).

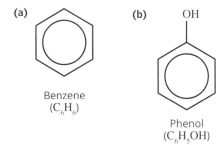

A benzene ring (a) forms the basis of the arene called phenol (b).

TABLE 1 Characteristic absorption bands of some functional groups

Functional group	Location	Wavenumber and intensity
C=O	in carboxylic acids	1650–1725 cm⁻¹, strong
C=O	in esters	1735–1750 cm⁻¹, strong
C=O	in ketones	1710–1725 cm⁻¹, strong
C–H	in alkanes	2850–2950 cm⁻¹, medium–strong
C–H	in alkenes, arenes	3000–3250 cm⁻¹, strong
O–H	in alcohols, phenols	3230–3550 cm⁻¹, strong
O–H	in carboxylic acids	2500–3000 cm⁻¹, strong

2 Use the information in the table to identify the functional groups in salicylic acid that correspond to the peaks marked with asterisks in the following IR spectrum.

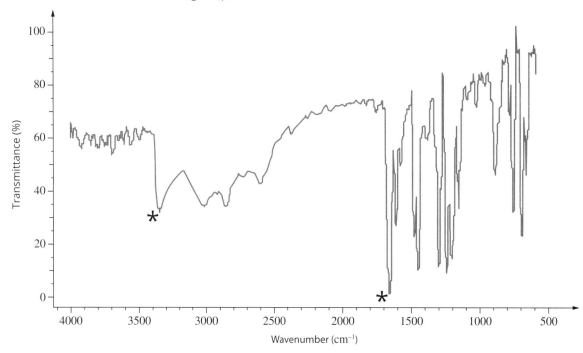

3 A ^{13}C nuclear magnetic resonance (NMR) spectrum gives information about the arrangement of carbon atoms in an organic molecule. The number of peaks in the spectrum indicates the number of carbon atoms in different chemical environments.

Examine the simplified ^{13}C NMR spectrum of salicylic acid below. How many different carbon atoms are present in salicylic acid? _____

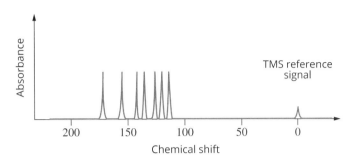

Determining the structure of salicylic acid

4 Complete the following summary of the information you have found about the structure of salicylic acid.

Molar mass ($g\,mol^{-1}$): _____

Molecular formula: _____

Functional groups present: _____

Number of carbon atoms in different environments in the molecule: _____

5 Draw a possible molecular structure for salicylic acid.

| RATING MY LEARNING | My understanding improved | Not confident ← → Very confident ○ ○ ○ ○ ○ | I answered questions without help | Not confident ← → Very confident ○ ○ ○ ○ ○ | I corrected my errors without help | Not confident ← → Very confident ○ ○ ○ ○ ○ |

ISBN 978 1 4886 1934 2   Pearson Chemistry 12 NSW | Skills and Assessment | Module 8   **181**

WORKSHEET 8.8

Optimising reactions in industry

In industrial processes, the conditions required for a fast rate of reaction and a high equilibrium yield are often in conflict with each other. This worksheet examines the conditions chosen for a particular industrial process.

Dimethyl ether (DME) is used as a propellant in cans of spray paints. It has similar properties to LPG and has been proposed as an alternative fuel for power generation, domestic uses and transportation. It does not contain any sulfur or nitrogen, burns with relatively low emissions of particulates and nitrogen oxides, and is harmless to humans, biodegradable and non-corrosive to metals. Table 1 contains some information about DME.

TABLE 1 Dimethyl ether (DME) data

Molecular formula	CH_3OCH_3
Recommended purity of DME as vehicle fuel	< 0.01% methanol and < 0.05% water
Energy value compared to LPG	similar
Cetane number (A fuel with a high cetane number starts to burn quickly after it is injected.)	10 times LPG
Boiling point of DME compared to LPG	−25°C compared with −42°C
Liquid density at 20°C compared to LPG	$0.67\,g\,mL^{-1}$ compared with $0.49\,g\,mL^{-1}$

There are three ways of producing DME, but the most recent and environmentally friendly process is a three-step synthesis involving a specially developed liquid slurry reactor containing a powdered catalyst (see figure below). Like many industrial processes, the reaction conditions must be carefully adjusted to ensure a relatively high yield of DME in a reasonable time.

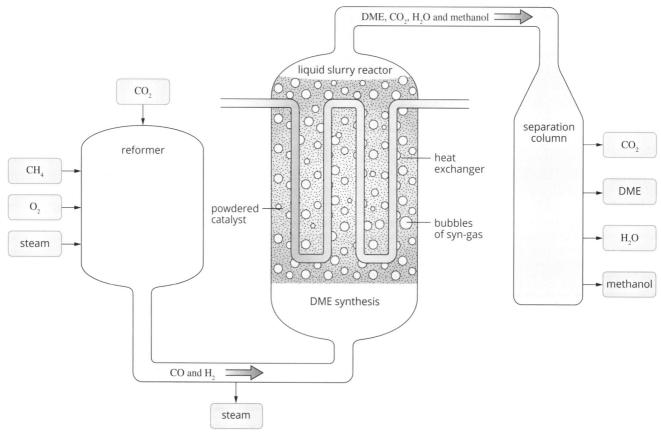

Flow chart of the three-step process for synthesising dimethyl ether (DME)

The steps in this process are:

- a highly efficient conversion of methane, oxygen and carbon dioxide into syn-gas (CO and H_2) and steam in a reformer
- DME synthesis in the liquid slurry reactor, where bubbles of syn-gas react as they rise through the catalytic slurry in an exothermic, temperature-sensitive process that produces DME and carbon dioxide (some methanol is also formed by a side reaction)
- purification to produce DME, CO_2, H_2O and methanol.

1 Use the flow chart and the information provided to write an equation for the main reaction that occurs in the liquid slurry reactor.

_____

2 Suggest why the heat exchanger is present in the reactor.

_____

In a pilot plant the exothermic reaction producing DME in the liquid slurry reactor takes place at 260°C and 5 MPa. At this temperature the conversion of syn-gas to DME is about 90%. The DME produced is 99.9% pure and contains less than 0.01% water and methanol. The catalyst is water-sensitive and gradually deactivates at temperatures higher than 300°C.

3 In the reactor, what would be the effect on the equilibrium yield of DME if you were to:

a decrease the pressure at constant temperature?

_____

b increase the temperature at constant pressure?

_____

4 With reference to reaction rates and equilibrium, discuss why the particular temperatures and pressure used in the reactor would have been chosen.

_____

_____

_____

5 Identify the wastes likely to be produced from this process and suggest a management process for each one.

_____

_____

6 What health and safety issues might be involved in this method of DME production? (You could use the internet to investigate this further.)

_____

_____

7 Given the information in this worksheet, state an advantage or disadvantage you can foresee for the use of DME as an alternative fuel to fossil fuels such as coal and diesel. (You could use the internet to investigate this further.)

_____

_____

RATING MY LEARNING	My understanding improved	Not confident ← → Very confident ○ ○ ○ ○ ○	I answered questions without help	Not confident ← → Very confident ○ ○ ○ ○ ○	I corrected my errors without help	Not confident ← → Very confident ○ ○ ○ ○ ○

Literacy review—understanding chemical ideas

1. Join each of the phrases on the left about carbon-13 NMR spectra with its matching phrase on the right. (Some phrases on the right will not be used.)

   a. The number of signals in a carbon-13 spectrum indicates...

   b. An NMR spectrum can be obtained for nuclei with...

   c. The chemical shift is...

   d. The chemical shift for each signal gives information about...

   e. NMR spectra are produced...

   A. when nuclei held in a magnetic field interact with radio waves.

   B. proportional to the number of H atoms in a particular environment.

   C. an odd number of protons or an odd number of neutrons.

   D. an even number of protons and an even number of neutrons.

   E. the number of different C chemical environments.

   F. the number of C atoms in the molecule.

   G. measured in ppm.

   H. the type of chemical environment of the C atom.

   I. when electrons held in a magnetic field interact with radio waves.

2. You are given two colourless liquids, A and B, and told that one is a primary alcohol and the other is a carboxylic acid.

   a. Write a general equation for a reaction that can occur between the two compounds.

   b. Describe two tests to show which liquid is the alcohol and which is the carboxylic acid.

   c. How could you quickly show they are saturated compounds?

3. A chemist is analysing an organic compound that is known to contain only C, H and O. Combustion analysis produced the following results: 64.80% carbon and 13.61% hydrogen.

   a. Calculate the percentage of oxygen in the compound, and determine the empirical formula of the compound.

b Use the mass spectrum (Figure a), infrared spectrum (Figure b) and carbon-13 NMR spectrum (Figure c) of the compound shown below to determine the following:

Relative molecular mass: _____

Molecular formula: _____

Functional group(s) present: _____

Number of different C atom environments: _____

(a)

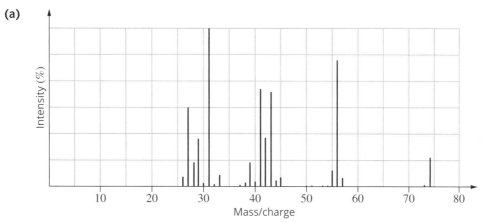

(b)

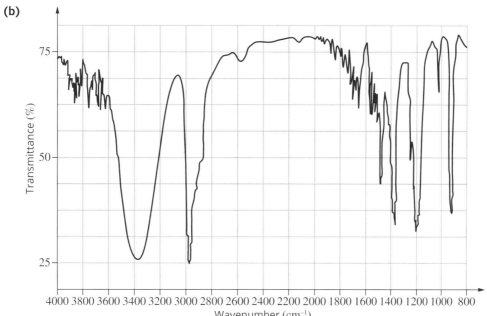

(c)

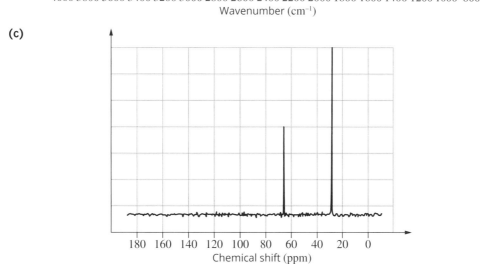

c Draw the structure and name the compound.

d For the structure you have drawn, how many signals would you expect in the ^{1}H NMR spectrum? Would you expect there to be any peak-splitting? Explain why or why not.

WORKSHEET 8.10

Thinking about my learning

On completion of Module 8: Applying chemical ideas, you should be able to describe, explain and apply the relevant scientific ideas. You should be able to interpret, analyse and evaluate data.

1 The table shows the areas of key knowledge covered in this module. Read each and reflect on how well you understand each concept. Rate your learning by shading the circle that corresponds to your level of understanding for each concept. It may be helpful to use colour as a visual representation. For example:

- green—very confident
- orange—in the middle
- red—starting to develop.

Concept focus	Rate my learning				
	Starting to develop ◄──────► Very confident				
Analysis of inorganic substances	○	○	○	○	○
Analysis of organic substances	○	○	○	○	○
Chemical synthesis and design	○	○	○	○	○

2 Consider points you have shaded from starting to develop to middle-level understanding. List specific ideas you can identify that were challenging.

_____

_____

_____

_____

_____

_____

3 Write down two different strategies that you will apply to help further your understanding of these ideas.

_____

_____

_____

_____

PRACTICAL ACTIVITY 8.1

Testing for ions in aqueous solutions

Suggested duration: 50–60 minutes (less if fewer tests are done)

INTRODUCTION

Several tests can be performed in the laboratory to determine the presence of cations and anions in ionic compounds. These include flame tests, testing the solubility of salts, and forming complexes with transition metal ions. In this experiment you will perform some of these tests for a number of ions and then use your results to determine the identities of the cations and anions in an unknown solution.

PURPOSE

To perform flame tests and solubility tests on a range of ions. You will also study the complexes formed by some transition metal cations. These observations will enable you to identify the cations and anions in an unknown solution.

PRE-LAB SAFETY INFORMATION		
Material used	**Hazard**	**Control**
$0.4 \, mol \, L^{-1}$ hydrochloric acid	corrosive; may cause burns and irritation to the respiratory system	Wear gloves, safety glasses and lab coat.
$2.0 \, mol \, L^{-1}$ ammonia solution	irritates eyes and respiratory system	Wear gloves, safety glasses and lab coat.
$0.4 \, mol \, L^{-1}$ sodium hydroxide solution	can cause burns; dangerous to eyes	Wear gloves, safety glasses and lab coat.
barium chloride solution	harmful if swallowed	Wear gloves, safety glasses and lab coat.
silver nitrate solution	can cause stains, on skin, clothing and benches	Wear gloves, safety glasses and lab coat.
potassium thiocyanate solution	may cause skin and eye irritations; harmful if ingested	Wear gloves, safety glasses and lab coat.
iron(III) nitrate solution	irritating to eyes, respiratory system and skin	Wear gloves, safety glasses and lab coat.
iron(II) chloride solution	irritating to eyes, respiratory system and skin	Wear gloves, safety glasses and lab coat.
copper(II) sulfate solution	hazardous if ingested; may cause irritation of skin, eyes	Wear gloves, safety glasses and lab coat.
sodium carbonate solution	slightly toxic if ingested	Wear gloves, safety glasses and lab coat.
calcium chloride solution	hazardous if ingested; may cause irritation of skin, eyes	Wear gloves, safety glasses and lab coat.
Please indicate that you have understood the information in the safety table.		

Name (print): _____

I understand the safety information (signature): _____

MATERIALS

Part A
- dropping bottles of testing solutions:
  - $2.0 \, mol \, L^{-1}$ NH_3 solution
  - $0.4 \, mol \, L^{-1}$ NaOH solution
  - $0.4 \, mol \, L^{-1}$ HCl solution
  - $0.1 \, mol \, L^{-1}$ $BaCl_2$ solution
  - $0.1 \, mol \, L^{-1}$ $AgNO_3$ solution
  - $0.1 \, mol \, L^{-1}$ KSCN solution
- icy-pole sticks for flame tests
- 5 dropping pipettes
- 2 test-tubes
- test-tube rack
- 5 semi-micro test-tubes
- semi-micro test-tube rack
- small, labelled dropping bottles containing $0.10 \, mol \, L^{-1}$ solutions of:
  - iron(III) nitrate
  - iron(II) chloride
  - copper(II) sulfate
  - sodium carbonate
  - calcium chloride
- safety gloves

Part B
- the same testing materials as for Part A
- small dropping bottle containing unknown solution A, B, C or D

PROCEDURE

Part A—Testing solutions

1 Table 1 shows the tests you will perform on solutions of five compounds: iron(III) nitrate, iron(II) chloride, copper(II) sulfate, sodium carbonate and calcium chloride. For each test, place approximately 4–6 drops of the solution of the compound and 4–6 drops of the testing solution in a semi-micro test-tube. Use clean dropping pipettes when transferring each solution.

2 Carefully observe whether a precipitate forms, the colour of the precipitate and if there is evidence of complex ion formation with the addition of KSCN and concentrated NH_3 solutions. Record your observations in Tables 1 and 2.

3 Perform flame tests on the solutions of the compounds by dipping a new icy-pole stick into each solution and holding it briefly in the flame. Record whether the flame changes colour and the colour of the flame in Table 1.

Part B—Identifying cations and anions in an unknown solution

You will be given a solution of an unknown ionic compound. Complete the following tests on the solution:

1 Using semi-micro test-tubes, test small volumes of your unknown solution using each of the testing solutions.

2 Using a new icy-pole stick, perform a flame test on the unknown solution.

3 Record your results in Tables 3 and 4.

RESULTS

Part A

TABLE 1 Tests for cations

Test	$Fe(NO_3)_3$	$FeCl_2$	$CuSO_4$	Na_2CO_3	$CaCl_2$
Add dilute NH_3 solution. If a precipitate forms add concentrated NH_3 solution.					
Add dilute NaOH solution.					
Add KSCN solution.					
Flame test					

TABLE 2 Tests for anions

Test	$Fe(NO_3)_3$	$FeCl_2$	$CuSO_4$	Na_2CO_3	$CaCl_2$
Add HCl solution.					
Add $BaCl_2$ solution.					
Add $AgNO_3$ solution. If precipitate forms, add NH_3 solution.					

....

PRACTICAL ACTIVITY 8.1

Part B

TABLE 3 Tests for cations

Test performed on unknown solution	Observation	Conclusions and equations (where appropriate)
Add dilute NH_3 solution. If a precipitate forms, add concentrated NH_3 solution.		
Add dilute NaOH solution.		
Add KSCN solution.		
Flame test		

TABLE 4 Tests for anions

Test performed on unknown solution	Observation	Conclusions and equations (where appropriate)
Add HCl solution.		
Add $BaCl_2$ solution.		
Add $AgNO_3$ solution. If a precipitate forms, add NH_3 solution.		

DISCUSSION

1 Why do metal ions produce distinctive flame colours?

2 List the cations in the solutions used in this experiment that can be identified by their flame colours.

··

PRACTICAL ACTIVITY 8.1

3 What is a complex ion?

_____

_____

4 List the cations that can be identified by reacting them with ammonia solution and forming complex ions.

_____

_____

5 Write balanced ionic equations in the table above for the tests that gave a positive result.

6 What is the identity of your unknown compound? Explain the reasons for your decision.

_____

_____

_____

_____

CONCLUSION

7 Summarise the methods for testing the identity of cations and anions in ionic compounds. Comment on the reliability and accuracy of your conclusions.

_____

_____

_____

RATING MY LEARNING	My understanding improved	Not confident ◄────► Very confident ○ ○ ○ ○ ○	I answered questions without help	Not confident ◄────► Very confident ○ ○ ○ ○ ○	I corrected my errors without help	Not confident ◄────► Very confident ○ ○ ○ ○ ○

PRACTICAL ACTIVITY 8.2

Gravimetric determination of sulfur as sulfate in fertiliser

Suggested duration: 70 minutes over 2 or 3 days

INTRODUCTION

Sulfur is an essential mineral for plants because it is needed for the synthesis of chlorophyll and for nitrogen fixation in legumes. The sulfur content of fertilisers is therefore an important consideration for farmers and home gardeners.

This practical activity determines the amount of sulfur present in a fertiliser in the form of sulfate ions. The sulfate is precipitated as barium sulfate from a solution containing a known mass of the fertiliser by adding an excess of barium chloride solution:

$$Ba^{2+}(aq) + SO_4^{2-}(aq) \rightarrow BaSO_4(s)$$

The proportion of sulfate ions, and therefore of sulfur, in the fertiliser is determined by collecting and weighing the precipitate that is formed during the above reaction.

PURPOSE

To find the percentage of sulfur (as sulfate) present in a brand of commercial fertiliser.

PRE-LAB SAFETY INFORMATION		
Material used	**Hazard**	**Control**
fertiliser	can cause skin and eye irritation	Wear gloves, safety glasses and a laboratory coat.
$0.5\,mol\,L^{-1}$ barium chloride solution	toxic, harmful if swallowed	Wear gloves, safety glasses and a laboratory coat.
$0.1\,mol\,L^{-1}$ silver nitrate solution	can stain skin, clothing and bench surface	Wear gloves, safety glasses and a laboratory coat.
$2\,mol\,L^{-1}$ hydrochloric acid	causes skin and eye irritation	Wear gloves, safety glasses and a laboratory coat.
heating of solution and crucible	burning and scalding	Wear gloves, safety glasses and a laboratory coat.

Please indicate that you have understood the information in the safety table.

Name (print): _____

I understand the safety information (signature): _____

PROCEDURE

1   Accurately weigh out 1.0 g of the finely ground fertiliser into a 100 mL beaker. Record the mass in Table 1 and, if a commercial fertiliser is being analysed, record the brand and its sulfur content as specified by the manufacturer.

2   Add 50 mL of deionised water and stir to dissolve as much of the sample as possible. Filter the mixture into a 600 mL beaker, washing the residue several times using deionised water.

3   Add about 3 mL of $2\,mol\,L^{-1}$ hydrochloric acid to the filtrate and add more water so that the total volume is about 200 mL. Heat the solution until it boils.

4   Add 15 mL of $0.5\,mol\,L^{-1}$ barium chloride solution drop by drop from a burette to the hot solution, stirring continuously. A white precipitate of barium sulfate will form.

MATERIALS

- 1.0 g fertiliser, finely ground using a mortar and pestle*
- 3 mL of $2\,mol\,L^{-1}$ hydrochloric acid, HCl
- 5 mL of $0.1\,mol\,L^{-1}$ silver nitrate solution, $AgNO_3$
- 20 mL of $0.5\,mol\,L^{-1}$ barium chloride solution, $BaCl_2$
- 200 mL deionised water
- 20 mL warm deionised water
- 2 × 100 mL beakers
- 600 mL beaker
- 10 mL measuring cylinder
- burette and stand
- filter funnel
- filter paper
- vacuum flask and vacuum pump (water-jet type)
- glass filter crucible (no. 4 porosity) and rubber adaptor**
- stirring rod
- wash bottle containing deionised water
- mortar and pestle
- Bunsen burner, tripod stand and gauze mat
- bench mat
- electronic balance
- oven

*   A suitable lawn food fertiliser for all analyses in this experimental investigation can be made by mixing 100 g $(NH_4)_2SO_4$, 5.4 g KH_2PO_4 and 1.5 g $FeSO_4 \cdot 7H_2O$. Various commercial lawn foods may be suitable commercial alternatives. Test them first, as some are better than others.

**   A Gooch crucible, rubber adaptor and filter paper to suit may be used instead. However, although the Gooch crucible is less expensive, filtration often takes longer and uses much more water. Filtration using a glass filter crucible usually takes only minutes and relatively little water is used.

5 Boil the mixture for a further minute, then remove it from the heat and allow the precipitate to settle. Ensure no sulfate ions remain in the solution by adding several more drops of barium chloride solution. If more precipitate forms, add 3 mL of barium chloride solution and test again for unreacted sulfate ions. If necessary the mixture can be left to stand overnight at this stage.

6 Weigh a glass filter crucible.

7 Collect the precipitate in the glass filter crucible using gentle vacuum filtration. (Filtration is faster if most of the liquid is filtered before the bulk of the precipitate is collected in the crucible.) Use about 10 mL of warm deionised water to wash any precipitate remaining in the beaker into the crucible.

8 Collect the last drops of filtrate in a 100 mL beaker and test for the presence of chloride ions by adding a few drops of silver nitrate solution to the filtrate. If the solution becomes cloudy, wash the precipitate with a further 10 mL of warm water and repeat the test.

9 Place the crucible and contents in an oven heated to 100–110°C and leave overnight.

10 Take out of oven and allow to cool in a dessicator.

11 Weigh the crucible and contents and record the mass in Table 1.

RESULTS

TABLE 1 Brand and mass results

Brand of fertiliser	
Mass of fertiliser sample (g)	
Sulfur as sulfate (content specified by manufacturer)	
Mass of fertiliser sample (g)	
Mass of crucible (g)	
Mass of crucible and contents (g)	

DISCUSSION

1 Determine the mass of the barium sulfate precipitate obtained.

2 Calculate the mass of sulfate ions present in the barium sulfate precipitate.

3 Determine the percentage by mass of sulfate in the fertiliser.

4 Determine the percentage by mass of sulfur (as sulfate) in the fertiliser.

5 How could the results obtained be affected if:

a the mixture in step 5 of the procedure was not tested with more barium chloride solution?

_____

b the filtrate was not tested with silver nitrate solution when the precipitate was washed in step 8?

_____

CONCLUSION

6 What sources of error might arise in a gravimetric analysis such as this? Comment on the reliability and accuracy of your results.

_____

_____

_____

7 If you analysed a commercial fertiliser, how well does your result for the percentage of sulfur present as sulfate agree with the manufacturer's value? Suggest reasons for any difference.

_____

_____

RATING MY LEARNING	My understanding improved	Not confident ← → Very confident ○ ○ ○ ○ ○	I answered questions without help	Not confident ← → Very confident ○ ○ ○ ○ ○	I corrected my errors without help	Not confident ← → Very confident ○ ○ ○ ○ ○

PRACTICAL ACTIVITY 8.3

Analysing precipitation titration data

Suggested duration: 30 minutes

INTRODUCTION

Precipitation titrations can be used to determine the concentration of ions in a solution when the ion forms a salt with limited solubility. An example is the determination of the concentration of chloride in a river water sample. A silver chloride precipitate is formed if silver nitrate solution is added to salty river water.

It can be difficult to determine the equivalence point in precipitation titrations. In the analysis of chloride in water, a solution containing chromate ions, CrO_4^{2-}, is added to the reaction mixture. When all the chloride has been precipitated as silver chloride, the first excess of Ag^+ ions results in the formation of brick-red coloured silver chromate, Ag_2CrO_4. The Ag_2CrO_4 effectively acts as an indicator of the equivalence point.

Because of the hazards associated with the chemicals used in this method, this activity analyses secondary-sourced data. (You might like to research the risks associated with the chemicals to see why this is so.) No materials are required for this activity.

PURPOSE

To determine the concentration of sodium chloride in a sample of river water.

PROCEDURE

1 Salty river water was heated until all the water was removed and only a residue remained.

2 The residue was dried completely in an oven at 110°C.

3 Three samples were weighed, then placed in separate conical flasks. About 100 mL of distilled water was added to each flask to dissolve the samples.

4 Small amounts of solid $NaHCO_3$ were added to each flask until all fizzing stopped. This ensured there was no acid present that would prevent the titration reaction from occurring.

5 About 2 mL of K_2CrO_4 solution was added to each flask and a titration performed using $0.01000\,mol\,L^{-1}$ $AgNO_3$ solution, titrating until the first permanent brick-red colour of $AgCrO_4$ was observed.

RESULTS

TABLE 1 Results of precipitation titration

Sample	Mass of sample (g)	Titre of $0.0100\,mol\,L^{-1}$ $AgNO_3$ (mL)
1	0.200	26.90
2	0.250	33.70
3	0.180	24.30

DISCUSSION

1   Write a balanced ionic equation for the reaction between the chloride ions in the samples and silver nitrate solution.

2   Calculate the amount, in mol, of $AgNO_3$ required to reach the equivalence point for each sample.

3   Calculate the amount, in mol, of sodium chloride in each sample, assuming that all the chloride is present in the river water as sodium chloride.

4   Calculate the percentage of sodium chloride, by mass, in each sample.

5   Average the percentage of sodium chloride in the samples.

CONCLUSION

6   State the percentage by mass of sodium chloride in the solid obtained from salty river water.

RATING MY LEARNING	My understanding improved	Not confident				Very confident	I answered questions without help	Not confident				Very confident	I corrected my errors without help	Not confident				Very confident

PRACTICAL ACTIVITY 8.4

Colorimetric analysis of iron in foods

Suggested duration: 25 minutes

INTRODUCTION

Iron is one of the minerals required by the body. It is used in the manufacture of the oxygen-carrying proteins haemoglobin and myoglobin. Without sufficient supplies of iron, a person can feel tired and listless, and may become anaemic. Most foods contain iron, but red meat, green vegetables, grains such as wheat and rice, seeds such as lentils and beans, and many fruits are rich sources of iron.

In this exercise the iron present in a sample of food is extracted by burning the food to remove elements such as carbon and hydrogen, and treating the residue to form a solution containing Fe^{3+} ions. To make the presence of the ions in solution visible, thiocyanate, SCN^-, ions are added. These react with the Fe^{3+} ions to form $FeSCN^{2+}$ ions, which give the solution a red colour:

$$Fe^{3+}(aq) + SCN^-(aq) \rightarrow FeSCN^{2+}(aq)$$

By comparing the intensity of the colour of this solution with the colours of a series of standards, the approximate concentration of iron in the food may be determined.

PURPOSE

To analyse the iron content of a sample of food using a colorimetric technique.

MATERIALS

- standard solutions containing 0.0050%, 0.0025%, 0.0013%, 0.0010% and 0.0005% iron
- 2.5 g food sample, e.g. raisins, spinach, silverbeet, parsley
- 5 mL 0.1 mol L^{-1} potassium thiocyanate solution, KSCN
- 10 mL 2 mol L^{-1} hydrochloric acid, HCl
- 5 mL deionised water
- crucible
- funnel
- 100 mL beaker
- 100 mL conical flask
- 10 mL measuring cylinder
- semi-micro spatula
- filter paper
- test-tube and stopper
- test-tube rack
- stirring rod
- crucible tongs
- Bunsen burner, tripod stand and pipe clay triangle
- bench mat
- electronic balance
- colorimeter, with data collection system if available
- safety gloves

PRE-LAB SAFETY INFORMATION

Material used	Hazard	Control
2 mol L^{-1} hydrochloric acid	corrosive; eye and skin irritant	Wear gloves, a laboratory coat and safety glasses.
FeSCN^{2+} standard solution	contains nitric acid and is irritating to skin and eyes	Wear gloves, a laboratory coat and safety glasses.
KSCN	may cause irritation to the eyes and skin; avoid contact	Wear gloves, a laboratory coat and safety glasses.

Please indicate that you have understood the information in the safety table.
Name (print): _____

I understand the safety information (signature): _____

PROCEDURE

1 Weigh a sample of a food of about 2.5 g in a crucible. Record its exact mass.

2 Heat the crucible, without a lid, until the food has been completely reduced to ash. Gentle heating is necessary at first to prevent excessive fumes, spitting and consequent loss of mass.

3 When cool, transfer the ash to a 100 mL beaker and, using a measuring cylinder, add 10 mL of 2 mol L^{-1} hydrochloric acid. Stir for 2–3 minutes.

4 Using the measuring cylinder, add 5 mL of deionised water to the beaker. Filter this solution into a 100 mL conical flask.

5 Using the measuring cylinder again, pour 5 mL of the filtrate into a test-tube and add 5 mL of 1.0 mol L^{-1} potassium thiocyanate solution. Stopper the test-tube and shake once or twice to mix.

6 Compare the red colour of the solution in the test-tube with the colours of the standard solutions provided by your teacher. It may be helpful to look at the colours against a white background and to look down the tubes when making your comparison. Estimate and record the concentration of iron in your solution. If time permits, repeat this procedure with a sample of a different food.

Using a colorimeter

A colorimeter (and an electronic data collection device if available) can be used to improve the accuracy of this analysis.

1   Fill a cell to three-quarters of its volume with deionised water and wipe the outside of the cell with a tissue. Following the manufacturer's instructions, calibrate the colorimeter to read zero transmittance when no light passes through the cell and 100% transmittance when blue light (470 nm) passes through the cell. Use blue light for the remainder of this experiment.

2   Discard the liquid from the cell, rinse the cell twice with the 0.0005% standard solution, and fill the cell to three-quarters of its volume.

3   Measure the absorbance and record the results in the Results table. In a similar fashion measure and record the absorbance of the other standard solutions.

4   Construct a graph of absorbance against concentration (using data collection software if possible). Since absorbance is directly proportional to concentration, draw a straight line of best fit through the data points and passing through the origin.

5   Measure the absorbance of the unknown solution and determine, using the graph, the concentration of iron in the unknown solution.

RESULTS

Mass of food sample: _____ g

Estimate of concentration by eye: _____ %

Standard solution concentration (% iron)	Absorbance
0.0050	
0.0025	
0.0013	
0.0010	
0.0005	
Unknown solution 1	

DISCUSSION

1   In this experiment, the iron in the ash from the food was dissolved in 15 mL of liquid (10 mL of hydrochloric acid and 5 mL of water). A 5 mL volume of this solution was then mixed with 5 mL of potassium thiocyanate and the absorbance measured.

   a   What is the concentration of iron in the 15 mL of liquid, in $mg\,L^{-1}$?

   b   Assume the 15 mL of liquid weighs 15 g (i.e. the density is $1.0\,g\,mL^{-1}$). Using your answer to part **a**, calculate the mass of iron in this volume of liquid. This is the mass of iron present in the 2.5 g food sample.

2 Calculate the percentage by mass of iron in the food sample.

3 Look up the food composition data tables published online by Food Standards Australia New Zealand to find the iron content of various foods.

   a Compare the values you and other class members obtained in this experiment with those listed in the tables. Suggest reasons for any discrepancies.

   b List four foods that have a particularly high iron content.

4 If this analysis was performed using a colorimeter, blue-green light would be used to measure the absorbance of solutions. Why is red light not used?

CONCLUSION

5 State the percentage by mass of iron in the food you analysed. Comment on the reliability and accuracy of your results.

Analysing UV–visible spectroscopy data

Suggested duration: about 40 minutes

INTRODUCTION

Caffeine is found in tea, coffee and cola drinks. Because it absorbs ultraviolet light readily, it can be analysed by UV–visible spectroscopy (also known as UV–visible spectrophotometry).

A typical label on a cola drink lists the following ingredients: carbonated water, sugar, caramel, phosphoric acid, flavours and caffeine. The caramel and flavours also absorb ultraviolet light and so could interfere with an analysis of the caffeine content of the drink. To avoid this problem, the caffeine is analysed using a technique called standard addition. The cola drink itself is used to prepare the standards. Different amounts of pure caffeine are added to identical portions of the sample.

In this activity you will use secondary-sourced data to determine the caffeine content of a cola drink. No materials are required.

PURPOSE

To determine the concentration of caffeine in a cola drink using data from UV–visible spectroscopy.

PROCEDURE

1   Cola drink was poured into four 100 mL volumetric flasks.

2   Standard 1 was prepared as follows:

   a 5.0 mg of caffeine was weighed accurately and added to the first volumetric flask.

   b The flask was shaken to dissolve the caffeine and more cola was added to bring the total volume to 100 mL.

3   Standards 2 and 3 were prepared in the same manner but using 10.0 mg and 15.0 mg of caffeine respectively.

   The sample was cola with no additional caffeine added.

   The cola sample and standards were analysed using a UV–visible spectrometer set to a wavelength of 275 nm.

RESULTS

TABLE 1 Absorbance of the standards and the sample

Standard and sample	Mass of caffeine (mg)	Absorbance
Pure cola	m	0.250
Standard 1	$m + 5.0$	0.405
Standard 2	$m + 10.0$	0.560
Standard 3	$m + 15.0$	0.720

DISCUSSION

Use Table 1 to answer the following questions.

1   What does the symbol m represent?

2 Plot a calibration curve of absorbance against mass of caffeine.

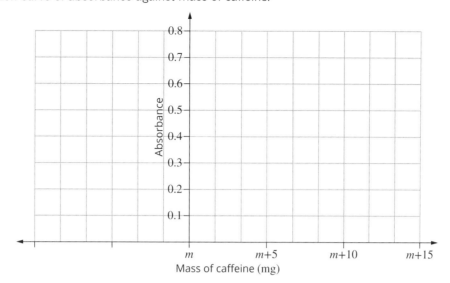

3 Draw a line of best fit through the points and extrapolate backwards to determine the intercept with the x-axis.

4 What mass of caffeine is present in 100 mL of this cola drink?

5 A single dose of 300 mg of caffeine can cause insomnia, restlessness, anxiety, palpitations, disturbances of vision and headaches. Would drinking a 1.25 L bottle of this cola drink be likely to cause these symptoms? Show your reasoning.

6 The molar mass of caffeine is $194 \, \text{g mol}^{-1}$. Calculate the molarity of the caffeine in the cola drink.

7 Why would the wavelength of 275 nm have been chosen?

8 Briefly describe the basic chemical principle that forms the basis of the operation of the instrument.

CONCLUSION

9 State the molarity of the caffeine in the cola drink.

| RATING MY LEARNING | My understanding improved | Not confident ◀ ▶ Very confident ⬡ ⬡ ⬡ ⬡ ⬡ | I answered questions without help | Not confident ◀ ▶ Very confident ⬡ ⬡ ⬡ ⬡ ⬡ | I corrected my errors without help | Not confident ◀ ▶ Very confident ⬡ ⬡ ⬡ ⬡ ⬡ |

PRACTICAL ACTIVITY 8.6

Analysing atomic absorption spectroscopy data

Suggested duration: about 40 minutes

INTRODUCTION

Iron is an essential component of the haemoglobin in blood. Pregnant and menstruating women in particular can have insufficient iron in their diets and may become anaemic. On the other hand, a high intake of iron can be dangerous for people with iron metabolism disorders such as hemochromatosis, because they cannot excrete excess iron efficiently. For both groups of people it is important to have information about the amount of iron in foods and medicines. The concentration of iron can be measured quickly, reliably and accurately by atomic absorption spectrometry (AAS).

No materials are required for this activity.

PURPOSE

To calculate the concentration of iron in a sample of breakfast cereal using data from atomic absorption spectroscopy.

PROCEDURE

1   The iron content in a sample of breakfast cereal was determined by the following technique. A 10.0 g sample of cereal was burnt to ash in a covered crucible. The ash was then mixed with concentrated nitric acid and diluted to 100 mL with water.

2   A sample of the solution was injected into the flame of an atomic absorption spectrophotometer.

3   The wavelength was adjusted to measure the light absorbed at 248.3 nm.

4   A series of standards containing various concentrations of iron were also analysed. The results are shown in Table 1.

RESULTS

TABLE 1 Results of standard solutions and sample

Sample or standard	Concentration of iron ($\mu g\,mL^{-1}$)	Absorbance
Cereal solution	unknown	0.403
Standard 1	0	0.030
Standard 2	2.5	0.198
Standard 3	5.0	0.342
Standard 4	7.5	0.481
Standard 5	10.0	0.620

DISCUSSION

1   Plot a calibration graph of absorbance against concentration of iron from the data in Table 1.

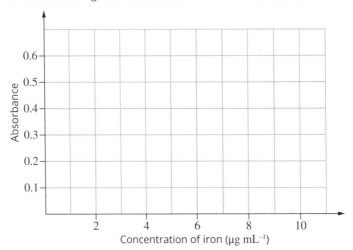

2 What could account for the small reading in the 'zero' Standard 1?

3 What was the concentration of iron, in $\mu g\,mL^{-1}$, in the cereal solution?

4 What mass of iron was present in the ashes of the 10.0 g of cereal?

5 What is the concentration of iron, in mg per 100 g, in the cereal?

6 If the mass of iron in 100 g calculated in question **5** is 56% of the recommended daily intake (RDI) of iron, what is the RDI in mg?

7 What mass of this cereal would you have to eat to obtain your RDI of iron?

8 Why would the wavelength of 248.3 nm have been chosen?

9 Briefly describe the chemical principles that form the basis of the operation of the instrument.

CONCLUSION

10 State the concentration of iron in the cereal, in mg per 100 g.

RATING MY LEARNING	My understanding improved	Not confident ◯ ◯ ◯ ◯ ◯ Very confident	I answered questions without help	Not confident ◯ ◯ ◯ ◯ ◯ Very confident	I corrected my errors without help	Not confident ◯ ◯ ◯ ◯ ◯ Very confident

PRACTICAL ACTIVITY 8.7

Testing for functional groups

Suggested duration: 45 minutes

INTRODUCTION

The organic chemicals used in this experiment undergo reactions typical of the different classes of organic compounds to which they belong. The chemicals and the classes they represent are cyclohexane (saturated hydrocarbon—see figure below); cyclohexene (unsaturated hydrocarbon—see figure below); 2-chloro-2-methylpropane (chloroalkane); ethanol (alcohol); and ethanoic acid (carboxylic acid).

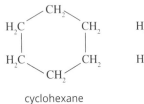

cyclohexane   cyclohexene

PURPOSE

To investigate the reactions and properties of saturated and unsaturated hydrocarbons, chloroalkanes, alcohols and carboxylic acids.

MATERIALS

- small dropping bottles of:
  - cyclohexane, C_6H_{12}
  - cyclohexene, C_6H_{10}
  - iodine in hexane, I_2
  - 2-chloro-2-methylpropane (tert-butyl chloride), $CH_3CCl(CH_3)CH_3$
  - ethanol, CH_3CH_2OH
  - $0.1 \, mol \, L^{-1}$ silver nitrate solution, $AgNO_3$
  - concentrated sulfuric acid, H_2SO_4
  - glacial ethanoic acid, CH_3COOH
  - $0.02 \, mol \, L^{-1}$ potassium permanganate solution, $KMnO_4$
  - $2 \, mol \, L^{-1}$ nitric acid, HNO_3
  - $1 \, mol \, L^{-1}$ sulfuric acid, H_2SO_4
- potassium hydroxide, solid, NaOH
- sodium hydrogen carbonate, solid, $NaHCO_3$
- deionised water
- 3 strips of blue litmus paper
- 2 strips of red litmus paper
- 250 mL beaker
- 8 semi-micro test-tubes
- 2 stoppers
- semi-micro test-tube stopper
- semi-micro test-tube rack
- semi-micro test-tube holder
- semi-micro spatula
- 2 dropping pipettes
- 2 small watch glasses
- matches
- beaker of hot water (almost boiling)
- disposable plastic gloves

PROCEDURE

Record your observations for the following tests in Table 1.

Part A—Reactions of saturated and unsaturated hydrocarbons

1   Shake five drops of cyclohexane with 10 drops of water in a test-tube. Note in the results table whether the saturated hydrocarbon is soluble in water. Repeat using the unsaturated hydrocarbon, cyclohexene.

2   Place two drops of cyclohexane on one watch glass and two drops of cyclohexene on another. Move the bottles of cyclohexane, cyclohexene and other organic chemicals well away from your work area. Light the two liquids with a match and record the appearance of each flame (colour, smoke, soot etc.).

3   Under a fumehood, place cyclohexane to a depth of 1 cm in one test-tube and cyclohexene to the same depth in another tube. Add two drops of a solution of iodine in hexane to each liquid. If there is no immediate reaction, stopper the tube and place it in sunlight for five minutes. Note your results.

Part B—Reactions of chloroalkanes

Use a fumehood during all of Part B.

1   Shake five drops of the chloroalkane, 2-chloro-2-methylpropane, with 10 drops of water. Note in the table whether the chloroalkane is soluble in water.

2   Mix two drops of 2-chloro-2-methylpropane and five drops of ethanol with half of a small pellet of solid potassium hydroxide. (The ethanol helps to dissolve the potassium hydroxide.) Warm the mixture in a beaker of hot water for one minute.

   Test for the presence of Cl^- ions by acidifying the mixture with $2 \, mol \, L^{-1}$ nitric acid, using litmus paper to test the acidity, and adding three drops of silver nitrate solution. Note whether a white precipitate of silver chloride forms.

Part C—Reactions of alcohols

1   Add five drops of ethanol to 10 drops of deionised water in a test-tube and shake the test-tube gently. Note whether the alcohol is soluble in water. Test the solution with red and blue litmus paper.

2   Add four drops of glacial ethanoic acid to eight drops of ethanol in a dry test-tube. Carefully add one drop of concentrated sulfuric acid. Heat the mixture in a beaker of hot water for two minutes and then pour it into a beaker of cold water. Note the fruity odour of the chemical formed.

3   Place five drops of ethanol, 10 drops of $1 \, mol \, L^{-1}$ sulfuric acid and two drops of potassium permanganate solution in a test-tube. Heat the mixture in the beaker of hot water for two minutes and note the colour change due to the formation of colourless Mn^{2+} ions.

Part D—Reactions of carboxylic acids

1   Shake five drops of glacial ethanoic acid with 10 drops of deionised water in a test-tube. Note whether ethanoic acid is soluble in water. Test the solution with red and blue litmus paper.

2   Add a small quantity of sodium hydrogen carbonate to the solution of ethanoic acid from step 1. Record your observations in the results table.

....

PRACTICAL ACTIVITY 8.7

RESULTS AND DISCUSSION

For each test, note the inferences that can be drawn from the observations and write equations, where appropriate.

TABLE 1 Test results and equations. Asterisks indicate specific tests for *C=C double bonds, **hydroxyl groups and ***carboxylic acids.

Test	Observations	Inferences	Equations (where appropriate)
A1 Solubility of cyclohexane and cyclohexene			
A2 Burning cyclohexane and cyclohexene			
A3* Action of iodine on cyclohexane and cyclohexene			
B1 Solubility of a chloroalkane			
B2 Action of KOH on a chloroalkane and test with $AgNO_3$			
C1 Solubility of ethanol in water; litmus test			
C2 Reaction of ethanol with ethanoic acid			
C3** Action of MnO_4^-/H^+ on ethanol			
D1 Solubility of ethanoic acid in water; litmus test			
D2*** Reaction of ethanoic acid with $NaHCO_3$			

CONCLUSION

Summarise the reactions and properties of alkanes, alkenes, chloroalkanes, alcohols and carboxylic acids in Table 2.

TABLE 2 Summary of reactions and properties

Homologous series	Reactions and properties
alkanes (saturated hydrocarbons)	
alkenes (unsaturated hydrocarbons)	
chloroalkanes	
alcohols	
carboxylic acids	

RATING MY LEARNING	My understanding improved	Not confident ← → Very confident ○ ○ ○ ○ ○	I answered questions without help	Not confident ← → Very confident ○ ○ ○ ○ ○	I corrected my errors without help	Not confident ← → Very confident ○ ○ ○ ○ ○

DEPTH STUDY 8.1

Investigating the applications of chemical ideas

Suggested duration: 4 hours (including writing time)

INTRODUCTION

This depth study requires you to design and conduct a research investigation that applies chemical ideas. You will develop a question about chemical or instrumental processes that can be used to test the composition or chemical structure of the chemicals present in a food or a water sample. You can collect and process data relevant to your question, and draw conclusions based on your evidence. You will communicate your results as a media report.

PLANNING YOUR INVESTIGATION

This research investigation will allow you to understand how chemical processes and techniques have been developed to analyse food or water supplies and to ensure they are of high quality. You will work in a scientific manner and develop skills used by research chemists. To start your investigation:

- Decide whether you are going to investigate food or water.
- Write a question about some aspect of your chosen area, and ask your teacher for approval.
- Write an aim that describes what you will investigate.
- Develop a hypothesis that predicts the result of the investigation.
- Decide on the audience for your media report.

You will then carefully design and plan your investigation with the assistance of your teacher, and consider the ethical and safety issues. You will need to consider which chemical processes you would use to test your question. You may consider any of the types of techniques that you learned about in this module: spectroscopy, precipitation, gravimetric analysis, test for ions or tests for organic compounds. You will need to explain how the techniques you select could be used and how accurate and precise the results would be. It is recommended that you are selective in your choice of techniques and clearly explain the reasons for your choices.

Finally, you will describe the results of your investigations to answer the question you initially proposed. Your results must be presented in the form of a media report for the public. Remember to explain the techniques clearly for your audience.

Research scientists constantly use logbooks where they record information, findings, equipment, ideas and concepts affecting their investigation. It is important and useful to set up a logbook, either in a notepad or in electronic form.

Some suggested questions, which you might decide to modify, are listed below.

- How can we determine the salinity of a sample of creek water and whether there are any heavy metals present at toxic levels?
- What techniques can be used to measure the concentration of ethanoic acid in a bottle of vinegar, and how can the presence of any alcohol be determined?
- Using spectroscopy, flame tests and tests for ions, how can the identity of a white powder found in a shipment of food be determined?
- What methods are available for testing for the presence and concentration of metal cations in a sample of oysters?
- How can the concentration of ions in a sample of tap water be measured?
- How might claims on a packet of biscuits such as 'contains no trans fats' and 'low in salt' be tested?
- How might the structure of an ester that is present in a fruit be determined?

QUESTIONING AND PREDICTING

Consider your chosen question and answer the following questions and any others that may also occur to you.

- What data do you need to answer your question?
- What chemical concepts do you need to understand?
- Which specific techniques will you use?
- Has this question been tested before?
- Do I need to do a literature review?

CONDUCTING YOUR INVESTIGATION

For each source that you access during this investigation, you should fill in a summary table such as the one below. Make as many copies of this table as you need.

Bibliographic information	
Summary of content (be concise and coherent) and tables of data	
Relevant findings and evidence	
Limitations, bias or flaws within the article	
Useful quotations	
Additional notes	

ANALYSING DATA AND INFORMATION

After you have completed your research summaries and are satisfied you have collected sufficient information, use the space below to plan the presentation of your results and the best way to produce your report. You should consider questions such as:

- What background chemistry concepts need to be included and explained in layman's terms?
- Which chemical terms need to be defined?
- What will you include in the introduction?
- What sub-headings will you need to use?
- What images, graphs and tables are relevant and helpful to the reader and should be included?

COMMUNICATING RESULTS

Your media report should contain no more than 1000 words, with photographs, diagrams and tables to illustrate the process you followed and the conclusions you drew from your results. Include:

- your question, prediction and aim
- the techniques you used
- the information you needed to answer the question
- data that you analysed, and calculations/graphs that you produced to answer the question
- images that will assist in communicating your answer to the question to your audience
- a bibliography.

Multiple choice

1 Which one of the following is always used in a gravimetric analysis?

A indicator

B burette

C volumetric flask

D balance

2 Which one of the following tests could be used to identify a primary alcohol?

A adding an acidified solution of potassium dichromate

B adding bromine solution

C adding a sodium carbonate solution

D adding litmus paper

3 A chemist wished to identify the molecular structure of an organic compound containing carbon, hydrogen and nitrogen. Which one of the following analytical techniques would not provide useful information about the structure of the compound?

A infrared spectroscopy

B atomic absorption spectroscopy

C carbon-13 nuclear magnetic resonance spectroscopy

D mass spectroscopy

4 An unknown compound does not produce a coloured flame when a sample is inserted in a Bunsen burner flame. When a solution of barium chloride is added to a sample of the compound dissolved in water, a white precipitate forms. Which one of the following could be the unknown compound? (You can refer to Table 8.1 on page 160.)

A calcium ethanoate (acetate)

B calcium sulfate

C silver ethanoate (acetate)

D silver sulfate

The following information refers to questions 5 and 6.

Polystyrene is one of the most widely used plastics. It is made from the monomer styrene, which in turn is synthesised from ethylbenzene by the reaction below. The reaction is endothermic.

$$C_6H_5CH_2CH_3(g) \rightleftharpoons C_6H_5CH=CH_2(g) + H_2(g)$$

5 Which one of the following sets of reaction conditions would favour the highest rate of reaction in an industrial synthesis of styrene?

A 250°C, 2000 hPa pressure

B 250°C, 1000 hPa pressure

C 400°C, 2000 hPa pressure

D 400°C, 1000 hPa pressure

6 Which one of the following sets of reaction conditions would favour the highest equilibrium yield in an industrial synthesis of styrene?

A 250°C, 2000 hPa pressure

B 250°C, 1000 hPa pressure

C 400°C, 2000 hPa pressure

D 400°C, 1000 hPa pressure

Short answer

7 Water pollution can be caused by phosphates that are added to detergents. The phosphorus in a 1.60 g sample of washing powder was precipitated as $Mg_2P_2O_7$. The precipitate was filtered and dried and had a mass of 0.0632 g.

a Calculate:

i the amount, in mol, of the $Mg_2P_2O_7$ precipitate.

ii the mass, in grams, of phosphorus in the sample.

iii the percentage of phosphorus in the sample.

b What would be the effect on the result if the precipitate was not completely dried?

_____

_____

8 The concentration of iron in bore water was determined by oxidising the iron to form Fe^{3+} and then complexing the Fe^{3+} ions with SCN^- ions, to form red-coloured $FeSCN^{2+}$ ions.

A sample of the bore water was then placed in a colorimeter equipped with a blue-green light filter and its absorbance measured. The absorbances of three standard solutions were also measured, as shown in the table below.

Iron standards ($mg\,mL^{-1}$)	Absorbance
2	3.0
4	5.8
6	8.8
Sample	4.4

a Construct a calibration curve of absorbance versus concentration of iron.

b Determine the concentration of iron in the sample in $mg\,mL^{-1}$.

c Explain why a blue-green filter is used, rather than a red filter.

_____

_____

9 A chemist finds a bottle labelled $C_3H_6O_2$. To confirm the identity of the compound in the bottle, she performs spectroscopic analyses on the compound. The mass spectrum of the compound is shown below.

a

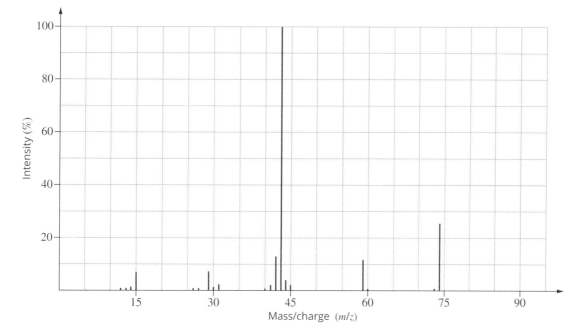

i Label the molecular ion peak with an asterisk (*).

ii Explain the origin of the peak at $m/z = 59$.

_____

_____

b The infrared (IR) spectrum of the compound is shown below.

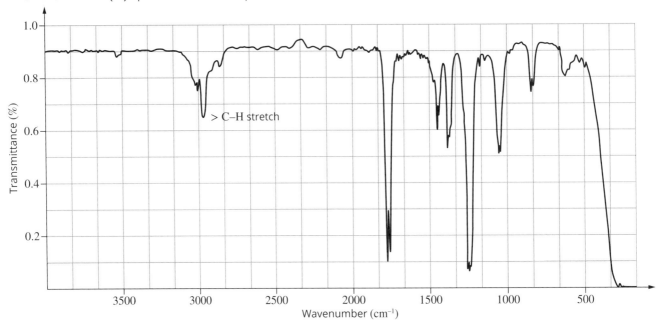

i Briefly explain what causes the absorption bands observed in an IR spectrum.

_____

_____

ii Based on the IR spectrum, state whether the compound is a carboxylic acid, an alcohol or an ester. Explain your answer.

_____

_____

c The carbon-13 NMR spectrum of the compound is shown below.

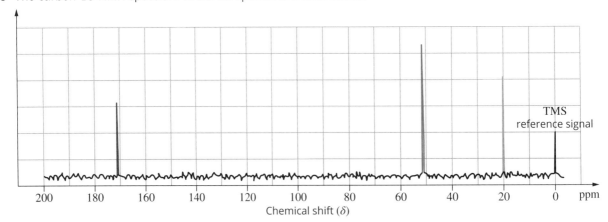

i Briefly explain what causes the signals observed in a carbon-13 NMR spectrum.

_____

_____

ii How many non-equivalent carbon atoms are present in the molecule? _____

d The high resolution ^{1}H NMR spectrum of the compound is shown below.

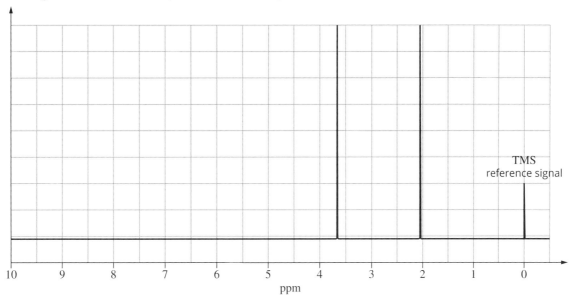

i How many non-equivalent hydrogen atoms are present in the molecule? _____

ii The signals in the spectrum are not split into multiple peaks. What does this indicate about the environment of the protons producing each signal?

e Draw the molecular structure of the molecule.

f Briefly describe a simple chemical test that could be used to decide if the chemical is a carboxylic acid or an ester.

_____

_____

_____

_____

10 Some industrial complexes incorporate small generators that produce ammonia, NH$_3$, from urea, (NH$_2$)$_2$CO. These generators employ the following chemical reaction:

$$(NH_2)_2CO(aq) + H_2O(l) \rightleftharpoons 2NH_3(aq) + CO_2(aq)$$
$$\Delta H \text{ is positive}$$

a Describe two methods by which the equilibrium yield of the reaction can be increased.

_____

_____

_____

_____

b Describe one method by which the rate of the reaction can be increased.

_____

_____

c Each hour a particular generator uses 25.5 kg of urea to produce 10.6 kg of ammonia. Calculate the percentage yield of ammonia.

d Describe three potential benefits of producing ammonia on-site, rather than transporting it from an industrial complex at another site.

_____

_____

_____

Groups

Periods

Key (example element box):

- ATOMIC NUMBER → 12
- RELATIVE ATOMIC MASS, ( ) indicates most stable isotope → 24.31
- SYMBOL → Mg
- BOILING POINT °C → 1090
- MELTING POINT °C → 650
- ELECTRONEGATIVITY → 1.3
- ELECTRON STRUCTURE → [Ne]3s²
- Magnesium

s BLOCK · p BLOCK · d BLOCK · f BLOCK

Z	Symbol	Name	Rel. atomic mass	Boiling pt °C	Melting pt °C	Electroneg.	Electron structure
1	H	Hydrogen	1.008	-252.9	-259	2.2	$1s^1$
2	He	Helium	4.003	-268.9	-272	–	$1s^2$
3	Li	Lithium	6.941	1342	180	1.0	$1s^2 2s^1$
4	Be	Beryllium	9.012	2468	1287	1.6	$1s^2 2s^2$
5	B	Boron	10.81	4000	2077	2.0	$1s^2 2s^2 2p^1$
6	C	Carbon	12.01	4827	3500	2.6	$1s^2 2s^2 2p^2$
7	N	Nitrogen	14.01	-195.8	-210	3.0	$1s^2 2s^2 2p^3$
8	O	Oxygen	16.00	-183	-219	3.4	$1s^2 2s^2 2p^4$
9	F	Fluorine	19.00	-188.1	-220	4.0	$1s^2 2s^2 2p^5$
10	Ne	Neon	20.18	-246	-249	–	$1s^2 2s^2 2p^6$
11	Na	Sodium	22.99	882.9	97.8	0.9	$[Ne]3s^1$
12	Mg	Magnesium	24.31	1090	650	1.3	$[Ne]3s^2$
13	Al	Aluminium	26.98	2519	660.3	1.6	$[Ne]3s^2 3p^1$
14	Si	Silicon	28.09	3265	1414	1.9	$[Ne]3s^2 3p^2$
15	P	Phosphorus	30.97	280.5	44.2	2.2	$[Ne]3s^2 3p^3$
16	S	Sulfur	32.07	444.6	115.2	2.6	$[Ne]3s^2 3p^4$
17	Cl	Chlorine	35.45	-34	-102	3.2	$[Ne]3s^2 3p^5$
18	Ar	Argon	39.95	-185.8	-189	–	$[Ne]3s^2 3p^6$
19	K	Potassium	39.10	758.8	63.4	0.8	$[Ar]4s^1$
20	Ca	Calcium	40.08	1484	842	1.0	$[Ar]4s^2$
21	Sc	Scandium	44.96	2836	1541	1.4	$[Ar]3d^1 4s^2$
22	Ti	Titanium	47.87	3287	1670	1.5	$[Ar]3d^2 4s^2$
23	V	Vanadium	50.94	3407	1910	1.6	$[Ar]3d^3 4s^2$
24	Cr	Chromium	52.00	2671	1907	1.7	$[Ar]3d^5 4s^1$
25	Mn	Manganese	54.94	2061	1246	1.6	$[Ar]3d^5 4s^2$
26	Fe	Iron	55.85	2861	1538	1.8	$[Ar]3d^6 4s^2$
27	Co	Cobalt	58.93	2927	1495	1.9	$[Ar]3d^7 4s^2$
28	Ni	Nickel	58.69	2913	1455	1.9	$[Ar]3d^8 4s^2$
29	Cu	Copper	63.55	2560	1085	1.9	$[Ar]3d^{10} 4s^1$
30	Zn	Zinc	65.38	907	419.5	1.6	$[Ar]3d^{10} 4s^2$
31	Ga	Gallium	69.72	2229	27.8	1.8	$[Ar]3d^{10} 4s^2 4p^1$
32	Ge	Germanium	72.64	2833	938.2	2.0	$[Ar]3d^{10} 4s^2 4p^2$
33	As	Arsenic	74.92	613	816.8	2.2	$[Ar]3d^{10} 4s^2 4p^3$
34	Se	Selenium	78.96	684.8	220.8	2.6	$[Ar]3d^{10} 4s^2 4p^4$
35	Br	Bromine	79.90	58.8	-7.1	3.0	$[Ar]3d^{10} 4s^2 4p^5$
36	Kr	Krypton	83.80	-153.4	-157	–	$[Ar]3d^{10} 4s^2 4p^6$
37	Rb	Rubidium	85.47	687.8	39	0.8	$[Kr]5s^1$
38	Sr	Strontium	87.61	1377	769	1.0	$[Kr]5s^2$
39	Y	Yttrium	88.91	3345	1522	1.2	$[Kr]4d^1 5s^2$
40	Zr	Zirconium	91.22	4406	1854	1.3	$[Kr]4d^2 5s^2$
41	Nb	Niobium	92.91	4741	2477	1.6	$[Kr]4d^4 5s^1$
42	Mo	Molybdenum	95.96	4639	2622	2.2	$[Kr]4d^5 5s^1$
43	Tc	Technetium	(98)	4262	2157	2.1	$[Kr]4d^5 5s^2$
44	Ru	Ruthenium	101.1	4147	2333	2.2	$[Kr]4d^7 5s^1$
45	Rh	Rhodium	102.9	3695	1963	2.3	$[Kr]4d^8 5s^1$
46	Pd	Palladium	106.4	2963	1555	2.2	$[Kr]4d^{10}$
47	Ag	Silver	107.9	2162	961.8	1.9	$[Kr]4d^{10} 5s^1$
48	Cd	Cadmium	112.4	766.8	321.1	1.7	$[Kr]4d^{10} 5s^2$
49	In	Indium	114.8	2072	156.6	1.8	$[Kr]4d^{10} 5s^2 5p^1$
50	Sn	Tin	118.7	2602	231.9	2.0	$[Kr]4d^{10} 5s^2 5p^2$
51	Sb	Antimony	121.8	1587	630.6	2.0	$[Kr]4d^{10} 5s^2 5p^3$
52	Te	Tellurium	127.6	987.8	449.5	2.1	$[Kr]4d^{10} 5s^2 5p^4$
53	I	Iodine	126.9	184.4	113.7	2.7	$[Kr]4d^{10} 5s^2 5p^5$
54	Xe	Xenon	131.3	-108.1	-112	2.6	$[Kr]4d^{10} 5s^2 5p^6$
55	Cs	Caesium	132.9	670.8	28.5	0.8	$[Xe]6s^1$
56	Ba	Barium	137.3	1845	727	0.9	$[Xe]6s^2$
57	La	Lanthanum	138.9	3464	920	1.1	$[Xe]5d^1 6s^2$
72	Hf	Hafnium	178.5	4600	2233	1.3	$[Xe]4f^{14} 5d^2 6s^2$
73	Ta	Tantalum	180.9	5455	3017	1.5	$[Xe]4f^{14} 5d^3 6s^2$
74	W	Tungsten	183.9	5555	3414	1.7	$[Xe]4f^{14} 5d^4 6s^2$
75	Re	Rhenium	186.2	5596	3454	1.9	$[Xe]4f^{14} 5d^5 6s^2$
76	Os	Osmium	190.2	5008	3033	2.2	$[Xe]4f^{14} 5d^6 6s^2$
77	Ir	Iridium	192.2	4428	2446	2.2	$[Xe]4f^{14} 5d^7 6s^2$
78	Pt	Platinum	195.1	3825	1768	2.2	$[Xe]4f^{14} 5d^9 6s^1$
79	Au	Gold	197.0	2836	1064	2.4	$[Xe]4f^{14} 5d^{10} 6s^1$
80	Hg	Mercury	200.6	356.6	-38.8	1.9	$[Xe]4f^{14} 5d^{10} 6s^2$
81	Tl	Thallium	204.4	1473	303.8	1.8	$[Xe]4f^{14} 5d^{10} 6s^2 6p^1$
82	Pb	Lead	207.2	1749	327.5	1.8	$[Xe]4f^{14} 5d^{10} 6s^2 6p^2$
83	Bi	Bismuth	209.0	1564	271.4	1.9	$[Xe]4f^{14} 5d^{10} 6s^2 6p^3$
84	Po	Polonium	(210)	962	254	2.0	$[Xe]4f^{14} 5d^{10} 6s^2 6p^4$
85	At	Astatine	(210)	366.8	301.8	2.2	$[Xe]4f^{14} 5d^{10} 6s^2 6p^5$
86	Rn	Radon	(222)	-61.8	-71.2	–	$[Xe]4f^{14} 5d^{10} 6s^2 6p^6$
87	Fr	Francium	(223)	676.8	27	0.7	$[Rn]7s^1$
88	Ra	Radium	(226)	1140	699.8	0.9	$[Rn]7s^2$
89	Ac	Actinium	(227)	3200	1050	1.1	$[Rn]6d^1 7s^2$
104	Rf	Rutherfordium	(261)	–	–	–	$[Rn]5f^{14} 6d^2 7s^2$
105	Db	Dubnium	(262)	–	–	–	$[Rn]5f^{14} 6d^3 7s^2$
106	Sg	Seaborgium	(266)	–	–	–	$[Rn]5f^{14} 6d^4 7s^2$
107	Bh	Bohrium	(264)	–	–	–	$[Rn]5f^{14} 6d^5 7s^2$
108	Hs	Hassium	(267)	–	–	–	$[Rn]5f^{14} 6d^6 7s^2$
109	Mt	Meitnerium	(268)	–	–	–	$[Rn]5f^{14} 6d^7 7s^2$
110	Ds	Darmstadtium	(271)	–	–	–	$[Rn]5f^{14} 6d^8 7s^2$
111	Rg	Roentgenium	(272)	–	–	–	$[Rn]5f^{14} 6d^9 7s^2$
112	Cn	Copernicium	(285)	–	–	–	$[Rn]5f^{14} 6d^{10} 7s^2$
113	Nh	Nihonium	(284)	–	–	–	$[Rn]5f^{14} 6d^{10} 7s^2 7p^1$
114	Fl	Flerovium	(289)	–	–	–	$[Rn]5f^{14} 6d^{10} 7s^2 7p^2$
115	Mc	Moscovium	(289)	–	–	–	$[Rn]5f^{14} 6d^{10} 7s^2 7p^3$
116	Lv	Livermorium	(292)	–	–	–	$[Rn]5f^{14} 6d^{10} 7s^2 7p^4$
117	Ts	Tennessine	(294)	–	–	–	$[Rn]5f^{14} 6d^{10} 7s^2 7p^5$
118	Og	Oganesson	(294)	–	–	–	$[Rn]5f^{14} 6d^{10} 7s^2 7p^6$

f BLOCK — Lanthanides

Z	Symbol	Name	Rel. atomic mass	Boiling pt °C	Melting pt °C	Electroneg.	Electron structure
58	Ce	Cerium	140.1	3443	799	1.1	$[Xe]4f^1 5d^1 6s^2$
59	Pr	Praseodymium	140.9	3520	931	1.1	$[Xe]4f^3 5d^0 6s^2$
60	Nd	Neodymium	144.2	3074	1016	1.1	$[Xe]4f^4 5d^0 6s^2$
61	Pm	Promethium	(145)	3000	1042	1.1	$[Xe]4f^5 5d^0 6s^2$
62	Sm	Samarium	150.4	1794	1072	1.1	$[Xe]4f^6 5d^0 6s^2$
63	Eu	Europium	152.0	1529	822	1.2	$[Xe]4f^7 5d^0 6s^2$
64	Gd	Gadolinium	157.3	3273	1313	1.2	$[Xe]4f^7 5d^1 6s^2$
65	Tb	Terbium	158.9	3230	1359	1.2	$[Xe]4f^9 5d^0 6s^2$
66	Dy	Dysprosium	162.5	2567	1412	1.2	$[Xe]4f^{10} 5d^0 6s^2$
67	Ho	Holmium	164.9	2700	1472	1.2	$[Xe]4f^{11} 5d^0 6s^2$
68	Er	Erbium	167.3	2868	1529	1.2	$[Xe]4f^{12} 5d^0 6s^2$
69	Tm	Thulium	168.9	1950	1545	1.3	$[Xe]4f^{13} 5d^0 6s^2$
70	Yb	Ytterbium	173.1	1196	824	1.1	$[Xe]4f^{14} 5d^0 6s^2$
71	Lu	Lutetium	175.0	3402	1663	1.0	$[Xe]4f^{14} 5d^1 6s^2$

f BLOCK — Actinides

Z	Symbol	Name	Rel. atomic mass	Boiling pt °C	Melting pt °C	Electroneg.	Electron structure
90	Th	Thorium	232.0	4875	1750	1.3	$[Rn]6d^2 7s^2$
91	Pa	Protactinium	231.0	4875	1572	1.5	$[Rn]5f^2 6d^1 7s^2$
92	U	Uranium	238.0	4131	1135	1.7	$[Rn]5f^3 6d^1 7s^2$
93	Np	Neptunium	(237)	3902	644	1.3	$[Rn]5f^4 6d^1 7s^2$
94	Pu	Plutonium	(244)	3228	640	1.3	$[Rn]5f^6 7s^2$
95	Am	Americium	(243)	2011	1176	1.3	$[Rn]5f^7 7s^2$
96	Cm	Curium	(247)	3110	1340	–	$[Rn]5f^7 6d^1 7s^2$
97	Bk	Berkelium	(247)	–	986	–	$[Rn]5f^9 7s^2$
98	Cf	Californium	(251)	–	900	–	$[Rn]5f^{10} 7s^2$
99	Es	Einsteinium	(252)	–	860	–	$[Rn]5f^{11} 7s^2$
100	Fm	Fermium	(257)	–	–	–	$[Rn]5f^{12} 7s^2$
101	Md	Mendelevium	(258)	–	827	–	$[Rn]5f^{13} 7s^2$
102	No	Nobelium	(259)	–	827	–	$[Rn]5f^{14} 7s^2$
103	Lr	Lawrencium	(262)	–	–	–	$[Rn]5f^{14} 6d^1 7s^2$